GENERAL ZOOLOGY

THE AUTHOR

Gordon Alexander has been a member of the Department of Biology, University of Colorado, since 1931. He became a full Professor in 1939, and headed the department from 1939 to 1958. In addition to teaching and conducting research, Dr. Alexander is curator of birds, University of Colorado Museum. He has traveled widely and served two years (1928–1930) as Visiting Professor of Biology, Chulalongkorn University, Bangkok, Thailand, under a joint project of the Government of Thailand and the Rockefeller Foundation. In 1957 he returned to Bangkok for a year's appointment as Fulbright Lecturer. At present Dr. Alexander is conducting research on animal distribution in relation to altitude.

Professor Alexander is a member of Sigma Xi, of the Ecological Society of America, of the Entomological Society of America, of the Society for the Study of Evolution, and of several ornithological societies. He was President of the Colorado-Wyoming Academy of Science during 1963–1964, and was Chairman of Local Arrangements for the 1964 national meeting of the American Institute of Biological Sciences.

He is author of *Biology* (a companion College Outline), *General Biology* (a standard textbook), and numerous articles on the biology of Thailand, on animal distribution in relation to altitude, and other aspects of biology.

COLLEGE OUTLINE SERIES

GENERAL
ZOOLOGY

GORDON ALEXANDER

Fifth Edition

BARNES & NOBLE, INC.   NEW YORK

Publishers   •   Booksellers   •   Since 1873

Preface

College courses in zoology are of two kinds, the so-called *survey* course and the *principles* course. The present *Outline* is designed as a supplement to standard textbooks used in courses of either type. The *survey* of the animal kingdom, constituting Part Two, is comprehensive enough to provide a valuable review for students in both survey and principles courses, and for advanced students who wish a convenient and condensed source of reference. The major biological *principles* are summarized in Parts One and Three.

It has not been possible to arrange the topics in this *Outline* to correspond with a common pattern in all textbooks, for there is no common plan. For that reason the student using this *Outline* to supplement a textbook must freely refer to the Tabulated Bibliography, the Table of Contents, and the Index. If several textbooks are being used, the best guide to equivalent pages is the Quick Reference Table. This *Outline* may, of course, also be used as a condensed textbook or syllabus in a course with a complete lecture plan. As a supplement in study or review one should, of course, also make use of the many excellent references that are not textbooks. A selection of these, classified to correspond with the various sections of this *Outline*, constitutes Appendix C.

The success of this book, which has been used by thousands of college and university students during the past twenty years, suggests that a major revision in organization is not necessary. In two respects, however, revisions in content have been necessary. In the first place, recent studies in the phylogeny of invertebrates have suggested some modifications of our former views of animal classification. I have suggested these different points of view in the text, where appropriate, but have not adopted new points of view to the exclusion of the old. The second type of revision is necessary because General Zoology today incorporates more basic biological principles than formerly. Recent biological discoveries, particularly in cell biology and in genetics, have had a major influence on thinking in all aspects of biological science. Consequently, the sections dealing with certain biological principles have been rewritten to bring them up to date.

Important material has been added to the last two editions in the form of study aids. The section How to Study Zoology is designed to provide general advice on how to get the most from a course in zoology. It is not designed merely as a guide to this *Outline* but includes advice on following lectures and doing laboratory work. Supplementing this section are Review Questions at the end of each chapter and a Sample Final Examination preceding the Index. The former are essay-type questions, but the latter is objective in form. The addition of these sections was suggested by the editorial staff of Barnes and Noble, whose advice in this and other matters is here gratefully acknowledged.

Most of the drawings were prepared by the author for this *Outline,* some of these being redrawn from published sources. To the several publishers who have generously permitted reproduction of copyrighted illustrations I extend my thanks. Specific acknowledgment is made in connection with each such figure. Cooperation of the textbook publishers in general has been very gratifying, making it easy for me to include page references to new textbooks and new editions.

Much of the general material of the *Outline of General Zoology* has appeared in somewhat similar form in my *Outline of General Biology,* where it has already benefited by suggestions from many individuals. To these I extend my thanks. In the preparation of the First Edition of this *Outline* I had the benefit of suggestions by Dr. Elmer G. Butler, Professor of Biology, Princeton University, and Dr. Robert W. Pennak, Professor of Biology, University of Colorado. While the *Outline* was still in manuscript Dr. Butler read and criticized Chapters XVI to XXI, inclusive; Dr. Pennak did the same for Chapters VII to XV, inclusive. I am particularly grateful to them, but of course assume myself the responsibility for any errors which may have reached print.

Suggestions and criticisms, from students or instructors, will be appreciated.

Boulder, Colorado   GORDON ALEXANDER

Table of Contents

PART THREE
BIOLOGICAL PRINCIPLES

How to Study Zoology

Zoology is a natural science. It therefore deals primarily with objects about us, not human ideas. For that reason books should be used to supplement and clarify observations on nature itself, not as a substitute for these observations. This is the significance of the oft-quoted motto of Louis Agassiz, "Study Nature, not books." A course in zoology without laboratory work would be like a course in Shakespeare without reading any of his plays. Hence, the following suggestions are based on the fact that lectures and readings are designed to simplify an understanding which has been gained, and could be gained again (though slowly), through direct observation of animals.

1. **Scheduling Your Time.** Course programs are set up to require approximately three hours per week of a student's time for every credit hour. Thus, a course which meets three lecture hours and one three-hour laboratory period each week and which probably gives four credit hours demands an average of six hours per week in outside study. Use such a figure in determining the time you should schedule for study, and distribute that time over several days. Concentrated study for periods of one or two hours is better than attempting to cram a week's study into one day.

2. **Learning the New Vocabulary.** Any science deals with exact expression — the right word, correctly spelled. In zoology a highly specialized and technical vocabulary is essential to complete comprehension of the subject matter. The new vocabulary is large, but it is not difficult to acquire if each new term is made a part of your vocabulary when it is first introduced. This means that its meaning (and its spelling) should be understood by use, not learned by rote. The best method of learning meaning and spelling together is to analyze the origin of such a word. Most zoological terms are of Greek or Latin origin, but that does not mean that one must study either language to learn the meanings of the roots of English words. The Greek root *proto,* meaning "first," is combined with the Greek *zoa,* meaning "animals," to form *Protozoa,* the name for the most primitive animals. The same first root plus *plasm,* meaning a "formed" material, becomes *protoplasm,* living material. The Greek root *bryo,* meaning "moss," combined with *zoa* gives us *Bryozoa,* the name of a group of animals with superficial resemblance to moss plants. These roots are not difficult to recognize or to learn, and the derivations of most new terms

can be found in a modern unabridged English dictionary. If you acquire the new vocabulary by learning its origins, you will soon find that you already know the roots for various new terms as they appear. Since certain roots recur frequently in zoological terms what may at first appear to be a complicated procedure becomes simplified.

3. **Getting the Most from Lectures.** Textbook assignments are made to correspond to lecture material. Therefore, you should read your assignments before going to class. Good lectures are not simply a rehash of textbook material, but, even if they were, one could get much more out of them after having done some reading on the subject ahead of time.

Useful lecture notes are very important. Record these legibly in permanent form (in ink) during the lecture. You should not have to waste time rewriting your notes afterward; instead, organize the material of the lecture at the time of the lecture. Even if the lecturer does not name them, the main topics should be obvious if you have read the assignment.

Discipline yourself to take down important points only. If you try to record every statement, you soon become so involved in the mechanics of the process that you listen for words instead of ideas.

4. **Getting the Most out of Textbooks.** The major problem in reading, assuming that the ordinary English vocabulary is understood, is concentration. Speed in reading the average textbook on zoology is not important. Rapid reading for ideas alone is definitely disastrous. The average assignment in a zoology textbook is short in number of pages but full of details which you must master. Therefore, you must read for retention of details as well as for an understanding of principles. On the other hand, memorizing facts without understanding them is of no value, so read for comprehension as well as retention.

A good study environment is necessary. Have a comfortable chair, an adequate desk or table, and good light. Distractions (human voices being the most serious) should be eliminated so far as possible. It may be better to study in a library reading room than in a dormitory.

Outlining the textbook is a good idea if your outline is not merely a copy of subdivisions already indicated in the text. Underlining key words and phrases, and using special notations in the margins, may prove as useful as a more formal outline. Nothing is gained by underlining several consecutive lines of type, however; that simply makes the passage more difficult to read.

5. **Getting the Most out of Laboratory Work.** Since it

is only in the laboratory that you have an opportunity to acquire first-hand information through your own observations, it is essential that you develop good laboratory habits. This means, first of all, the habit of working alone rather than depending upon others. This is good practice in general, of course, but in the laboratory it is essential if an appreciation of the objective and critical approach of the scientific method is to be acquired.

Use carefully the materials you examine or dissect. Read the directions for the work of each laboratory period before beginning work, and follow instructions in the sequence suggested. The arrangement of directions is usually designed to give maximum value from the materials being studied. Preserved animals used for dissection should not be allowed to dry out. If they are to be used again store them in appropriate containers, completely submerged in the preservative. Handle prepared microscope slides with care. They should be focussed under the low power of a microscope before changing the focus to high power. A microscope should never be carried with a loose slide on the stage.

Keep your dissecting instruments sharp. They should be cleaned and dried carefully each time before being put away. The acquisition of skill in their use should be one of your aims. This means using scissors and forceps much more frequently than they are used by most students.

The primary record of observations in the laboratory is made in drawings. These indicate to the instructor that you have done the work, help fix the observation in your mind in a way that dissection alone can never do, and give you a record to use when you review the work. I do not believe that prepared outline drawings which a student labels have much value for either of the first two purposes. I am convinced, furthermore, that the student's complaint, "But I can't draw," has little validity. A person can't draw if he can't write his name; he can't draw if he is unable to use a ruler to measure with or as a guide in drawing a straight line; and of course he can't draw if he can't observe. Poor drawings in the zoological laboratory are usually due to inaccurate observations. Such drawings are supposed to be, first of all, accurate in all proportions. If you measure a series of critical dimensions and transfer these, in proper proportions, to the drawing paper you can usually fill in the details free-hand with a close approximation to accuracy. Attempting to draw a complete dissection free-hand, without taking measurements, usually leads to inaccuracy. One who has had training in drafting will find that such training is of more value in the zoological laboratory than is free-hand drawing.

Good drawings require, of course, suitable instruments and

appropriate paper. Line drawings in pencil, without any shading, are usually called for. Such drawings should be made with a very sharp, hard pencil (3H or 4H) on paper with a hard, moderately smooth surface. Have a ruler available for taking dimensions and for making faint guide lines to be used in lettering the labels. Printed labels are usually required, and they certainly make for greater legibility and more attractive appearance. The process of lettering, being purely mechanical, can be learned by anyone. The forms of the letters correspond to those on a printed page, so one need not learn special lettering styles unless such are specifically required.

Drawings made from objects under the microscope present special problems. Transfer of such images to the drawing paper becomes relatively simple, however, when you learn to use both eyes at once. Look through the microscope at the focussed object with the left eye but keep the right eye open. Now bring a sheet of drawing paper close to the base of the microscope on the right side. With a little practice you will soon be able to see the drawing paper and the object under the microscope superimposed. The process of drawing will then become little more than the process of "tracing" the object as seen in the field of the microscope.

6. **Supplementary Study.** Much can be gained by examining library sources in addition to standard textbooks. Assuming that the books are on open shelves, in the widely used Dewey Decimal System of library classification, the most useful references are under 570 (Biology), 580 (Botany), 590 (Zoology), and 612 (Medicine). In the Library of Congress System, the most valuable references will be under QH (Biology), QL (Zoology), QP (Physiology), R (Medicine), and S (Agriculture). Subject catalogues may be consulted where one may not browse along the shelves.

Museums, as sources of supplementary study, should not be overlooked. Some university and college museums have a special section devoted to a survey of the animal kingdom. Such a section, in particular, is a useful place to review the characteristics of different groups.

Man's environment contains many species of animals. As a student in zoology you can gain a great deal by carrying over into everyday life what you learn of animals in the formal course. There are actually many opportunities to do so — in the parks, in fish markets, on the farm, or along the beach.

7. **Reviewing the Course.** An adequate review of a course in zoology involves going over the textbook, lecture notes, and laboratory notes. Recognize the major generalizations of the course, but don't forget the details which justify the generalizations. In

reviewing the characteristics of different phyla or lower groups of animals try to follow a definite pattern or outline. Such an outline, applicable to all groups, might be the following: Metabolism, Irritability, Reproduction (each of these headings suggesting both structures and functions), Distribution, Evolutionary Relationships.

8. **Writing the Final Examination.** Examinations have several purposes. For students the most important are two: they stimulate review, which makes for better retention; and they test recall of facts and comprehension of principles. In answering the examination take nothing for granted. Assume that you are writing the examination for someone who knows none of the answers. The instructor is not expected to read between the lines. Your answers must therefore be complete and clear.

Planning for an examination should come early. If you keep up throughout the term, the examination should have no terrors. A review of a few hours, scheduled before the last night, should then prove adequate. Cramming may be better than nothing, but it has little to recommend it. Relax the night before an examination and get a good night's sleep.

At the beginning of the examination look over all questions first and plan your method of answering. This saves time in the long run. In an objective examination answer first those parts that are most familiar; don't spend time trying to recall material that does not come to mind readily until you have answered the "easy" questions. This will give you a feeling of confidence, and it will give you more time in which to recall subconsciously the less familiar material. If properly answered, an essay-type examination, contrary to general opinion, requires reference to numerous details. The material must be organized, however, not merely written down in the order in which ideas come to mind. Before starting to answer an essay question, therefore, write or mentally devise an outline to be followed.

Remember, too, that the form in which an examination is handed in is important. It makes a better impression in ink than in pencil, because it is easier to read — especially by artificial light. The writing should be legible, and this legibility is a result not merely of carefully formed letters but of adequate spacing between words and sentences. It is not inconsistent with rapid writing. Finally the terminology must be exact, the spelling must be perfect, and the grammar must be correct; these are basic requirements.

Tabulated Bibliography of Standard Textbooks

This *Outline* is keyed to standard textbooks in two ways.

1. If you are studying one of the following textbooks consult the cross references here listed to find which pages of the *Outline* summarize the appropriate chapter of your text. (Roman numerals refer to the textbook chapters, Arabic figures to the corresponding pages of this *Outline*.)

2. If you are using the *Outline* as your basis for study and need a fuller treatment of a topic consult the pages of any of the standard textbooks as indicated in the Quick Reference Table on pages xx-xxi.

Braungart, D. C., and Buddeke, R. *An Introduction to Animal Biology.* 6th ed. Mosby, 1964.
I (221-222, 255-259); II (7-31); III (21-22, 36-37); IV (53-64); V (30-31, 37-44); VI (65-68); VII (68-74); VIII (76-84); IX (99-107); X (90-98); XI (109-119); XII (120-137); XIII (138-143); XIV-XV (144-149); XVI-XVII (146, 150-152); XVIII (159-167); XIX (168-179); XX (180-182, 185-204); XXI (207-220); XXII (229-237).

Breneman, W. R. *Animal Form and Function.* 2nd ed. Ginn, 1959.
I (7-20); II-III (20-27, 36-37); IV (53-64); V (47-52, 221-223); VI (16-31); VII (65-68); VIII (68-74); IX (76-82); X (83-84); XI (31-32); XII (99-107); XIII (138-143); XIV (108-137); XV (90-98); XVI (55-61, 79-84); XVII (144-185); XVIII (185-203); XIX (239-249); XX (207-219); XXI (230-237, 249-251).

Cockrum, E. L., and McCauley, W. J. *Zoology.* Saunders, 1965.
I (1-4, 160-166); II (7-12, 17-18, 30-32); III (18-23); IV (23-26, 36-44); V (207-218); VI (221-223); VII (53-64); VIII (65-82); IX (82-89, 99-143); X (88, 90-98, 144-149); XI (190-196); XII (185-190, 196-202); XIII (227-233); XIV (233-237); XV (224-228); XVI (160-163, 182-183); XVII (163-164, 184, 194-196); XVIII (166-167, 202-204); XIX (164-166, 196-202); XX (144-150); XXI (150-158); XXII (159-167); XXIII (168-171); XXIV (173-179); XXV (180-185); XXVI (219-220, 245-248); XXVII (238-246); XXVIII (246-251); XXIX (255-259).

Dillon, L. S. *Principles of Animal Biology.* Macmillan, 1965.
I (1-4); II (7-14); III (17-20); IV (20-27); V (221-223, 233-234); VI (8); VII (53-64); VIII (65-68); IX (49-52); X (68-87, 99-107); XI (90-98, 109-145); XII (146-236); XIII (185-190); XIV (196-201); XV (201-202); XVI (190-192, 193-196); XVII (192-193); XVIII (36-39, 202-204); XIX-XX (39-44, 202-204); XXI-XXII (207-220); XXIII-XXV (238-251).

Elliott, A. M. *Zoology.* 3rd ed. Appleton-Century-Crofts, 1963.
I (1-4, 255-259); II (7-16); III (17-23); IV (29-35); V (229-237); VI (47-52, 220-223); VII (53-64); VIII (65-74); IX (76-82); X (82-87); XI (138-143); XII (99-107); XIII (109-137); XIV (90-98); XV (144-203); XVI (185-190); XVII (196-202); XVIII (190-192); XIX (193-194); XX (194-196); XXI (192-193); XXII (35-40, 202-203); XXIII (40-43, 203-204); XXIV (23-28); XXV (207-220); XXVI-XXVII (238-251).

Guthrie, M. J., and Anderson, J. M. *General Zoology*. Wiley, 1957.
I (1-4); II (7-28); III (29-30, 190-195); IV (185-190, 196-202); V (36-44, 202-204); VI (207-220); VII (33-34, 47-52, 221-223); VIII (53-64); IX (65-68); X (68-75); XI (76-82); XII (82-89); XIII (138-143); XIV (99-107); XV (108-137); XVI (90-98); XVIII (144-204); XIX (229-237); XX (238-251).

Hegner, R. W., and Stiles, K. A. *College Zoology*. 7th ed. Macmillan, 1959.
I (1-4); II (7-28); III (56-59); IV (53-55); V (59-60); VI (60-64); VII (59-63); VIII (29-52); IX (65-68); X (68-74); XI (74-75); XII (76-82); XIII (82-85); XIV (86-89); XV (99-107); XVI (109-111, 114-119); XVII (108-112); XVIII (120-137); XIX (113-114); XX (138-143); XXI (90-98); XXII (144-149); XXIII (160-166); XXIV (150); XXV (150-158); XXVI (151-152); XXVII (159-167); XXVIII (168-172); XXIX (173-179); XXX (180-204); XXXI (185-190); XXXII (190-196); XXXIII (196-202); XXXIV (202-204); XXXV (207-220); XXXVI (238-251); XXXVII (224-237); XXXVIII (255-259).

Hickman, C. P. *Integrated Principles of Zoology*. 3rd ed. Mosby, 1966.
I-II (1-4, 47-52, 221-223); IV (7-20, 23-26); V (20-23); VI (29-44); VIII (53-64); IX (65-68); X (68-74); XI (74); XII (76-82); XIV (82-87); XV (84); XVI (87-89); XVII (99-107); XVIII-XIX (108-119); XX (120-136); XXI (138-143); XXII (90-98); XXIII (144-145); XXIV (144-149); XXV-XXVI (150-158); XXVII (159-160, 168-171); XXVIII (160-167); XXIX (173-179); XXX (180-185); XXXI (185-190); XXXII (190-196); XXXIII (196-201); XXXIV (201-204); XXXV (41-44); XXXVI (207-218); XXXVII (218-220); XXXVIII-XXXIX (238-251); LL (224-237); XLIII (255-259).

Milne, L. J., and Milne, M. *Animal Life*. Prentice-Hall, 1959.
I (1-3); II (2, 34-35); III (47-49); V (7-28); VI (9-12); VIII (144-149); IX (152, 162-163, 176, 190-194); X (154-155, 163-164, 192-196); XI (185-190); XII (201-202); XIII (155-157, 196-199); XV (90-98); XVI (108-137); XVII (99-107); XVIII (138-143); XIX (65-89); XX (53-64); XXI (23-27); XXII (36-44); XXIII (207-220); XXIV-XXV (224-237); XXVI-XXVII (238-251).

Pettit, L. C. *Introductory Zoology*. Mosby, 1962.
I (1-4); II (7-33); III (47-51); IV (53-68); V (68-82, 84); VI (82-87); VII (88-89, 99-107, 138-144); VIII (108-119); IX (120-136); X (90-97, 144-158); XI (159-171); XII (173-179); XIII (180-185); XIV (185-190); XV (190-196); XVI (192-193, 202-204); XVII (196-202); XVIII (207-220); XIX (224-251); XX (219-220, 245-248); XXI (255-259).

Silvernale, M. N. *Zoology*. Macmillan, 1965.
I (1-31, 221-223, 233-234); II (53-64); III (65-68); IV (68-74); V-VI (76-82); VII (82-85); VIII (99-107); IX (138-143); X (108-137); XI (90-98); XII (30-32, 144-149); XIII (160-167); XIV (182-185); XV (185-204); XVI (150-158); XVII (159-160); XVIII (168-171); XIX (173-179); XX (180-185) XXI (207-220); XXII (238-251).

Storer, T. J., and Usinger, R. L. *General Zoology*. 4th ed. McGraw-Hill, 1965.
I (1-4); II (160-167); III (7-31); IV (9-13, 20-23); V (185-190); VI (190-192); VII (194-196); VIII (192-194); IX (201-202); X (196-201); XI (36, 105, 202-204); XII (207-220); XIII (224-228); XIV (238-251); XV (47-52, 221-223); XVI (53-64); XVII (65-68); XVIII (68-74); XIX (76-82); XX (82-84); XXI (74, 84, 86-90); XXII (90-98); XXIII (138-143); XXIV (99-107); XXV (108-119); XXVI (120-137); XXVII (108-119); XXVIII (144-149); XXIX (150); XXX (150-158); XXXI (151-152); XXXII (159-167); XXXIII (168-172); XXXIV (173-179); XXXV (180-185); XXXVI (185-204).

Storer, T. I., and Usinger, R. L. *Elements of Zoology.* 2nd ed. McGraw-Hill, 1961.
I (1-4, 255-259); II (159-167); III (7-28); IV (29-35, 185-190); V (12-13, 190-192); VI (194-196); VII (193-194); VIII (192-193); IX (201-202); X (196-201); XI (36-44, 202-204); XII (207-220); XIII (224-237); XIV (238-251); XV (47-52, 221-223); XVI (53-64); XVII (65-75); XVIII (76-85); XIX (86-98); XX (138-143); XXI (90-107); XXII (108-119); XXIII (120-137); XXIV (144-149); XXV (150-158); XXVI (159-172); XXVII (173-179); XXVIII (180-185); XXIX (185-204).

Villee, C. A., Walker, W. F. Jr., and Smith, F. E. *General Zoology.* 2nd ed. Saunders, 1963.
I (1-4, 255-259); II (7-16); III (17-34); IV (12-14, 20-23); VI (36-44); VII (47-48, 221-223); VIII (53-64); IX (65-68); X (76-82); XI (76-82); XII (82-87); XIII (49-52); XIV (138-143); XV (99-107); XVI (108-137); XVIII (88-89); XIX (90-98, 144-145); XX (144-149); XXI (159-167); XXII (150-158); XXIII (159-160, 168-172); XXIV (173-179); XXV (180-185); XXVI (185-190); XXVII (190-194); XXVIII (194-196); XXIX (192-193, 202); XXX (199-201); XXXI (196-199); XXXII (201-202); XXXIII (202-204); XXXIV-XXXV (207-220); XXXVI-XXXVII (238-251); XXXVIII (245-248); XXXIX (229-237); XL (224-228); XLI (231-233).

Weisz, P. B. *The Science of Zoology.* McGraw-Hill, 1966.
I (1-4); III (7-8, 17-18); IV (8-14, 18-20); V (20-23). VI (23-26); VII (29-35, 47-52); VIII (129-131, 160-162, 164-166, 185-190, 196-202); IX (132-133, 162-166, 190-196); X (36-41); XI (41-44, 166-167); XII (207-218); XIII (246-251); XV (238-246); XVI (224-228, 235); XVII (233-237); XVIII (229-233); XIX (53-64); XX (65-68); XXI (68-74); XXII (76-82); XXIII (82-88); XXIV (88-89); XXV (138-143); XXVI (99-109); XXVII (109-114); XXVIII (112, 114-143); XXIX (90-98, 144-145); XXX (144-149); XXXI (150-158); XXXII (159-185).

Winchester, A. M., and Lovell, H. B., *Zoology.* 3rd ed. Van Nostrand, 1961.
I (1-4); II (17-27); III (7-15); IV (20-23); V (21-23, 29-32); VI (221-223); VII (53-64); VIII (65-68); IX (68-74); X (76-82); XI (82-85); XII (99-107); XIII (109-110, 114-119); XIV (110-114); XV (120-122, 129-133); XVI (133-136); XVII (122-129); XVIII (74, 86-89, 108-109); XIX (138-143); XX (90-97); XXI (144-148); XXII (160-165, 185-190, 196-201); XXIII (162-164, 190-196); XXIV (164-166, 192-193, 201-202); XXV (150-158); XXVI (159-171); XXVII (173-179); XXVIII (180-185); XXIX (224-228); XXX (229-237); XXXI (36-41); XXXII (207-220); XXXIII (38, 41-44); XXXIV (238-251).

QUICK REFERENCE TABLE TO STANDARD TEXTBOOKS

All Arabic figures refer to pages

Chapter in this Outline	Topic	(1) Braungart & Buddeke	(2) Breneman	(3) Cockrum & McCauley	(4) Dillon	(5) Elliott	(6) Guthrie & Anderson	(7) Hegner & Stiles	(8) Hickman	(9) Milne & Milne	(10) Pettit	(11) Silvernale	(12) Storer & Usinger (G. Z.)	(13) Storer & Usinger (E. of Z.)
I	Zoology	23	1	3	3	3	3	1	6	1	15	3	3	3
II	Protoplasm	27	15	37	12	47	22	14	38	30	32	18	42, 64	42
III	Cells	32	20, 82	15, 45	29	67, 645	10, 35	20	46	29	38	12	41	46
IV	Organization of Animal Body	79	95, 181	22	94, 145	95	58, 510	78	77		44		48, 78	50, 217
V	Reproduction	44, 69	27	67	380	601	128	79	651	187, 217	405	331	160, 676	130
	Embryology	77	89	80	423	621	145	81	79, 683	196	48, 414	341	171	141
VI	Animal Classification	25	66	123	94	148	214	7	9	10	53	29	269	215
VII	Protozoa	46	39	138	103	159	228	30	109	177	67	35	285	230
VIII	Porifera	81	108	164	132	202	273	92	145	174	95	55	313	244
	Coelenterata	90	120	168	161	207	284	102	157	170	101	65	321	248
	Ctenophora			180		225	310	130	185		109	69	365	276
IX	Platyhelminthes	110	146	181	168	226	314	133	190	168	112	87	339	257
	Nematoda	122	165	196	173	245	348	149	222		131	107	354	263
	Acanthocephala and Nematomorpha			198		241	354	160	222, 237		124, 130	119	367	276
X	Miscellaneous Minor Phyla			202, 248	175	244	344, 357	163	221, 242	166	126, 142, 149		369	277
XI	Echinodermata	148	282	249	205	335	486	303	372	147	240	195	393	270

QUICK REFERENCE TABLE TO STANDARD TEXTBOOKS (Cont.)

INTRODUCTION

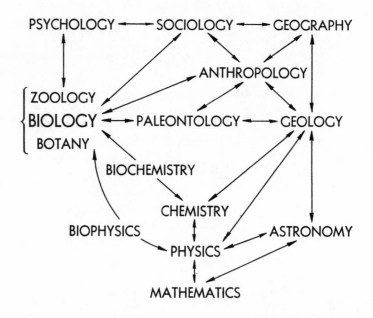

Fig. 1. Diagram illustrating the relations between biology, including zoology and botany, and other sciences.

CHAPTER I

ZOOLOGY

DEFINITION OF ZOOLOGY

Zoology is the science of animals. Zoology and *botany* (the science of plants) together constitute *biology*. The most important principles of biology apply with equal validity to plants as well as animals. These general biological principles are, naturally, part of the scope of zoology proper. The science includes, in addition, many facts and principles which relate to animal life alone.

ZOOLOGY IN RELATION TO OTHER SCIENCES

Zoology draws extensively upon chemistry and physics in its interpretations of life activities; there exist borderline sciences in which each of these fields is combined with biology, viz., biochemistry and biophysics. Zoology is intimately related to geology, because both sciences are concerned with the history of past animal life (paleontology). Certain zoological principles are fundamental to the sciences of psychology, sociology, anthropology, and geography, all of which may be considered more specialized than zoology itself. (Fig. 1).

REASONS FOR STUDYING ZOOLOGY

Zoology is a part of one's cultural background, as well as a science basic to certain technical fields. Through it the average individual, the layman, may:

1. Learn the meaning of the scientific method.
2. Understand how ideas may be acquired from natural objects rather than books.
3. Acquire or expand an aesthetic appreciation of nature.
4. Through a study of animal types, see the broad sweep of organic evolution.

5. Learn something practical to the individual about man as an animal organism.

Zoology is basic to the technical fields of medicine, agriculture, certain aspects of geology, and conservation.

THE SCIENTIFIC METHOD IN ZOOLOGY

Although non-scientific fields often make use of the "scientific method," it is chiefly associated with the sciences. There it is predominantly the method by which theories are acquired to explain observed phenomena. Its usual steps, though not consciously followed by the investigator, are as follows:

Question: Observation leads to the recognition of a phenomenon not previously explained. What is its cause?

Hypothesis: The scientist analyses available data (may, in fact, accumulate more), and from these develops a *hypothesis* ("scientific guess") as to the cause of the observed phenomenon.

Testing: The hypothesis is tested by devising controlled experiments, or by analysis of additional observations (many hypotheses in zoology cannot be tested experimentally). If the hypothesis is not verified, another is developed and tested.

Application: Verification of a hypothesis — which may then be called a *theory* — leads to its application to new situations. When it proves to have wide application, it may be called a *scientific law*.

SUBDIVISIONS OF ZOOLOGY

Subdivisions of Zoology based upon Study of Individual Animals.

Morphology is the study of the structures of organisms. It involves a static viewpoint. Morphology is further subdivided as follows:

1. *Anatomy*, the study of gross structures, in general those visible to the naked eye.

2. *Histology*, the study of tissues.

3. *Cytology*, the study of cells.

Physiology is the study of function. It involves a kinetic viewpoint; organisms and their parts are considered from the standpoint of their activities.

Embryology is the study of development. In this subdivision, one considers the structures of the individual as changing in form. Consequently the viewpoint is kinetic; but the structures may at definite points in development, for purposes of study, be treated as if they were static.

Subdivisions of Zoology based upon Studies of Relations between Animals.

Taxonomy is the science of animal and plant classification. With hundreds of thousands of different kinds of animals, the zoologist must, for convenience, classify them in different groups to indicate different degrees and kinds of similarity or relationship.

Distribution in space. *Ecology* is the study of the relations between organism and environment. *Zoogeography* or *animal geography* is the science which deals with animal distribution in the larger geographical divisions of the earth.

Heredity and evolution. *Genetics* is the study of the similarities and differences existing between parents and offspring, and the factors which control the same. *Organic evolution* is the term applied to the progressive development of more complex forms of life from simpler ones. It is to the race what embryology is to the individual. The principles which govern inheritance must, of necessity, also be involved in evolution.

UNITY AND DISTRIBUTION OF ANIMAL LIFE

Although animals occur all over the face of the earth, from tropical deserts to arctic snows, in the depths of the ocean, underground, and in the air, or as parasites in the bodies of other animals, they are fundamentally alike in structure and function.

There may be more than a million different kinds of animals, and yet there are fundamental likenesses between even those seemingly most unlike each other. These principles of fundamental unity in structure and function have been discovered through a comprehensive study of animal life in general—one of the purposes of a course in zoology. Such a course of study inevitably leads one to realize that the fundamental unity, in spite of great variation in the adaptations with which animals meet different environments, suggests a common origin from which animals have evolved along several different paths. These different environments, however, have certain common traits. Animals cannot function in an environment very different in temperature, light, and chemical composition from that at the surface of the earth. Probably no other planet in our solar system can support animal life. Animal life certainly cannot exist in interplanetary space, and if life exists in other planetary systems, as is quite possible, we shall not be able to reach it. Man cannot reach the nearest star that might have such a planetary system in less than a million years of travel at the highest speed of present satellites!

ADVICE TO THE BEGINNING STUDENT

Remember that any science deals with exact expression. In zoology this is evident in a highly specialized and technical vocabulary, which is not at all difficult to acquire, but which is absolutely essential to complete comprehension. Terms should become a part of the student's vocabulary at the time they are introduced. For the benefit of those who have difficulty in retaining the meanings of such terms there is a brief glossary at the end of this volume.

REVIEW QUESTIONS

1. What is the scope of zoology? What are its relations to other sciences?
2. Name and give the scope of the subdivisions of zoology.
3. What is the scientific method?

Part One

PRINCIPLES OF ORGANIZATION OF THE ANIMAL BODY

CHAPTER II

PROTOPLASM

PROTOPLASM, THE LIVING SUBSTANCE

All living things are characterized by the presence of a complex substance called *protoplasm*. Protoplasm is that which is "alive" in animals and plants. It was first recognized as a living substance by the French zoologist, Dujardin, in 1835; first called "protoplasm" by the Bohemian zoologist, Purkinje, in 1839. The term was brought into general use among scientists by the German botanist, von Mohl. Protoplasm was called the "physical basis of life" by T. H. Huxley.

DEFINITION OF PROTOPLASM

Protoplasm is a complex, polyphasic colloid occurring only in living organisms. It is the substance of life. Protoplasm is not a definite chemical compound, but consists of water in which are dissolved inorganic and organic compounds and in which are suspended colloidal particles of various shapes, sizes, and arrangements. Protoplasm has no constant composition; it is not a compound, but a mixture whose composition varies not only in different organisms but even in different parts of the same organism.

DISTINCTIONS BETWEEN LIVING AND NON-LIVING MATTER

Properties of Protoplasm. Fundamentally, the characteristics of living as opposed to non-living matter are the characteristics of protoplasm. Its complexity, its organization in structural units called cells (Chapter III), its ability to maintain itself through internally regulated chemical processes, to respond to stimuli, to grow throughout (by intussusception rather than by accretion), to reproduce itself — these are the characteristics of living matter.

7

Are Virus Proteins Alive? The distinctions are a bit vague when we consider a virus. Such a disease-causing entity may be capable of "reproducing" itself at an enormous rate in the body of its host, and yet be a chemical compound—nucleic acid associated with a protein. We may perhaps justifiably consider such compounds the link between living and non-living matter.

Theories of the Source of the Attribute We Call "Life". We do not yet know what it is that makes protoplasm "alive." The theories proposed at various times have been:

1. MECHANISTIC THEORIES.

    a. Life is due to a single compound characteristic of protoplasm.

    b. Life is a result of the peculiar aggregations of compounds occurring in protoplasm.

2. VITALISTIC THEORY. Life is a transcendent force not inherent in the chemical composition of protoplasm.

These theories are now only of historic interest. Most biologists today believe that life is simply the manifestation of the combinations of compounds that occur in protoplasm.

CHARACTERISTICS OF PROTOPLASM

Living matter exhibits certain physical and chemical properties, but in addition to these has other properties that are

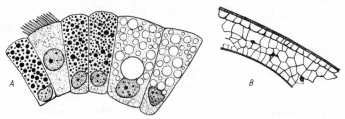

Fig. 2. Protoplasmic structure. A. In cells lining the oviduct of a canary (modified from Groebbel after Schumacher). B. In a protozoan, *Vorticella* (redrawn after Hartmann).

unique. The latter are here referred to as "biological characteristics," since they have no real counterparts in the non-living world.

Physical Characteristics of Protoplasm. Protoplasm is a viscous liquid, capable of changing its state from that of a watery solution to a jelly-like semi-solid. Its viscosity is usually between 800 and 8,000 times that of water (Seifriz). It is translucent, and colorless (but usually appears pale blue-gray). As indicated above, it is a complex polyphasic colloid, *i. e.,* it contains many different insoluble materials in suspension. Some of these, granules and droplets, can be seen with the compound microscope, in either living or killed and stained protoplasm. (Fig. 2.) The fact that protoplasm possesses marked elasticity as well as fluidity is accepted by colloid chemists as good evidence for an ultramicroscopic structure of rod-like colloidal particles arranged as in a brush heap. The particles are loosely associated, but free to change their relations. Some colloidal constituents of protoplasm are known, however, to have their particles (micelles) oriented in parallel rows.

Chemical Characteristics of Protoplasm. Certain chemical elements always occur in protoplasm; certain others never do. No elements are unique in living matter. This is one of several reasons for believing that life first appeared on this planet through the formation of increasingly complex biological compounds from inorganic compounds already present. The most common elements occur in certain types of compounds which are associated typically with living organisms. It must be remembered, however, that protoplasm averages 75 per cent water. *Organic chemistry* began as the study of the chemistry of compounds associated with living organisms, but has become the chemistry of carbon compounds. The chemistry of living organisms is now called *biological chemistry* or *biochemistry.*

1. ELEMENTS.

    a. *Invariably present:* hydrogen, carbon, nitrogen, oxygen, phosphorus, sulfur.

    b. *Usually present but not invariably so:* sodium, magnesium, chlorine, potassium, calcium, iron.

    c. *Present in special cases:* lithium, boron, fluorine, aluminium, silicon, manganese, copper, zinc, bromine, iodine.

2. COMPOUNDS.

    a. *Carbohydrates* are compounds of carbon, hydrogen, and oxygen—they are sugars or condensation products of sugars. The hydrogen and oxygen are usually present in the proportions of water. Carbohydrates in our foods are made up of hexoses (6-carbon sugars). [Examples: glucose, $C_6H_{12}O_6$; cane sugar, $C_{12}H_{22}O_{11}$; starch, $(C_6H_{10}O_5)_n$.] Pentoses (5-carbon sugars) occur in nucleotides. (Example: ribose, $C_5H_{10}O_5$.)

b. *Lipids* (Fats) and *Phospholipids*.

(1) *True fats*, except for food storage, are relatively uncommon. These are glyceryl esters of fatty acids, *i.e.*, they are compounds of one molecule of glycerol and three molecules of fatty acids (Fig. 3, B). They contain only carbon, hydrogen, and oxygen. (Example: olein, $C_{57}H_{104}O_6$).

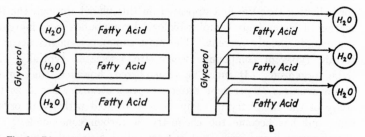

Fig. 3. Diagrams illustrating the chemical structure of a true fat. A. Hydrolysis (digestion) of a fat into one molecule of glycerol and three of fatty acid. B. Dehydration synthesis of a fat, from one molecule of glycerol and three molecules of fatty acid, by removal of three molecules of water.

(2) *Phospholipids* have the formula of a true fat in which one fatty acid is replaced by a phosphorus-containing radical. Lecithin ($C_{42}H_{84}PO_9N$), a phospholipid, is an important constituent of various types of cells.

c. *Steroids* are complex ring compounds of, chiefly, carbon and hydrogen, plus some oxygen. Cholesterol ($C_{27}H_{45}OH$) and other steroids are important in metabolism.

d. *Proteins* are compounds of carbon, hydrogen, oxygen, and nitrogen. The latter occurs in the amino radical ($-NH_2$), which is characteristic of amino acids. These are the "building stones" of proteins. Elements other then the four mentioned occur, particularly sulphur and phosphorus. (Examples: salmine, $C_{30}H_{57}N_{17}O_6$; hemoglobin, $C_{758}H_{1203}N_{195}S_3FeO_{218}$).

e. *Nucleotides* and *Nucleic Acids.*

(1) A nucleotide consists of a nitrogen-containing portion (chemically a particular purine or pyrimidine), a pentose sugar (ribose or deoxyribose), and phosphate (Fig. 4A). Most nucleotides occur as constituents of nucleic acids. Certain modified nucleotides are important in the mobilization of chemical energy in cells: ADP (adenosine diphosphate) and ATP (adenosine triphosphate); the latter is transformed from the former by the addition of a high-energy phosphate group.

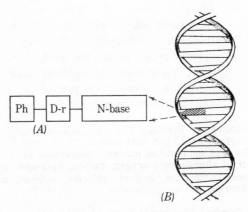

Fig. 4. (A) General structure of a nucleotide in DNA (Ph, phosphate; D–r, deoxyribose; N–base, nitrogenous base—purine or pyrimidine). Its orientation in the DNA molecule corresponds to the cross-hatched portion of (B), which represents part of a DNA molecule. The DNA molecule is a double spiral, its central axis the bonds connecting the N-bases of adjacent nucleotides. The outer ribbons here represent connections between nucleotides in the long axis, these bonds being between the sugar of one and the phosphate of the next.

(2) Nucleic acids are complex compounds made up of many nucleotides (Fig. 4B). When the nucleotides contain ribose, the nucleic acid is RNA (ribose nucleic acid), which is involved in protein synthesis; when the sugar is deoxyribose, the nucleic acid is DNA (deoxyribose nucleic acid), which is a major constituent of cell nuclei. Only four different nitrogenous bases (two purines and two pyrimidines) occur in a nucleic acid. In both RNA and DNA, the purines are adenine and guanine. In RNA, the pyrimidines are cytosine and uracil; in DNA, they are cytosine and thymine. The nucleotides in the double spiral of the nucleic acid molecule are linked between these bases, but the only possible linkages are between adenine and thymine (or uracil in RNA) and between guanine and cytosine.

f. *Inorganic constituents.* Water is the most abundant constituent of protoplasm, and is essential to it. Inorganic compounds of the various elements previously named occur, the most abundant being chlorides, carbonates, phosphates, and sulphates. For normal functioning of protoplasm certain elements must be present in rather definite proportions.

According to Seifriz, "The composition of the human body is 65 per cent water, 15 per cent protein, 14 per cent fat, 5 per cent salt, and 1 per cent unidentified matter, representing the following elements (in order of abundance): oxygen, carbon, hydrogen, nitrogen, calcium, phosphorus, potassium, sodium, chlorine, sulphur, magnesium, iron, iodine, fluorine, silicon, manganese, arsenic, etc."*

Biological Characteristics of Protoplasm. Living matter differs from non-living matter chiefly in its greater complexity. However, the following properties of living matter have no true counterparts in the physical or chemical properties of non-living matter.

1. METABOLISM consists of the chemical reactions in proto-

---

* Quoted by permission from *Protoplasm*, by William Seifriz, published by the McGraw-Hill Book Company, Inc.

plasm. These involve the preparation of food, and its use by the organism—either as a source of energy or in building up new protoplasm. In green plants, but not in animals, this includes food manufacture by *photosynthesis.* (Organisms that make their own food are *autotrophic;* those that, like animals, depend on other organisms for it, are *heterotrophic.*) Animals acquire their food directly or indirectly from plants; they may then digest it to simpler form, oxidize it to release energy, or condense it into storage products or new protoplasm. All these processes are made possible by special catalytic proteins called *enzymes. Vitamins* function in association with enzymes, and *hormones* are important in various aspects of the regulation of metabolism.

a. *Digestion* is the process by which food is prepared for absorption. Digestion consists chemically of the hydrolysis of foods. By the addition of water, the food molecules are "split" into still smaller molecules. Enzymes aid in this process—being catalytic agents.

    Example. In the digestion of a fat, three water molecules are added for each molecule of fat. (Fig. 3, A).

b. *Respiration* is the process by which the end products of digestion are oxidized to release energy for the various activities of the organism. This is accomplished by a complex chain of reactions involving many steps and many enzymes. The first steps are *anaerobic* (without free oxygen) and only the last involve free oxygen. The energy released from the food is picked up by ADP, which is converted by this process to ATP, the source of energy for all cellular functions. The steps in the oxidation of glucose, condensed in one "short-hand" equation, may be represented as follows:

$$C_6H_{12}O_6 + 6\ O_2 \rightarrow 6\ H_2O + 6\ CO_2 + \text{energy}.$$

One must keep continuously in mind the fact that the release of energy from food is the basic process that makes all animal activities—all life itself—possible.

(Note: The process of photosynthesis in green plants is fundamentally the opposite metabolic reaction. Energy is stored in food, this energy having come from the sun.)

    c. *Assimilation* is the use of food for the synthesis of new protoplasm. This process is the reverse of digestion, for the simple compounds are combined in more complex forms — although the new forms which they have may be different from those in which they were received by the organism. Chemically, the process is the reverse of hydrolysis, viz., dehydration. The water molecules added in digestion are removed in synthesis.

2. GROWTH of protoplasm takes place by *intussusception*. In other words, increase in size of a mass of protoplasm is not due to the adding of layers on the outside (accretion), but to the addition of new materials throughout its substance. It grows in all parts, more or less simultaneously.

3. REPRODUCTION in simple form occurs when a bit of protoplasm has attained a certain size. This mass then divides into two parts, each of these capable of further growth. Reproduction involving duplication of large organisms by the indirect process of fusion of sex cells is a further manifestation of this same characteristic of protoplasm.

4. IRRITABILITY is the faculty of responding to outside conditions. Anything in the outside world capable of causing such a response is a stimulus. Different common stimuli are: pressure, change in temperature, light waves, sound waves. Protoplasm is capable of conducting the impulse initiated by such a stimulus from one part of its mass to another.

5. MOVEMENT is one of the evident responses of protoplasm to stimuli. Movement, however, is inherent in living organisms and is not dependent upon external forces. The energy for movement—as the energy for growth, reproduction, and irritability—is derived from respiration.

6. ORGANIZATION. Protoplasm exists only in particular structural units, the *cells*. (Chapter III).

METHODS OF STUDYING PROTOPLASM

Units of protoplasm (cells) are usually quite small, and the various materials suspended in the protoplasm are still smaller; protoplasm is, therefore, best studied under high powers of magnification. For this the compound microscope is used, with magnifications ordinarily from about one hundred to one thousand diameters, or the electron microscope, an expensive research instrument that requires special preparation of tissues, with magnifications of 50,000 diameters or more. Many characteristics of protoplasm may be studied in living organisms of small size. Permanent preparations of protoplasm, in which it is coagulated and preserved in as nearly the normal condition as possible, for class study, involve the following steps:

1. KILLING. The protoplasm is killed as quickly as possible, to avoid any changes in the relations of its parts. The agents used are selected for great toxicity and power of rapid penetration.

2. FIXATION. The protoplasm is coagulated in as nearly the normal condition as possible. Often the same reagent acts both as a killing and fixing agent.

3. DEHYDRATION. Water is removed from the protoplasm, very gradually, and replaced by another liquid. Alcohol is the most commonly used dehydrating agent.

4. CLEARING. The protoplasm is rendered transparent, so that it may readily be examined by transmitted light.

5. SECTIONING. After being impregnated with and embedded in paraffin or celloidin, thin sections of the material are cut. The sections are usually from five to twenty microns in thickness. (A micron is .001 millimeter, or about .00004 inch.)

6. MOUNTING. The thin sections are freed from paraffin or celloidin and mounted under thin glass slips or cover-glasses on microscope slides, in a mounting medium, usually a gum which hardens on standing.

7. STAINING. Ordinarily some time during the dehydration process, the protoplasm is treated with one or more dyes of known chemical properties. These give maximum contrast between structures, and aid greatly in their examination.

These steps are those used in preparing the slides you examine in the laboratory with the ordinary light microscope. Preparation of materials for examination with the electron microscope involves similar steps but greater refinements. It is not possible to examine living protoplasm with the electron microscope, but light microscopes can be used. Particularly valuable results have come from examination of living material with the phase-contrast microscope.

REVIEW QUESTIONS

1. What are the physical properties of protoplasm?
2. Which chemical elements and compounds are most characteristic of protoplasm?
3. Describe the various phases of metabolism.
4. Distinguish chemically between digestion and synthesis, and illustrate with examples.
5. What is respiration, and what is its purpose?
6. What are the steps in the preparation of microscope slides for permanent study?
7. What technical limitations are associated with optical examination of protoplasm?

CHAPTER III

CELLS

DEFINITION OF A CELL

Protoplasm exists in the forms of masses, usually minute, which are known as *cells*. The term cell was first applied by Robert Hooke, in 1665, who applied it to the empty chambers which he saw in cork. A typical cell, as recognized today, consists of a central differentiated portion, the *nucleus,* and a surrounding portion, the *cytosome.*

THE CELL THEORY, CONCEPT, OR PRINCIPLE

Although Theodor Schwann, a German zoologist publishing in 1839, and Matthias Schleiden, a German botanist publishing in 1838, are generally credited with the first statement that all organisms consist of cells, this concept, the *cell theory* or *cell principle,* was actually stated several years earlier by other biologists, including Lamarck and Dutrochet. During the late 70's and early 80's of the last century, the complex process of cell division was discovered and analyzed (by Strasburger, Flemming, and others). This led to the expansion of the cell theory to furnish the basis for modern interpretations of development and inheritance. Even physiology, today, has become fundamentally the study of the functions of cells. As recognized today, the concept implies that those forms of life in which the protoplasm is continuous are of but one cell, and that other plants and animals consist of many cells and their products.

MORPHOLOGY OF ANIMAL CELLS

Size. The smallest animal cells are protozoan blood parasites, having a diameter of about two microns. The largest animal cell is the "yolk" of the largest bird's egg — the ostrich, if we exclude extinct species.

Shape. Cells freely suspended in liquid surroundings are spherical (by the laws of surface tension). In groups, inequalities of pressure from the different sides result in irregularities of form. If all cells in a given mass are of the same size and subject to equal pressure from all sides, they will be flattened against each other. It has been suggested that such a cell may have fourteen faces, eight of these triangular, six of them square.

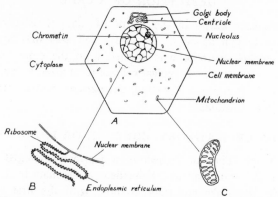

Fig. 5. A. A typical animal cell as seen in section under the high power of the compound (light) microscope. B. A diagrammatic representation of the nuclear membrane and the cytoplasm adjacent to it as observed with the electron microscope. C. A diagrammatic section through a mitochondrion as observed with the electron microscope.

Cell Structures. The major parts characteristic of a typical cell are (1) the surrounding *cell membrane*, (2) the *cytoplasm*, (3) *cytoplasmic inclusions*, and (4) the *nucleus* (Fig. 5, A).

1. THE CELL MEMBRANE. The outside boundary of all cells is determined by a thin but definite membrane. This is of protoplasm, and is alive just as much as is the protoplasm within the cell.

   (Note: This is not a *cell wall*; a cell wall is a rigid, non-living envelope, characteristic of plant, not animal cells.)

2. THE CYTOPLASM occupies the region between cell membrane and nucleus. Its structure, as determined by electron microscopy, is characterized by a network of minute, constricted or dilated vesicles, the *endoplasmic reticulum* (Fig. 5, B), which extends throughout the cytoplasmic matrix. Portions of the reticulum may bear on their surfaces minute granules,

the *ribosomes*, which contain RNA and are involved in protein synthesis.

3. CYTOPLASMIC INCLUSIONS are various types of structures suspended in the cytoplasmic matrix.

    a. *Mitochondria*, which appear under the light microscope as granules of various shapes and sizes, are, as observed with the electron microscope, complex double-layered structures, the inner layer in intricate folds (Fig. 5, C). Mitochondria are centers of activity of respiratory enzymes.

    b. The *Golgi body* is a localized group of granules and rods, or a network whose micro-structure is vesicular and membranous. It apparently plays a role in cell metabolism.

    c. *Centrioles* (central bodies) are self-duplicating division centers, from which radiate at the time of cell division the cytoplasmic strands involved in mitosis. They are ordinarily seen as granules, but with the electron microscope each appears to consist of nine tubules arranged in a cylinder.

    d. *Vacuoles* are relatively large liquid globules suspended in the cytoplasm. They are more typical of plant than animal cells. Unicellular animals may possess *contractile vacuoles,* which periodically discharge liquid from the organism. *Food vacuoles,* which consist of solid particles of food surrounded by the film of water ingested with them, occur in unicellular animals, and also in the cells of certain more complex animals. Food vacuoles function as temporary digestive structures.

    e. *Plastids* are characteristic of plant rather than animal cells. They are relatively large cytoplasmic bodies. *Chloroplasts*, the plastids of green plants, are the centers of photosynthetic activity.

4. THE NUCLEUS is a specialized mass of protoplasm, usually spherical, near the center of the cell. It normally occupies

a position symmetrical with reference to the polarity of the cell. In its absence (as in mature human red blood corpuscles) the power of cell reproduction is lost. In some cells the nucleus is elongated or branched; in others it may consist of several distinct parts.

a. *The nuclear membrane* is a protoplasmic membrane surrounding the nucleus. The electron microscope has demonstrated that it contains pores, that it is a double layer, and that its outer layer is continuous with the endoplasmic reticulum (Fig. 5, B). Exchanges between nucleus and cytoplasm take place across this membrane. It disappears in most cells during cell division.

b. The characteristic feature of the interior of the nucleus is a network of granular filaments called the *chromatin* network. Chromatin is chiefly nucleoprotein, the nucleic acid involved being DNA. During nuclear division the chromatin becomes condensed into characteristic units, the *chromosomes*. These appear as discrete structures only during the process of cell division.

c. *Nucleoli* are small, usually spherical bodies in the nucleus. They are concentrations of RNA and protein. One or more are present in most cells. They disappear during cell division.

PHYSIOLOGY OF ANIMAL CELLS

Properties of the Cell Membrane. The cell membrane is of living protoplasm. It exhibits differential permeability (sometimes incorrectly referred to as "semipermeability"), *i. e.,* certain substances in solution are able to penetrate it; others are not. In general, substances which dissolve fats penetrate with great rapidity. This suggests that the membrane contains fats or fat-like substances in concentration—perhaps lecithin, a phosphorized fat which is a common constituent of cells. Carbon dioxide and ammonia penetrate the membrane with great rapidity, but strong acids and bases apparently do not until they have killed the membrane. After death the cell membrane becomes freely permeable to all substances in solution. If the concentration of a solute to which the living membrane is impermeable is greater inside a cell than outside, this results in a high osmotic pressure in the cell — which tends to draw water into the cell. Animal cells exposed to water containing little salt, in contrast to sea water or blood, tend to absorb water too rapidly. In such cells, or in the organisms of which they are a part, may occur structures for the regulation of the osmotic pressure of the cells or of the fluids bathing the cells. The contractile vacuoles of one-celled animals function in this way.

Cell Metabolism. The most important function of all organisms is nutrition — the acquiring and using of food — and this function is evident in every individual cell. Metabolism is made up, essentially, of all the chemical processes involved in nutrition. All its phases are catalyzed by enzymes specific for the various reactions. Metabolism involves two sets of opposite chemical reactions. Those reactions in which materials are broken down into simpler forms, and in which there is a net release of energy, are collectively called *catabolism;* those in which more complex materials are synthesized from simple compounds, with energy required from outside the reaction, constitute *anabolism.* Catabolic reactions include digestion and respiration; anabolic reactions include food condensation and the synthesis of simple foods. Animal cells are not capable of synthesizing simple foods but must depend upon green plants for this phase of metabolism.

1. DIGESTION. Foods which are taken into a cell before complete digestion are acted upon by enzymes secreted by and contained in the cell. These enzymes catalyze (aid or hasten) the hydrolysis of foods, but are themselves not used up in the reactions. A given hydrolyzing enzyme aids in the digestion of only one kind of food. The digestion of a double sugar to two molecules of simple sugar is illustrated by the following equation:

$$C_{12}H_{22}O_{11} + H_2O \rightarrow 2\ C_6H_{12}O_6$$

2. RESPIRATION is the process of cellular oxidation by which most of the available energy stored in the food molecule is released for use by the cell. The simple equation previously given to represent it (Chapter II) is correct only in that it indicates that water and carbon dioxide are end products

and energy is released. The process is actually a very complex chain of reactions involving many enzymes. Its many steps may be condensed in the following summary, which lists the major events in the oxidation of a simple sugar molecule ($C_6H_{12}O_6$):

a. Phosphorylation of the sugar molecule, by which it acquires the necessary activation energy, as well as two phosphate groups, from ATP.

b. The sugar diphosphate breaks into two molecules of phosphoglyceraldehyde. (Subsequent steps involve each of these molecules separately.)

c. Phosphoglyceraldehyde is converted into pyruvic acid ($C_3H_4O_3$) by loss of hydrogen (*dehydrogenation*) and by loss of phosphate.

d. Pyruvic acid is converted into a 2-carbon compound by loss of carbon dioxide (*decarboxylation*) and hydrogen. This 2-carbon compound is then combined with a 4-carbon compound to form citric acid. (This is the beginning of the Krebs cycle.)

e. Citric acid (a 6-carbon compound) is converted back into the 4-carbon compound by a series of reactions referred to as Krebs cycle or the citric acid cycle. Steps in this cycle include both decarboxylation and dehydrogenation.

f. The hydrogen that has been given off in various steps has been picked up by a chain of *hydrogen acceptors*, the last in the chain delivering it to oxygen, with which it combines to form water. (This is the only phase of cellular oxidation that requires free oxygen.)

Release of chemical energy, for subsequent use by the cell, takes place in steps c, d, e, and f. In each case the released energy is used to convert adenosine diphosphate (ADP) into its more energy-rich form, adenosine triphosphate (ATP). When the cell subsequently uses this energy for any of its requirements the ATP is converted back into ADP as the energy is used.

3. FOOD CONDENSATION. Simple sugars are condensed within

animal cells to form complex carbohydrates such as glycogen; glycerol and fatty acids are combined to form fats; and amino acids are condensed to form protein molecules. In each case the reaction is chemically the opposite of digestion. Synthesis of glycogen from simple sugar is illustrated by the following equation:

$$n\ C_6H_{12}O_6 \rightarrow (C_6H_{10}O_5)_n + n\ H_2O$$

4. FOOD SYNTHESIS. Animal cells are unable to synthesize simple foods—sugars, glycerol, fatty acids, amino acids. These are acquired, directly or indirectly, from green plants, which can synthesize simple sugars and from these manufacture the other simple foods. The basic process, photosynthesis, involves a complex chain of enzymatic reactions by which water and carbon dioxide provide the raw materials, and sunlight the source of energy in the synthesis of simple sugar. Oxygen is released as a waste product. *Chlorophyll*, the green pigment in the chloroplasts, is essential to the process. The following equation represents a simple, shorthand condensation of the process:

$$6\ CO_2 + 6\ H_2O + \text{energy from sun} \rightarrow C_6H_{12}O_6 + 6\ O_2.$$

REPRODUCTION OF ANIMAL CELLS

When a cell has attained a certain size, which seems to be fairly definite for the particular kind, it divides. This process constitutes cell reproduction. It was formerly thought to consist of a rather simple fragmentation of the nucleus into two approximately equal parts, followed by division of the cytosome. It is now known that, typically, a cell always divides by a very complicated indirect method known as *mitosis.*

Mitosis.

1. DEFINITION. Mitosis is indirect cell division. It involves the disappearance of the nucleus as a definite body, but is accompanied by the exact division of its essential parts.

2. PHASES OR STEPS. Mitosis should be thought of as one continuous process, beginning with a single growing (or "resting") cell, and ending, without a significant pause, only when that cell has become two independent ones.

For convenience in discussing the process, it is commonly divided into four steps. These are essentially the same in plants and animals, but vary somewhat among different organisms. As outlined below, the process occurs in most animal cells. (Fig. 6).

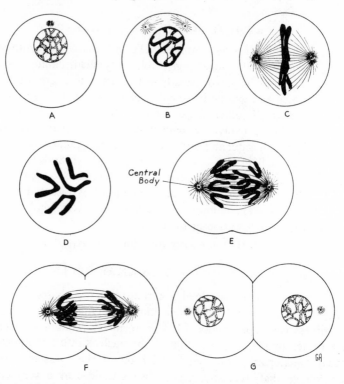

Fig. 6. Mitosis in animal cells, as illustrated in embryo cells of the parasitic worm, *Ascaris*. A. growing or "resting" cell; B, prophase; C, end of prophase, beginning of metaphase, chromosomes at equator of spindle; D, polar view of chromosomes at equator of spindle; E, anaphase; F, early telophase; G, the two daughter cells in the growing stage.

a. *Prophase.* All changes in the cell from the beginning of division to the establishment of the chromosomes on the equator of the spindle. (Fig. 6, B, C). These changes are:

(1) Migration of the halves of the central body to opposite poles of the nucleus, 90° from their original position.

(2) Condensation of the chromatin into the *spireme,* a more or less spiral thread usually not continuous.

(3) Beginning of the formation of the *amphiaster* or *spindle* — completed with the disappearance of the nuclear membrane.

(4) Formation of the *chromosomes* from the spireme. In a given species the number of chromosomes in all cells is typically the same. In the example illustrated (Fig. 6, D) the number is four; in man, it is usually forty-six.

(5) Disappearance of the nuclear membrane. In some cells the nuclear membrane persists, however, and mitosis occurs within it. (Fig. 7, B).

(6) Migration of the chromosomes to the *equatorial plate* of the spindle.

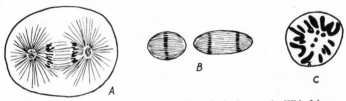

Fig. 7. Variations in the appearance of the mitotic figure. A. Whitefish egg in anaphase. B. Two stages in the mitotic division of the micronucleus of a protozoan, *Stylonychia* (from Hartmann, after Bütschli). C. Polar view of the equatorial plate of a dividing spermatogonium (*Stenobothrus,* a grasshopper); all chromosomes in homologous pairs except the sex chromosome, marked X; (redrawn from Hartmann, after Belar).

b. *Metaphase.* The division and separation of the daughter chromosomes on the spindle. The actual division (a longitudinal split) may be evident even in the spireme, but the daughter halves are not completely separated until this stage. A phase including relatively little activity. (Fig. 6, C, D).

c. *Anaphase.* The changes associated with the migration of the chromosomes to the poles of the spindle—the positions of the new nuclei. The chromosomes move as if pulled by the contraction of the spindle fibers attached to them. (Fig. 6, E).

    d. *Telophase.* The processes of reorganization of the two daughter cells.

      (1) The chromosomes come into contact, either by swelling or branching, to form the nuclear network of the resting nucleus.

      (2) The central body usually divides preparatory to the next cell division.

      (3) The daughter cells separate. The spindle fibers disappear, and the cells are separated by a constriction. (Fig. 6, F, G).

3. MECHANISMS OF MITOSIS. Several theories exist, none entirely satisfactory, to explain the movements of the chromosomes and the division of the cell on a physico-chemical basis.

    a. It is obvious that fibers of some kind are attached to the chromosomes and that these seem to pull the chromosomes toward the poles. The mitotic spindle resembles a polarized magnetic field of force, but evidently is not one—experimental studies showing that such an interpretation is impossible.

    b. Diffusion streams occur during mitosis, especially in embryonic animal cells. Changes in protoplasmic viscosity occur, and are probably of considerable importance.

Amitosis.

1. DEFINITION. Direct nuclear division, the nucleus fragmenting or pinching in two; usually not followed by division of the cytosome.

2. OCCURRENCE. Amitosis is a very rare form of cell division, found only in specialized or degenerate cells. It occurs frequently as a means of nuclear subdivision, resulting in an increase in the nuclear surface of a cell, but is only rarely associated with cell reproduction.

Meiosis.

All cells of a particular animal species have the same number of chromosomes. This number, characteristic of the species, it kept constant in all cells of one organism by mitosis. The chromosome number could not be kept uniform from one generation to the next, however, unless the number were halved in the cells that unite in sexual reproduction. A sperm cell and an egg cell have, in each case, only half the number of chromosomes characteristic of the species. This reduced number is acquired by a special process, meiosis, which involves two successive cell divisions. (See Fig. 13, p. 38)

DIFFERENCES BETWEEN ANIMAL AND PLANT CELLS

Morphology. The smallest unicellular plant organisms are considerably smaller than the smallest animal cells, whereas the maximum size of animal cells considerably exceeds that of plant cells. Typically, however, plant and animal cells are of about the same size. Plant cells in general possess a rigid cell wall, surrounding the cell membrane. It is composed principally of cellulose. The cytosome often contains plastids, particularly the chloroplastids, which are involved in photosynthesis.

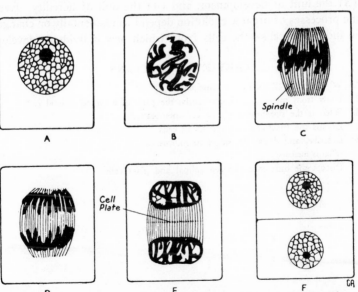

Fig. 8. Mitosis in plant cells, as illustrated in the onion root tip. Somewhat diagrammatic. A, growing or "resting" cell; B, prophase; C, metaphase; D, anaphase; E, telophase; F, the two daughter cells in the growing stage. The absence of centrosomes, and the presence of the cell-plate (E), are characteristics of mitosis in flowering plants.

Physiology. The cell wall, being rigid, prevents the free expansion of the living cell contained within it. Consequently, the absorption of water, due to the high osmotic pressure of the protoplasm, results in the development of the characteristic *turgor* of plant cells. Carbohydrates, fats, and proteins can be synthesized by the plant cell from simple inorganic compounds. Specific enzymes are involved in these processes, and the energy for the reactions is derived from sunlight or exothermic chemical reactions.

Reproduction. In the cells of flowering plants, centrosomes are absent. During telophase of mitosis, the daughter cells do not separate by the formation of a constriction but by the growth of a structure, the *cell-plate,* on the equator of the disintegrating spindle. (Fig. 8).

THE SIGNIFICANCE OF CELLS

The importance of the cell concept or principle may be seen from the fact that the cell is (1) the unit of structure, and (2) the unit of function in all organisms. It is also, as will appear later, (3) the unit of development, and (4) the unit of heredity. Even the processes of organic evolution depend fundamentally on changes in individual cells—the cells from which new individuals develop.

REVIEW QUESTIONS

1. What is the cell theory, or principle?
2. Draw from memory, and label fully, the parts of a typical animal cell.
3. What is the significance of the cell membrane?
4. Discuss the functions common to all cells.
5. Describe, and draw, the stages in mitosis.
6. What is meiosis?
7. Discuss the difference between animal and plant cells.

CHAPTER IV

ORGANIZATION OF THE ANIMAL BODY

INTRODUCTION

Differences between Animals and Plants. Animals, in contrast to plants, may usually, but not always, be characterized by (1) powers of locomotion, (2) pronounced and rapid response to external stimuli, (3) a tendency to grow to a definite rather than an indeterminate size, (4) requirement of complex foods, and (5) soft body tissues.

The Organismal Concept. Either as a single cell or as a group of cells, the individual animal behaves as a unit. It has organization: the parts are subordinate to the whole, whether they are parts of cells or whole cells. This is the *organismal concept,* one of the most important concepts in biology.

Colonies and Individuals. An organism, whether one-celled or many-celled, may exist as a separate *individual* or as one of an aggregate or group more or less dependent upon each other. Such a group is a *colony.* It should be kept in mind that a colony of unicellular animals is comparable to a colony of multicellular ones, and not to a single multicellular organism.

(Note: It may be true in some colonies, however, that subservience of individuals to needs of the whole colony is so pronounced that the whole colony may reasonably be considered one organism.)

DIVISION OF LABOR

The different positions of the parts of a cell, or the cells of a multicellular animal, naturally result in different functional requirements. The ways in which these various structures contribute to the unified action of the whole organism constitute "division of labor."

Intracellular Organelles. In one-celled animals (Protozoa, Chapter VII), different functions may be accomplished by highly specialized intracellular structures, all parts of the single cell. These are called *organelles* (diminutive for organ). Such structures may, for example, be adapted for protection, movement, food ingestion, and digestion. (For illustrations of highly differentiated organelles see Fig. 9).

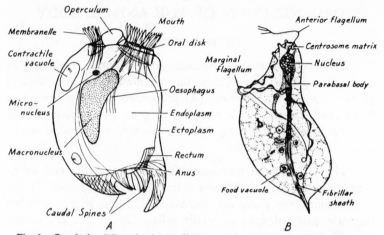

Fig. 9. Complexly differentiated unicellular animals. A. *Diplodinium dentatum* (Stein), a ciliate protozoan parasite from the stomach of cattle (after Kofoid and MacLennan). B. *Gigantomonas lighti* Connell, a flagellate protozoan parasite from the intestine of termites (after Connell).[1]

Germ Cells and Somatic Cells. The primary division of labor among cells of metazoa (many-celled animals) is evident in the separation of *germ cells* (reproductive in function) from *somatic cells* (non-reproductive). That portion of the animal which is continuous from one generation to the next is, of course, the germ cell line. This concept of germ cell continuity is the principle of *the continuity of the germ-plasm,* associated with the name of August Weismann.

Tissues. In many-celled animals, cells are differentiated into types adapted for different functions. A group of cells of similar structure and function constitutes a *tissue.* The major types of animal tissues, as found in higher animals, are illustrated in Figure 10. These are ordinarily classified as (1) *epithelial* (Fig. 10, A—C), (2) *muscular* (Fig. 10, D—F), (3) *connective and supporting* (Fig. 10, G—L), and (4) *nervous* (Fig. 10, M, N). *Blood* may be recognized as a distinct type, or as connective tissue. In the more primitive animals all such tissues may not be differentiated. We may find, for example, a single

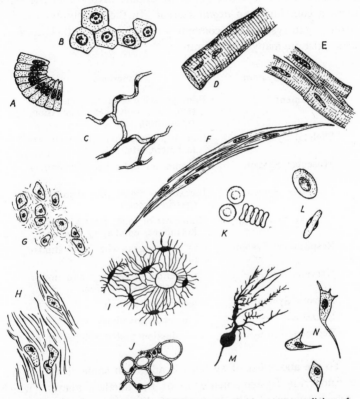

Fig. 10. Animal tissues. A-C, epithelial tissue; A, from mucous lining of frog's intestine; B, liver cells of cat; C, epithelial lining of lung alveoli of rabbit. D-F, muscle tissue; D, striated muscle from grasshopper femur; E, cardiac (heart) muscle; F, smooth muscle from wall of frog intestine; G-L, connective and supporting (including blood) tissue; G, cartilage tissue; H, fibrous connective tissue in stomach wall of frog; I, section through Haversian system (bone tissue); J, adipose (fat) tissue from fat-body of frog; K, human erythrocytes (red blood corpuscles); L, frog erythrocytes. M,N, nerve cells (neurons), the processes from the cell bodies being incomplete; M, Purkinje cell from cerebellum of rabbit (Golgi method of staining); N, nerve cell bodies from spinal cord of rabbit.

cell functioning in the reception of stimuli and in contraction — corresponding to nervous and muscular tissues combined. With increasing complexity specialized functions become separated in different types of cells.

Organs. A group of cells or tissues may be combined for a definite function or group of functions. Such a structure is called an *organ*. Its constituent cells may be largely of one kind of tissue, as in a muscle; or they may be of many types of cells, as in the eye. A group of organs involved in the same function constitutes an *organ system*. In the vertebrates the following organ systems are commonly recognized, and their counterparts exist in many invertebrates:

Organ System	Functions
Integument	Body covering — protection, sensation, secretion, heat insulation, respiration, etc.
Skeletal System	Support, protection, muscular attachment, etc.
Muscular System	Locomotion and other body movements.
Digestive System	Ingestion, digestion, absorption, egestion, secretion.
Circulatory System	Transport of food, wastes, oxygen, hormones, combating disease.
Respiratory System	Gas exchanges with the atmosphere.
Nervous System	Conduction of sensory and motor impulses, coordination.
Sensory System	Reception of stimuli.
Excretory System	Removal of metabolic wastes.
Reproductive System	Reproduction and development of offspring.

To the above list of systems is added, in some classifications, the Endocrine System, made up of the ductless glands (which secrete hormones). The function of this system is chemical coordination. As a system it is less localized, and therefore less easily defined, than any other system of organs.

Colonial Division of Labor — Polymorphism. Social animals may be specialized within a colony for reproduction, protection, and work, as in a colony of ants or termites. The conditions in which different individuals of the same species are specialized for different functions is *polymorphism*. Even non-colonial animals may be said to illustrate *dimorphism* in their frequent specialization in two sexual groups, male and female.

BODY FORM

Kind of Symmetry. Animals may show no plane of symmetry, being asymmetrical, or they may possess spherical, radial, biradial, or bilateral symmetry to a greater or lesser degree. This refers, of course, to external form; many internal organ systems of an externally symmetrical animal may be asymmetrical.

1. SPHERICAL SYMMETRY. The symmetry of a ball. Any section through the center divides the organism into symmetrical halves. Examples: certain marine protozoa of the Class Rhizopoda.

2. RADIAL SYMMETRY. The symmetry of a wheel. Any vertical section through the center divides the organism into symmetrical halves. Examples: jelly-fish, sand-dollar.

3. BIRADIAL SYMMETRY. The symmetry of an oval. Only two sections, vertical ones at right angles to each other, divide the organism into symmetrical halves; there is only one axis whose poles differ from each other — the oral-aboral axis. Example: sea-walnut or comb-jelly.

4. BILATERAL SYMMETRY. The symmetry of a plank in which the two ends differ. Only one section, a vertical one in the longitudinal axis, divides the organism into symmetrical halves; there are two axes whose poles differ from each other — dorsal-ventral and anterior-posterior. Examples: earthworm, man.

Number of Germ-layers. Metazoa develop from either two or three germ-layers (embryonic cell layers). Those of the former type are usually called *diploblastic,* of the latter type, *triploblastic.* The three layers of triploblastic animals are, in order from outside in, the *ectoderm, mesoderm,* and *endoderm.* Scattered cells between the two layers of diploblastic animals make the classification of doubtful value. (Fig. 11).

Development of a Coelom or Body-Cavity. In the more advanced triploblastic animals a cavity develops within the mesoderm, lined with mesoderm. This is the true *body-cavity* or *coelom*. In some animals the mesoderm lining is incomplete. The cavity is then a false coelom or *pseudocoel*. (Fig. 11).

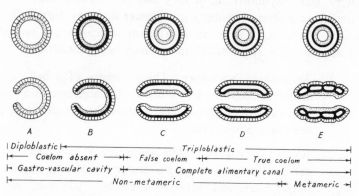

Fig. 11. Diagram illustrating the evolution of body form among Metazoa. Upper row, cross sections; lower row longitudinal or oral-aboral sections. Stippled layer, endoderm; cross-hatched layer, ectoderm; solid black layer, mesoderm; clear space outside endoderm, coelom. Examples of phyla illustrating the stages shown: A, Coelenterata; B, Platyhelminthes; C, Nematoda; D, Echinodermata; E, Annelida.

Metamerism. Several groups of animals are character-ized by more or less complete segmentation of the body. This condition is known as *metamerism,* each segment being a *metamere.* The metameres show various degrees of independence from each other, but are subordinate for the most part to the whole organism. (Fig. 11).

Homology and Analogy. In the interpretation of the fundamental relationships of animals it is necessary to distinguish between similarities which are the accidental result of similar function, *analogies,* and similarities which are fundamental in development and structural relations, *homologies.* Organs which are fundamentally the same in development and structure may, nevertheless, be modified for widely different functions; they are, however, homologous, and suggest a common origin for the animals which possess them.

DESCRIPTIVE TERMINOLOGY

Planes and Sections of the Animal Body. In a bilaterally symmetrical animal, a cut which follows any vertical plane parallel with the longitudinal axis is a *longitudinal section.* If exactly in the mid-longitudinal axis, it is a *sagittal section.* Sections in the vertical plane at right angles to the long axis are *transverse* or *cross sections.* Sections in the horizontal plane are *horizontal* or *frontal sections.* (Fig. 12).

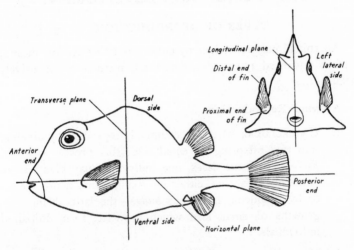

Fig. 12. Diagram illustrating descriptive terminology. An explanation of the names of *sections* occurs in the accompanying text. (The fish is a trunk-fish, after Evermann and Marsh).

Names of Directions. The forward end is *anterior,* the opposite end, *posterior.* The back is *dorsal,* the lower surface, *ventral.* The sides are *lateral.* The point of attachment of a structure is its *proximal* end, the free end is *distal.* (Fig. 12). All these terms are adjectives.

REVIEW QUESTIONS

1. What are the principal differences between plants and animals?
2. What is an organism? Discuss the colony in relation to organisms.
3. Discuss the different types of division of labor found among animals.
4. Draw from memory, and label, the different types of animal tissues.
5. What are the organ systems, and their functions?
6. Define symmetry, metamerism, coelom, diploblastic, triploblastic.
7. What is the distinction between homology and analogy? Which condition is of more significance in determining zoological relationships?

Chapter V

REPRODUCTION AND DEVELOPMENT

TYPES OF REPRODUCTION

An animal may reproduce by either sexual or asexual means; in more advanced types of animals the method is exclusively sexual.

Asexual Reproduction.

1. UNICELLULAR ANIMALS commonly reproduce by dividing into two offspring of equal size; this process is called *fission*. In some cases, one individual may give rise to numerous offspring, either by dividing into many *spores,* or by producing numerous *buds* — the latter being outgrowths of small size which grow to form full-sized individuals.

2. MULTICELLULAR ANIMALS. Here asexual reproduction usually involves development of offspring from a relatively small part of the parent. New individuals may form as outgrowths from the parent, buds; they may form from the fragments of a parent that has broken into pieces; they may develop from resistant structures formed in an animal's body before the onset of unfavorable conditions — *gemmules* of fresh-water sponges, or *statoblasts* of fresh-water bryozoa.

Sexual Reproduction. Analogies with sexual reproduction are found in certain reproductive processes of protozoa, *e. g.,* conjugation; although the more frequent mode of reproduction in unicellular animals is asexual. The process in higher animals is characterized by the fusion of two mature reproductive or germ cells *(gametes)* to form a single cell, the *fertilized egg* or *zygote.* The gametes have developed in parents of different *sex.* The *male* gamete is a *sperm cell (spermatozoan);* the *female* gamete, an *egg cell* or *ovum.* Each gamete develops by a process called *maturation* or *gametogenesis,* in an organ called a *gonad.* The gonad of the male is the *testis;* of the female, the *ovary.* The fusion of the gametes (more specifically their nuclei) constitutes *fertilization.* The zygote becomes the mature animal through the process of *embryology (embryogeny).*

1. GAMETOGENESIS OR MATURATION is the process by which gametes are formed. Structurally, the male gamete is modified for active movement and for penetration of the egg. The female gamete contains a large amount of food material (yolk) for the developing embryo, and is passive in movement. In both, during the process of gametogenesis the number of chromosomes is reduced by half. In somatic cells and immature germ cells the number characteristic of the species is said to be *diploid.* Chromosomes in the diploid number are represented in pairs. During the process of reduction the members of the chromosome pairs are separated, with the result that in the reduced number only one of each pair is represented. The reduced number is called *haploid.* From the standpoint of inheritance (see Chapter XXVI) it is more important that the members of the chromosome pairs are segregated than that the number is reduced; it is true, however, that the halving of the chromosome number maintains constant the number of chromosomes characteristic of a given species. (Fig. 13).

   a. *Spermatogenesis.* Following the period of cellular multiplication, by which the number of germ cells in the testis is increased, occurs the growth period. The growing cell (destined to form spermatozoa) becomes the *primary spermatocyte.* It divides, forming two *secondary spermatocytes.* Each of these divides forming two *spermatids.* Each spermatid, by a process of differentiation without any division, becomes a sperm cell or spermatozoan. Two cell divisions have occurred, together constituting *reduction division* or *meiosis.* End result: four functional sperm cells, each with the haploid number of chromosomes. (Fig. 13).

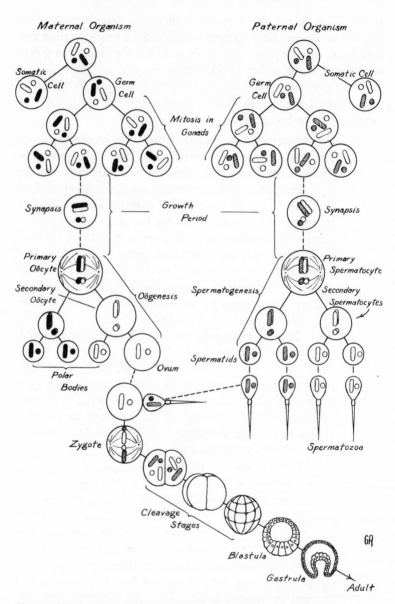

Fig. 13. Diagram illustrating maturation or gametogenesis (oögenesis in female, spermatogenesis in male) and the stages of embryogeny in animals. Also illustrated is the continuity of chromosomes from the gametes which form two parents, through the germ-cells in the gonads of these individuals, to the embryo which is their progeny. A reduction division is represented here as occurring during the first maturation division; meiosis actually involves the second maturation division as well as the first.

b. *Oögenesis.* Following the period of multiplication in the ovary occurs the growth period, the enlarged cell being the *primary oocyte.* It divides unequally, forming one (large) *secondary oocyte* and a (small) *polar body.* The size difference is not due to nuclear size difference but to cytoplasmic. The polar body may or may not divide again; its fate is unimportant. The secondary oocyte divides to form a second small polar body and the mature egg cell or ovum. The divisions thus result in one functional mature germ cell, the ovum, and two or three non-functional polar bodies. The ovum has the haploid number of chromosomes. (Fig. 13).

2. FERTILIZATION of the egg is completed when the two *pronuclei,* one from the sperm cell, one already in the ovum, fuse. The sperm may penetrate the egg cell before the first polar body is formed, between formation of first and second polar bodies, or after the egg is mature; in no case does the sperm pronucleus fuse with the egg pronucleus until maturation is complete. The time at which *penetration* occurs is characteristic for different species. Fertilization merges immediately into the first division of the zygote, the chromosomes from the two pronuclei being combined on the mitotic spindle, restoring the diploid number of chromosomes, and giving to the new individual equal numbers of chromosomes from paternal and maternal parents. The new individual receives from each parent one member of each pair of chromosomes constituting the diploid number. (Fig. 13).

3. ACCESSORY PROCESSES, designed to insure fertilization, occur. If fertilization occurs outside the female's body, both egg and sperm cells may be shed, more or less simultaneously, into the surrounding medium (in most cases water). In some cases where fertilization is external, behavior patterns exist which insure a greater percentage of fertile eggs. In the earthworm, eggs are discharged into a cocoon, into which are then ejected sperm cells received previously during copulation with another worm.

In frogs, males clasp the female during spawning, so that the sperm cells as discharged come immediately into contact with the egg mass. In animals in which fertilization is internal, the male discharges the sperm cells directly into the genital tract of the female during *copulation.* In some forms, this involves merely the apposition of the genital openings, neither being specialized. In others, the male discharges packets of sperm cells which are later picked up by the cloaca of the female (*e. g.,* salamanders). An *intromittent organ* or *penis,* introduced into the female genital tract during copulation, may convey packets of sperm cells (*e. g.,* grasshoppers) or sperm cells in a liquid medium produced by various accessory glands (*e. g.,* higher vertebrates).

4. Variations in the Reproductive Process.

    a. *Metagenesis.* Alternation of generations, or *metagenesis,* so characteristic of plants, occurs among a few animals. It involves an alternation of a sexually-reproducing with an asexually-reproducing generation. It is best illustrated in colonial coelenterates like *Obelia.* (See Chapter VIII). The animals of the *Obelia* colony are formed asexually, by budding; certain of these buds produce, also by budding, the medusae; the medusae reproduce sexually, the fertilized eggs developing into polyps which, by budding, produce new colonies (Fig. 27). Metagenesis occurs also among the parasitic flatworms. (Chapter IX).

    b. *Variations from Normal Sexual Reproduction.*

        (1) *Hermaphroditism.* One individual, a *hermaphrodite,* may produce both eggs and sperm cells. The eggs may be fertilized by sperm cells of the same animal *(self-fertilization)* or by those of another *(cross-fertilization).* (Examples: *Hydra,* flatworm, earthworm, snail.)

        (2) *Parthenogenesis* is reproduction through the development of an unfertilized egg — so-called virgin reproduction. (Examples: bees, plant-lice.) *Artificial parthenogenesis* has been brought

about by chemical or physical methods in many species of animals.

(3) *Pedogenesis.* Reproduction by an animal in a young or larval condition. (Examples: liver-fluke, tiger salamander, or axolotl.)

EMBRYOLOGY

Definition of Embryology. Strictly speaking, the whole course of development from the fertilized egg throughout life constitutes *embryology.* Ordinarily, embryology is considered the process of development from the fertilized egg to a stage approximating the adult condition, *e. g.,* to hatching in birds, or birth in mammals. (Some authors prefer to call the process of development *embryogeny,* reserving the word embryology for the study of the process.)

General Principles. The zygote divides by a sequence of mitosis characteristic for each animal, this constituting a differentiation pattern which produces the adult form. The process of early development is governed by the nature of the egg.

Kinds of Egg Cells. The nucleus of egg cells is usually eccentric, its position being the side on which polar bodies are formed — the *animal pole.* The cytoplasm is concentrated toward the same side, the yolk being concentrated nearer the opposite pole — the *vegetative pole.* If the yolk is small in amount and rather evenly distributed, the egg is *homolecithal.* If it is large in amount and concentrated toward one pole, the egg is *telolecithal.* In insect eggs, the nucleus with a little cytoplasm lies in the yolk, which is central, the whole being surrounded by a layer of cytoplasm. Such an egg is *centrolecithal.* In the first case, *cleavage* (cell division) may be *equal* and *total* (or *entire*), the cells formed being completely divided and of about equal size. In telolecithal eggs, cleavage may be confined to a disc-like region at the animal pole *(discoidal);* in centrolecithal eggs, cleavage may be confined to the surface but extend over all of the egg *(superficial).* Entire cleavage is said to be *holoblastic;* discoidal or superficial cleavage is *meroblastic.*

Stages in Embryology (Embryogeny). The following stages merge one into another; they are given different names for convenience only. (Fig. 13).

1. EARLY CLEAVAGE. The early stages of cell division. The cells as they divide remain attached; the original mass does not increase in size, it simply subdivides. The zygote forms two cells, each of these two making four; in some cases this geometric progression continues some time: $2 — 4 — 8 — 16 — 32$; but in most cases, greater division rates at the animal pole disturb the regularity. Embryos of approximately sixteen cells look like mulberries; hence, the name *morula* for a stage with this appearance.

2. BLASTULA. Continued cleavage results in the formation of a hollow ball of cells, the *blastula,* its cavity being the *blastocoel* or *segmentation cavity.*

3. GASTRULA. More rapid division of cells at animal than at vegetative pole results in a pushing in or *invagination* of the cells near the vegetative pole. This results in a reduction in the size of the blastocoel as the outer cells push inward, the embryo becoming a ball of cells whose cavity *(gastrocoel* or *archenteron)* opens to the outside but is surrounded elsewhere than at the opening (the *blastopore)* by two layers of cells, the outer *ectoderm* and the inner *endoderm.* In some animals invagination does not occur, but the endoderm is formed by *delamination* — an internal layering-off from the cells of the blastula. The internal cavity in such embryos becomes secondarily open to the outside (e. g., *Hydra).* From an evolutionary standpoint, the gastrula represents the stage which the adult coelenterate attains. (Chapter VIII).

4. MESODERM FORMATION. Between ectoderm and endoderm, cells proliferate to occupy the segmentation cavity. These form the third germ-layer, the *mesoderm.* The platyhelminthes attain this stage in evolution but go no further. (Chapter IX).

5. COELOM FORMATION. Mesoderm cells may separate into two layers, an outer *(somatic)* and an inner *(splanchnic),*

leaving a space between which becomes the true *body-cavity* or *coelom.* The coelom may be separated by transverse partitions into segmentally-arranged cavities (*e. g.,* earthworm).

6. ORGANOGENY. With the beginning of coelom formation, *organogeny* or differentiation of organs commences. (Example: formation of nervous system from ridges of ectoderm.) Derivations of the embryonic germ-layers are in general, as follows:

From ectoderm: Integument, nervous system, lining of mouth and anus.

From endoderm: Lining of alimentary canal (except mouth and anus), and its appendages (*e. g.,* lungs, bile ducts, etc.).

From mesoderm: Internal skeleton, muscles, heart and blood vessels,· kidneys, gonads, muscular and connective tissue layers of alimentary canal and its appendages.

Accessory Processes. In some animals the young are retained in an expanded portion of the oviduct, the *uterus,* during a period of development. They may merely be protected, having no nutritional dependence on the maternal organism, as in some fishes and reptiles; or they may receive nourishment from the mother, as in most mammals. The organ which provides for nutrition in mammals is the *placenta,* of partly foetal (embryonic) and partly maternal tissue. Food and oxygen may diffuse through the placental membranes from the maternal into the foetal blood, and waste material may diffuse in the opposite direction; but there is no direct connection between mother and foetus, either in the circulatory or the nervous system. The connection between the embryo and the placenta is provided by the *umbilical cord.*

Metamorphosis. Many animals attain adult form only after passing through a series of stages more or less unlike the adult. If these stages are very unlike the adult, development is said to be indirect *(complete metamorphosis);* if these stages are present but in general quite like the adult, development is said to be direct *(incomplete metamorphosis).* Common examples of the former are (1) frogs and toads — which pass through a tadpole stage, and (2) bees and butterflies — which have larval and pupal stages. (Among insects having complete metamorphosis, four stages may be recognized: egg, larva — during which stage there may be several molts, pupa, adult.) A common example of incomplete metamorphosis is furnished by the grasshopper, which passes through a series of nymphal stages all of which look somewhat like the adult. The differences are in body proportions, and presence and nature of wings or wing-pads. One may also consider the fresh-water mussel an example of this type of development. In this, the young mussel or *glochidium* lives as a parasite on the gills of certain fishes.

REVIEW QUESTIONS

1. Compare the methods of reproduction of unicellular and multicellular animals.
2. What are the fundamental characteristics of sexual reproduction?
3. Give the steps in gametogenesis, distinguishing between the processes of spermatogenesis and oögenesis.
4. What is the normal course of embryological development from fertilization on?
5. Give examples of various types of complexities in animal development.
6. Define: gonad, gamete, zygote, spermatid, polar body, blastula, gastrula, mesoderm, archenteron, telolecithal, animal pole, metagenesis, hermaphroditism, parthenogenesis.

PART TWO

SURVEY OF THE ANIMAL KINGDOM

Chapter VI

ANIMAL CLASSIFICATION

HISTORY OF CLASSIFICATION

Animal classification of a sort is as old as an interest in animals, but early attempts at scientific classification were merely devices for combining animals of apparent similarity into groups. The purpose was convenience. Modern classification, the science of *taxonomy,* has convenience as one of its purposes, naturally; but of major importance is its effort to bring out relationships of common descent—the evolutionary relationships. Such a purpose, of course, was not evident until the nineteenth century, and particularly not until after the publication of Charles Darwin's *Origin of Species,* in 1859. However, the technical basis of modern animal classification goes back much further, even antedating the work of Linnaeus, who is ordinarily credited with its introduction. Carolus Linnaeus, the Swedish botanist, in the 1750's introduced into general use the principle of scientific names now universally used, each species being designated by two names of Latin form, the genus and the species. This we call the *binomial system of nomenclature.* The close relationship of one species to another is, first of all, indicated by using the same generic name for both. Hence, the Linnaean system, while not on an evolutionary basis, lent itself well to this second and more important function of taxonomy. (See Chapter XXIII).

CATEGORIES OF CLASSIFICATION

The species is considered the unit of animal classification, all animals of the same "kind" belonging to the same species. (For a fuller account of taxonomy see Chapter XXIII). Closely related species constitute a *genus.* Similar genera (plural of genus) are combined to form a *family;* similar families, to form an *order;* similar orders, to form a *class;* and similar classes, to form a

47

phylum. Thus, the song sparrow, *Melospiza melodia,* is in the same genus with *Melospiza lincolni,* Lincoln's sparrow. With the chipping sparrow, juncos, and cardinal (none in the genus *Melospiza*) and many other species of finch-like birds, they comprise the family, Fringillidae. This family is combined with other families of the so-called song-birds (thrush family, Turdidae; jay family, Corvidae; and others) to constitute the order, Passeriformes. All orders of birds constitute the class, Aves, which, with the classes of mammals, reptiles, fishes, etc., forms the phylum, Chordata. The complete classification of an animal species involves at least the six categories given above. Intermediate categories are frequently added for convenience; thus a *superorder* may be a group of related orders which do not constitute an entire class; a *subfamily* is a group of related genera which do not constitute an entire family. The genus and species names together, the former always capitalized and the latter always spelled with an initial lower-case letter, constitute the *scientific name* of the species. The name of the person who first used the species name may follow that of the scientific name; zoological writers should, in fact, give author names with scientific names. The author's name is enclosed in parenthesis if the genus name differs from the one originally used with the species name. The author's name always refers to the man who named the species — not necessarily the genus. To illustrate: The name of the white-winged junco, *Junco aikeni* Ridgway, is in the genus of the original description by Ridgway; *Melospiza melodia* (Wilson) was called *Fringilla melodia* in Wilson's original description.

Examples:

Phylum:	Chordata	Chordata
Class:	Aves	Aves
Order:	Passeriformes	Anseriformes
Family:	Fringillidae	Anatidae
Genus:	Melospiza	Branta
Species:	melodia	canadensis
Scientific name:	Melospiza melodia	Branta canadensis
Common name:	Song sparrow	Canada goose

CRITERIA OF INCREASING COMPLEXITY

The major categories of classification are commonly arranged in an order corresponding roughly to an evolutionary scale — the simpler animals being listed first, the more complex last. Certain major characteristics constitute the most important criteria for this increasing complexity. These are suggested in the following parallel columns:

Less Complex	More Complex
One-celled	Many-celled
Asymmetry or radial symmetry	Bilateral symmetry
Diploblastic	Triploblastic
Coelom absent	Coelom present
Non-metameric	Metameric
But one opening in digestive tract	Digestive tract a continuous tube through body
Absence or simplicity of a given organ system	Presence and complexity of a given organ system

PHYLOGENETIC LINES

All major animal groups or phyla do not form one logical sequence, of course, and any linear arrangement of their names is somewhat arbitrary. The most advanced phyla are all quite complex, but they are also quite different from each other, and they have arrived at their present characteristics by diverse evolutionary routes. They have had a common ancestry, but their development has been along different channels, or *phylogenetic lines*.

The two most important phylogenetic lines seem to be associated with different methods of coelom formation in the embryo. Phyla in which the coelom originates as a space in the mesoderm have evolved in the direction of the mollusks and arthropods, while the chordates represent the end of a line in which the coelom arises as pouches from the embryonic gut.

CHARACTERISTICS OF THE PHYLA

The number of phyla recognized by any particular author depends upon the extent to which classes may be combined with

TABLE I. MAJOR CHARACTERIST

Phylum	Germ-Layers	Coelom	Segmentation
Protozoa	(Unicellular)	(Unicelluar)	(Unicellular)
Porifera	Two, plus mesenchyme	Absent	Absent
Coelenterata	Two, plus mesenchyme	Absent	Absent
Ctenophora	Triploblastic	Absent	Absent
Platyhelminthes	Triploblastic	Absent	Absent
Nematoda	Triploblastic	Pseudocoel	Absent
Acanthocephala	Triploblastic	Pseudocoel	Absent
Nematomorpha	Triploblastic	Pseudocoel	Absent
Rotatoria	Triploblastic	Pseudocoel	Absent
Gastrotricha	Triploblastic	Pseudocoel	Absent
Tardigrada	Triploblastic	Coelom	Four fused segments
Chaetognatha	Triploblastic	Coelom (3 compartments)	Absent
Bryozoa	Triploblastic	Pseudocoel or coelom	Absent
Brachiopoda	Triploblastic	Coelom	Absent
Echinodermata	Triploblastic	Coelom	Absent
Annelida	Triploblastic	Coelom (segmental compartments)	Numerous similar segments
Onychophora	Triploblastic	Vestigial coelom	Segments similar
Arthropoda	Triploblastic	Vestigial coelom	Segments similar or unlike
Mollusca	Triploblastic	Coelom	Absent
Chordata	Triploblastic	Coelom (2-4 compartments, usually)	Segments unlike

Digestive System	Other Significant Morphological Characteristics
Intracellular	One-celled animals (= acellular animals)
Collar-cells, intracellular	Canal system through which water circulates; no specialized organ systems.
Gastrovascular cavity	Radial symmetry; stinging cells in ectoderm; mesogloea between ectoderm and endoderm.
Gastrovascular cavity	Biradial symmetry; paddle plates as locomotor organs.
Gastrovascular cavity (complete canal in Nemertea)	Bilateral symmetry; body usually flattened; flame cells in excretory system.
Complete canal	Elongated cylindrical body; cilia entirely absent; excretory system present.
No digestive organs	Hook-bearing proboscis; excretory system present.
Complete canal (mouth may be absent)	Body thread-like; excretory system absent.
Complete canal	Microscopic in size; ciliated oral disk.
Complete canal	Microscopic in size; cilia on ventral surface.
Complete canal	Four pairs of non-jointed legs.
Complete canal	Small, arrow-worms; excretory system absent.
Complete canal	Small size; usually colonial; lophophore present; no circulatory system.
Complete canal	Enclosed between dorsal and ventral shells; lophophore present; circulatory system present.
Complete canal (anus may be non-functional)	Radial symmetry, with five antimeres; usually a hard spiny covering.
Complete canal	Closed blood vascular system; ventral chain of segmental ganglia; paired nephridia.
Complete canal	Soft integument; paired nephridia; tracheae; open blood vascular system.
Complete canal	Chitinous exoskeleton; paired, jointed appendages; open blood vascular system.
Complete canal	Soft body, usually with shell; respiratory organs in mantle cavity; closed blood vascular system.
Complete canal	Notochord; dorsal tubular nerve cord; pharyngeal respiratory system.

each other or recognized as separate phyla. Consequently a zoologist cannot say that there is any given number of animal phyla. The phyla recognized in this Outline are included in the report of a special committee of Section F (Zoology), American Association for the Advancement of Science, published in 1948 (see reference: Pearse, A. S.). These phyla, with their major characteristics, are summarized in Table I. This table will be a useful reference in connection with Chapters VII-XXI inclusive.

REVIEW QUESTIONS

1. How are animals classified? Give an example.
2. What are the fundamental criteria for distinguishing between simple and more advanced types of animals?
3. Name and briefly characterize the animal phyla.

Chapter VII

PROTOZOA

CHARACTERISTICS OF THE PHYLUM PROTOZOA

Protozoa are animals consisting of a single cell. They are much more complex in structure than single cells of many-celled animals (and therefore are called "acellular" by some zoologists), but the entire organism is enclosed within a single plasma membrane. They are small, ranging from less than ten microns to, rarely, a quarter inch in length. They inhabit fresh water, the ocean, damp soil, and the bodies of other animals.

CLASSES OF THE PHYLUM PROTOZOA

The Protozoa are commonly divided into five classes, as follows:

Class Mastigophora (Flagellata). Locomotion by means of one to several flagella. (Examples: *Euglena, Trypanosoma*).

Class Sarcodina (Rhizopoda). Locomotion by means of pseudopodia. (Examples: *Amoeba, Entamoeba*).

Class Sporozoa. Usually no means of locomotion. Spore-producing parasitic protozoa. (Examples: *Plasmodium, Babesia*).

Class Ciliata (Infusoria). Locomotion by means of cilia. (Examples: *Paramecium, Balantidium*).

Class Suctoria. Cilia present in young stages; mature individuals without special means of locomotion. This class is sometimes included under Ciliata. (Example: *Sphaerophrya*).

EXAMPLES OF THE PHYLUM PROTOZOA

Class Mastigophora (Flagellata). The most frequently studied example of this class is Euglena, which, because it possesses chlorophyll (see page 20), is just as often classified as a plant (one of the algae, in that case) as an animal. Other examples of importance are found among the disease-producing flagellates, *e.g.,* the cause of African sleeping sickness.

1. EUGLENA is a genus of green flagellates whose species occur commonly in ponds, often forming extensive green surface scums. (Fig. 14).

   a. *Morphology.* It is usually spindle-shaped, but variable; from 25 to more than 100 microns long. A single *flagellum,* at the anterior end, extends from

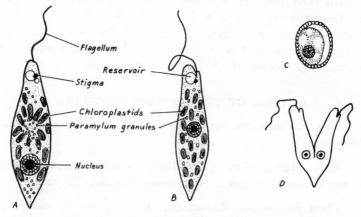

Fig. 14. Euglena. A, *Euglena viridis* Ehrbg., (redrawn after Doflein); B, *Euglena gracilis* Klebs; C, cyst of *Euglena viridis* (redrawn from Doflein after Tschenzoff); D, dividing Euglena, diagrammatic.

a "gullet." Opening into the latter is a *reservoir,* into which open several small *contractile vacuoles.* A red *stigma,* or "eye-spot," is in the anterior portion, near the reservoir. Chloroplastids are usually numerous. Granules of *paramylum,* a carbohydrate stored food, occur in the cytoplasm. The nucleus is single, the chromatin concentrated centrally in it. (Fig. 14, A, B).

   b. *Physiology.* Nutrition *autotrophic* (manufacturing its own food) or *saprophytic* (absorbing dissolved food from the surrounding medium). Euglena is able to manufacture food only in the presence of light, but can maintain itself in darkness, for long periods, saprophytically. Under the latter circumstances the green color disappears — it becomes *etiolated*. It does not ingest solid food, the "gullet" being. misnamed. Respiration takes place through the surface membrane. Locomotion is brought about by the flagellum. Under certain conditions Euglena shows positive *phototaxis,* turning and swimming toward a source of light. A form of rhythmic contraction (euglenoid movement) occurs occasionally; it is not a method of locomotion. Euglena forms *cysts* in which individuals may survive drying and other unfavorable conditions. (Fig. 14, C).

c. *Reproduction.* Asexual, by *longitudinal fission,* division beginning at the anterior end. (Fig. 14, D).

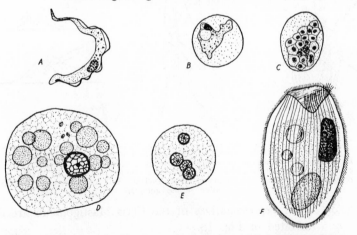

Fig. 15. Protozoa causing diseases of man. A. *Trypanosoma gambiense* Dutton, cause of African sleeping sickness. B,C, *Plasmodium vivax* Grassi and Feletti, cause of tertian malaria, in human red blood corpuscles; B, amoeboid form; C, spore-formation. D,E, *Entamoeba histolytica* Schaudinn, cause of amoebic dysentery; D, active form, containing red corpuscles in various stages of digestion; E, cyst. F. *Balantidium coli* (Malmsten), cause of balantidial dysentery. All approximately X1500. (Redrawn after Doflein.)

2. The TRYPANOSOMES are a group of flagellates occurring as parasites in the blood of vertebrates. They are characterized by the possession of a flagellum which arises near the posterior end, extends forward as the border of an *undulating membrane,* and emerges as a free

filament at the anterior end. *Trypanosoma gambiense* Dutton (Fig. 15) is the cause of African sleeping sickness. It is about twenty-five microns in length. In man it lives and reproduces (by fission) in the blood and other body fluids, including the cerebrospinal fluid. It is conveyed from one human host to another by the agency of a blood-sucking fly, *Glossina palpalis* Linn., one of the tsetse-flies. (Fig. 16). Rapid reproduction of the trypanosome occurs in the digestive canal of the fly. The area in which man may be infected is limited to the geographic range of the fly, the *insect vector* of sleeping sickness, to parts of central and west Africa.

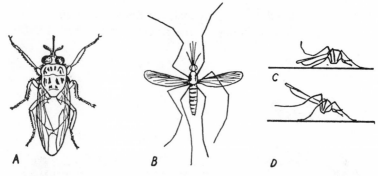

Fig. 16. Insect vectors (carriers) of protozoan diseases in man. A. The tsetse fly, *Glossina palpalis* L., carrier of the organism of African sleeping sickness. B. A mosquito of the genus *Anopheles,* carrier of malarial organisms. C, diagrammatic profile of a *Culex* mosquito, not a carrier, at rest; D, profile of *Anopheles,* a carrier. (A, redrawn after Doflein; B-D redrawn from Doflein after various authors.)

3. Other representatives of the Class Mastigophora are illustrated in Fig. 18.

Class Sarcodina (Rhizopoda). The amoeboid protozoa possess a body of indefinite shape, changing in outline by the movements of flowing processes of protoplasm, *the pseudopodia* ("false-feet"). *Amoeba,* a free-living animal, is the best known example. Some of the other free-living forms are not naked, like *Amoeba,* but enclosed within a shell-like case, *e.g.,* the foraminifera, which, as fossils, are valuable in determining the age of rock strata. There are also parasitic rhizopods, one being the cause of amoebic dysentery in man.

1. AMOEBA, a genus of naked, free-living rhizopods. (Fig. 17).

   a. *Morphology.* The species of *Amoeba* most commonly studied vary from approximately 200 to 300 microns in diameter; the external form is asymmetrical, continuously changing during locomotion. The cytoplasm is divided into an external clearer

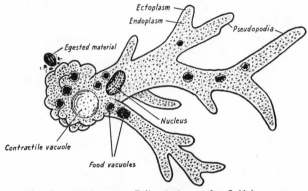

Fig. 17. *Amoeba proteus* Pallas (redrawn after Leidy).

   region, the *ectoplasm,* and an inner, more opaque region, the *endoplasm.* The single, definite nucleus is a flattened sphere. There is typically one contractile vacuole. Numerous food vacuoles are ordinarily present.

   b. *Physiology.* Locomotion is by flowing extensions of protoplasm, the pseudopodia. These seem to be formed by temporary liquefactions of the viscous outer portion of the endoplasm — the *plasmagel.* The more liquid *plasmasol* is extruded, as the liquefaction takes place, to form the pseudopodium. Solid food is ingested (*holozoic* nutrition) by pseudopodia, which flow around the food, enclosing it and some of the surrounding medium in the food vacuole thus formed. Digestion occurs within the cytoplasm, in food vacuoles. Undigested material may be egested at any part of the cell surface. Respiratory exchange takes place through the entire surface. The contractile vacuole excretes water chiefly, maintaining a high internal osmotic pressure. The *Amoeba* responds, through positive and negative movements, or contraction, to a variety of different stimuli.

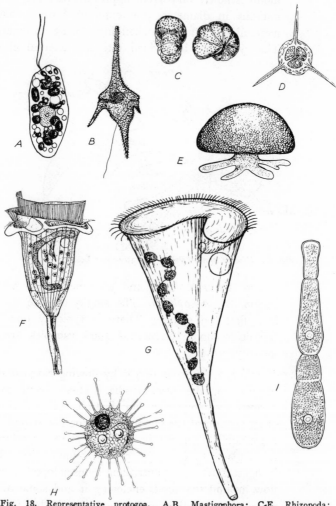

Fig. 18. Representative protozoa. A,B, Mastigophora; C-E, Rhizopoda; F,G, Ciliata; H, Suctoria; I, Sporozoa. A, *Chilomonas paramecium* Ehrbg., (after Mast and Pace); B, a dinoflagellate, *Ceratium hirundinella* (O. F. Müller) (redrawn from Doflein after Lauterborn); C, a foraminiferan, *Anomalina grosserugosa* Gümbel (after Gümbel); D, a radiolarian shell, *Archibursa tripodiscus* Haeckel (after Haeckel); E, a species of *Arcella* (redrawn after Doflein); F, *Carchesium polypinum* Ehrbg., (redrawn after Doflein); G, *Stentor coeruleus* Ehrbg., (redrawn after Doflein); H, *Sphaerophrya magna* Maupas (redrawn from Doflein after Maupas); I, a gregarine, *Gregarina blattarum* (Siebold) (from Doflein after R. Hertwig).

c. *Reproduction* is asexual, by fission. A form of sporulation (multiple fission) has also been observed.

2. ENTAMOEBA HISTOLYTICA Schaudinn is the causative organism of amoebic dysentery. It is a naked amoeba, twenty to thirty microns in diameter, which lives in the human intestine. There it invades the intestinal wall by destruction of cells. The red blood corpuscles which escape from the blood capillaries in the bleeding thus induced are engulfed by *Entamoeba*. Reproduction is by fission. Cysts, containing four nuclei, are produced. (Fig. 15, C). These leave the body in the feces. Contaminated water is the chief means of transfer of the infection to a new host. Transfer by *carriers* who are food-handlers is possible, and this may explain the occurrence of a few infected persons in every hundred, on the average, in the United States.

3. Other representatives of the Class Rhizopoda are illustrated in Fig. 18.

Class Sporozoa. The Sporozoa are parasitic protozoa which reproduce by the formation of *spores,* a type of rapid, multiple reproduction. The most important of these for man are the causative organisms of the different types of malaria.

1. PLASMODIUM (Figs. 15 and 19) is the genus to which the organisms causing human malaria belong. Several species occur which are causes of different types of malaria. The organisms, which live in the red corpuscles of the human blood stream, are extremely small — one species attaining a maximum diameter of about five microns. The life cycle is complicated, only asexual reproduction (by sporulation) occurring in the primary host (man), but sexual reproduction taking place in the insect vector of malaria (the secondary host), a mosquito of the genus *Anopheles*. (Fig. 16). For details of the life cycle of Plasmodium see Fig. 19.

2. OTHER SPOROZOA are illustrated in Figs. 18 and 20. The latter figure illustrates the life cycle of the causative

organism of Texas fever of cattle. This is transmitted
by the cattle tick. (Fig. 20).

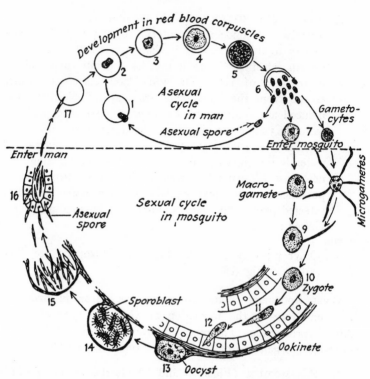

Fig. 19. Diagram of the life cycle of the malarial parasite (*Plasmodium*) showing
the asexual cycle in man (1-6, 17) and the sexual cycle in a mosquito of the genus
Anopheles (in stomach 8-12, cyst on stomach wall 13-15, in salivary gland 16).[1]

Class Ciliata (Infusoria). The cilia-bearing protozoa are
chiefly free-living. They are common in ponds. The most frequently studied example is *Paramecium*.

1. PARAMECIUM is a genus of moderately large, spindle- or
   cigar-shaped protozoa, rather uniformly covered with cilia.
   (Fig. 21).

   a. *Morphology. Paramecium* is about 250 microns long,
      asymmetrically cigar-shaped. A spiral *oral groove*

leads from the anterior end to the *gullet,* about half
way back. The ectoplasm is thin, containing numerous *trichocysts,* structures which (presumably in de-
fense) are exuded and hardened as threads. One

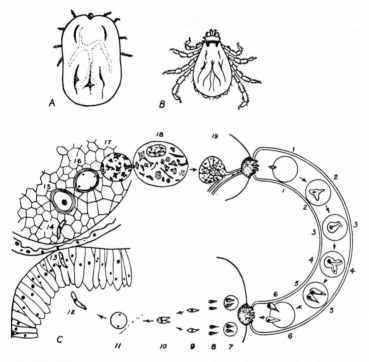

Fig. 20. Life cycle of the organism causing Texas fever in cattle. A, gorged
female, and B, male, of *Margaropus annulatus* (Say), the cattle tick which transmits the organism. C, diagram illustrating life cycle of *Babesia bigemina* (Smith
and Kilbourne), a sporozoan, in the blood of cattle and in the tick; 1-6, asexual
division in erythrocytes of cattle; 7-12, sexual cycle in gut of tick; 13-14, zygote
passes through stomach wall and oviduct wall into ovum; 15-18, spores formed
may occur in cells destined to become part of the salivary gland (19), and hence
have ready access to the blood of cattle through the bite of the tick. (A,B, from
Salmon and Stiles; C from Dennis in the University of California Publications
in Zoology, vol. 36, reprinted with the permission of the University of California
Press.)

large *macronucleus* is present, and one or two small
micronuclei (one in *Paramecium caudatum* Ehrbg.,
the species usually studied). There are typically two
contractile vacuoles, and numerous food vacuoles.
(Fig. 21).

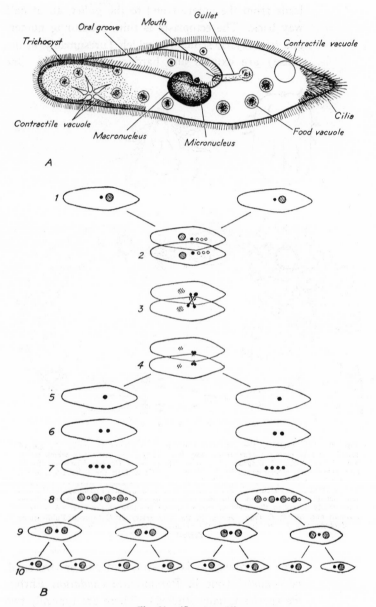

A

B

Fig. 21. (See page 63).

b. *Physiology.* Nutrition is holozoic, bacteria and other small food particles being ingested through the gullet and formed into food vacuoles. These follow a definite course through the cytosome during the process of digestion, and the undigested portion is egested at a definite region on one side, the *anus.* The contractile vacuoles regulate osmotic pressure, and probably aid in excretion. Respiratory exchanges take place through the surface membrane. In response to certain stimuli, *Paramecium* gives what is called the *avoiding reaction* — consisting of backing away at an angle and swimming forward in a new path. The ordinary path in forward progression is a spiral, the animal rotating on its long axis while following the spiral path.

c. *Reproduction.* In asexual reproduction, *Paramecium* divides by *transverse fission,* the macronucleus dividing amitotically, the micronucleus or -nuclei, mitotically, within the nuclear membrane. (Fig. 7, B). A form of sexual reproduction occurs, *conjugation,* in which nuclear exchanges occur between two individuals which then separate and rapidly divide into, in each case, four small individuals. (Fig. 21). A nuclear reorganization comparable to this process but involving only a single individual also takes place in *Paramecium.* This process is *endomixis.*

2. OTHER FREE-LIVING CILIATES are illustrated in Fig. 18. *Balantidium coli* (Malmsten), which occasionally parasitizes man (living in the intestine and inducing dysentery-like symptoms) is illustrated in Fig. 15.

Fig. 21. *Paramecium caudatum* Ehrbg. A. Details of morphology. B Stages in conjugation, diagrammatically represented. Macronuclei are large cross-hatched circles; micronuclei are small circles, black if persistent, hollow if disintegrating. The individuals at 1 fuse (2) by a protoplasmic bridge; the macronuclei disintegrate (3,4); each micronucleus divides twice, forming four; three of these disintegrate (2), the fourth dividing (3), half of the divided micronucleus migrating into the other conjugant and fusing (4) with the non-migratory daughter micronucleus; the animals separate, each with a fusion micronucleus (5) which divides three times, eventually forming four micro- and four macronuclei (8); three of the former disintegrate (8); the individual then divides twice, the macronuclei being segregated while the micronucleus forms four by dividing twice (9, 10). Each ex-conjugant gives rise to four small individuals, each with completely reorganized nuclear constitution.

Class Suctoria. Protozoa of this class are, in the adult stage, if free-living attached to some object by a stalk. Some species parasitize other protozoa. Tentacles, piercing or suctorial, or of both types, are present on the adult, but cilia are absent, although the latter occur on the (free-swimming) embryos. Nutrition is holozoic. Reproduction is typically by the formation of buds. (Fig. 18).

REVIEW QUESTIONS

1. Give the characteristics of the Phylum Protozoa and its five classes.
2. Why may Euglena be considered a plant? an animal?
3. Give the classification, characteristics, and life-histories of the protozoa causing African sleeping sickness, amoebic dysentery, malaria, Texas fever.
4. What are the similarities and differences between Amoeba and Paramecium?
5. How does reproduction take place in protozoa?

CHAPTER VIII

PORIFERA, COELENTERATA, CTENOPHORA

The phyla included in this chapter are the most primitive of the Metazoa, but they do not constitute a natural group. The Porifera (sponges) represent a very primitive group of radially symmetrical or asymmetrical animals not in the main line of evolution of the Metazoa. They are sometimes distinguished from the remaining Metazoa (which constitute the Branch Enterozoa) as the Branch Parazoa. The Coelenterata (Cnidaria) and Ctenophora are closely related and are occasionally considered members of the same phylum, though not in this Outline. The former are radially, the latter, biradially, symmetrical; the former have two germ-layers (are "diploblastic"); the latter, by some interpretations, are triploblastic.

CHARACTERISTICS OF THE PHYLUM PORIFERA

The Porifera are the sponges; they are mostly marine, but some occur in fresh-water. They are sessile, inactive organisms in the adult stage. A sponge contains a central cavity (the so-

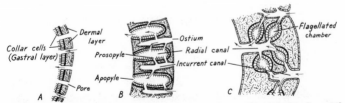

Fig. 22. Diagrams illustrating the different degrees of complexity in canal systems of sponges. The cross-hatched layer is the gastral layer, consisting of collar cells; it is separated from the dermal layer (stippled) by a heavy black line. In each case only a small segment of the wall of the sponge is illustrated, with gastral cavity to the left. Direction of water movement is indicated by arrows. A, ascon type of olynthus; B, sycon type (as in *Grantia*); C, leucon type. The latter type is extremely variable. (Modified from various sources.)

called cloaca or gastral cavity) surrounded by a body wall penetrated by a series of canals of varying degrees of complexity. (Fig. 22). The internal cavity opens to the outside by the osculum, an opening at the distal end. Microscopic food particles, the source of nutrition, are removed from the currents of water passing through the canal system by the flagellated collar cells. A skeleton of spicules (of lime, silica [glass], or spongin) supports the organism. There are no specialized organ systems. A single "sponge" may be a colony of individuals all of which have budded from one parent. Sponges are diploblastic, the two germ-layers not being ectoderm and endoderm but epidermis and collar cells, respectively, with scattered cells between. Reproduction takes place sexually (they are hermaphroditic), and by budding. Regenerative ability is possessed to a remarkable degree by certain sponges.

CLASSES OF THE PHYLUM PORIFERA

Class Calcarea. Marine sponges with spicules of lime. (Examples: *Leucosolenia, Grantia.*)

Class Hexactinellida. Marine sponges with six-rayed siliceous spicules. (Example: Venus' flower-basket.)

Class Demospongia. Marine and fresh-water sponges with spicules or fibers of spongin or silica (if of the latter material they are not six-rayed) or both. (Examples: *Spongilla,* in fresh-water; sponges of commerce.)

(Note: According to more recent classification, the second and third classes are combined into one, the Class Noncalcarea.)

EXAMPLES OF THE PHYLUM PORIFERA
Grantia.

1. MORPHOLOGY AND PHYSIOLOGY. *Grantia* is a genus of simple cylindrical sponges, about an inch long, common along the Atlantic coast. The canal system is of the *sycon* type, *i. e., incurrent* and *radial canals* parallel each other, and are connected by minute pores *(prosopyles).* The incurrent canals have smooth lining cells; the radial canals are lined with flagellated *collar cells,* which ingest food. Water passes through *ostia* (incurrent pores), incurrent canals, prosopyles, radial canals (flagellated chambers), *apopyles, cloaca* or *gastral cavity,* and out through the *osculum,* and in that order. (Figs. 22 and 23). The skeleton consists of calcareous mon- and triaxon *spicules.*

2. REPRODUCTION. Asexual reproduction occurs by the formation of buds near the base of the parent, which then separate as independent individuals. In sexual reproduction both types of gametes are produced by one Grantia, *i. e.*, it is hermaphroditic. The zygote divides several times, forming a blastula-like structure (Fig. 23, C), from which the *amphiblastula* (early embryo) develops. This embryo escapes from the osculum of the parent. It then invaginates in such fashion that its outer flagellated cells now line the inner cavity; it becomes attached, and develops into the mature sponge. Hence, although essentially diploblastic, the ectoderm of the embryo comes to occupy the inner part of the adult, while the outer covering is derived from endoderm. This is characteristic of sponges in general.

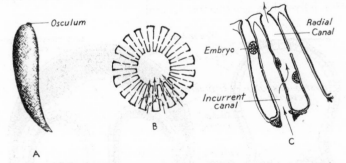

Fig. 23. *Grantia.* A. External appearance. B. Diagram of a cross section. C. Portion of body wall in cross-section, enlarged. Direction of water-movement is indicated by arrows. Water leaves the gastral cavity by the osculum. (Compare B and C with Fig. 22, B).

Leucosolenia. This sponge is similar to Grantia, but somewhat smaller, more slender, and with a slightly less-complicated canal system — although the latter is really of the sycon type.

Commercial Sponges. The sponges of commerce are complex in canal structure (leucon or rhagon type), and with a fibrous skeleton of spongin, an organic material. The spongin is stiff when dry, but pliable when wet. This skeleton of spongin constitutes the commercial "sponge" — the living material having died, disintegrated, and been washed away during the process of cleaning for the market. Most commercial sponges come from the Mediterranean, West Indies, and Florida. In all these areas a definite industry exists, with many boats and men employed to collect and clean the sponges.

CHARACTERISTICS OF THE PHYLUM COELENTERATA (CNIDARIA)

Most coelenterates are marine; a few inhabit fresh water. They have two cell layers, outer epidermis and inner gastrodermis, the latter lining the gastrovascular cavity, its single opening functioning as both mouth and anus. Stinging cells are present in the epidermis (hence the name Cnidaria). Between epidermis and gastrodermis is the jelly-like mesogloea, sometimes with scattered cells. Two body forms occur, the polyp and the medusa. (Fig. 24). These may develop alternately during the life cycle. Examples: *Hydra*, jelly-fishes, sea-anemones, corals.

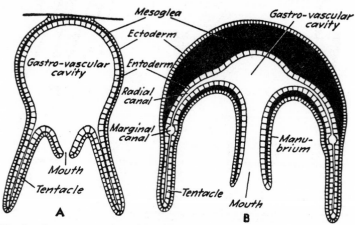

Fig. 24.   Diagram illustrating the morphological similarities and differences between a polyp (A) and a medusa (B).[1]

Polyp. The general form is cylindrical, one end (proximal) attached; the distal end contains a mouth surrounded by tentacles. This form may occur in colonies. Gonads are external or internal. (Fig. 24A).

---

[1] Reprinted by permission from *Animal Biology*, by R. H. Wolcott, published by the McGraw-Hill Book Company, Inc.

Medusa. The general form is umbrella- or bell-shaped. The mouth is in the manubrium, which corresponds to the handle of the "umbrella" or the clapper of the "bell." The digestive cavity has four main branches in the umbrella portion, the radial canals. These open into the circular canal around the rim. Tentacles hang from the margin of the umbrella surface. Gonads are suspended under the radial canals — opening internally in some medusae, externally in others. (Fig. 24B).

CLASSES OF THE PHYLUM COELENTERATA

Class Hydrozoa. Mostly colonial, and of rather small size. Polyp form usually predominant; it may be the only body form. Polyps of some species produce medusae, by budding. Medusae of this group possess a velum (a circular shelf within

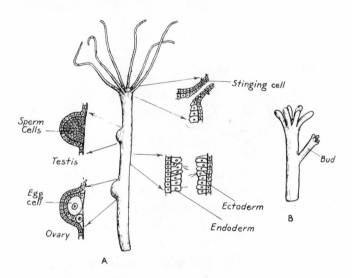

Fig. 25. *Hydra.* A. Expanded individual, bearing gonads. Internal structures are shown in longitudinal section, enlarged, projected from four regions (indicated by arrows). B. A partially contracted individual, bearing a bud.

the umbrella), and the margin of the umbrella surface lacks notches. (Examples: *Hydra, Obelia, Gonionemus,* Portuguese man-of-war.)

Class Scyphozoa. Medusa form predominant, although a polyp-like stage is present. Medusae without velum, and with

the margin of the umbrella notched. Of moderately large size—
an inch to several feet in diameter. (Example: jelly-fish.)

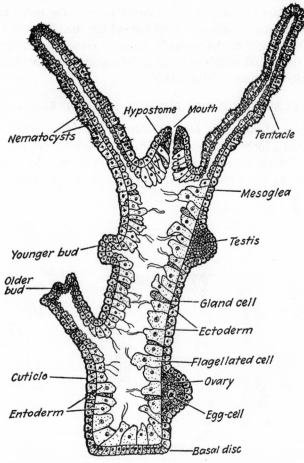

Fig. 26. Somewhat diagrammatic longitudinal section of a hydra,
with two buds on the left, and a spermary and ovary on the right.[1]

Class Anthozoa. Polyp form only, the polyp possessing
a gullet or stomodaeum, and vertical partitions (mesenteries) which
divide the gastrovascular cavity into compartments. (Example:
sea-anemones, corals.)

1 Reprinted by permission from *Animal Biology*, by R. H. Wolcott, published by the
McGraw-Hill Book Company, Inc.

EXAMPLES OF THE PHYLUM COELENTERATA

Class Hydrozoa.

1. HYDRA, a genus of fresh-water polyps, has no medusa stage. The common species are about one-quarter to one-half inch long. They possess some six to ten *tentacles,* surrounding an elevation, the *hypostome,* in which the mouth is located. Hydras are highly contractile, containing cells which function as combined sensory and muscular elements. *Cnidoblasts* (stinging cells) containing *nematocysts* capable of suddenly extruding a barbed thread or entangling thread occur in the ectoderm. They are particularly numerous on the tentacles. Reproduction is sexual, or by budding. In the former case, gonads appear as external swellings. (Figs. 25, 26).

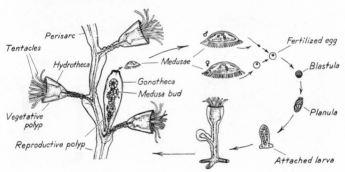

Fig. 27. *Obelia,* one of the colonial Hydrozoa. At the left, a portion of a colony, which reproduces asexually, by budding; at the right, diagrammatically shown, the sexual portion of the life cycle.

2. OBELIA is a marine colonial hydrozoan of very small size. A colony of polyps develops asexually from a zygote, the polyps being of two kinds — *vegetative* (feeding) and *reproductive.* Each polyp is surrounded by a transparent covering, the *hydrotheca* about vegetative, the *gonotheca* about reproductive polyps. All polyps are connected with each other by a hollow stem and branches. Reproductive polyps produce medusae by budding. These swim away when mature. They are sexually reproductive. Thus there is an alternation of asexual and sexual methods of reproduction, this alternation of reproductive methods being called *metagenesis.* (Fig. 27).

3. GONIONEMUS is a genus of marine (brackish-water) hydrozoa with a fairly large medusa (over one-half inch in diameter). The medusa is similar to that of Obelia. It is studied in American laboratories chiefly because its size is of advantage in seeing the characteristics of the hydrozoan medusa.

Class Scyphozoa. The true jelly-fishes are medusae with a notched margin, no velum, radial canals with complex branches, and gonads in pouches of the gastric cavity. *Aurelia,* a common genus along the Atlantic coast, is about three to four inches in

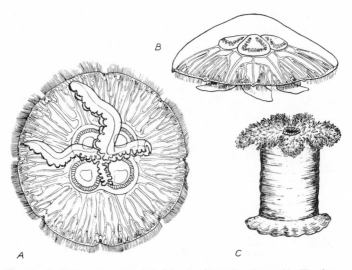

Fig. 28. A. Oral surface of a jelly-fish, *Aurelia aurita* (Lamarck). The four oral arms, two of which have been cut, radiate from the mouth opening, which is concealed. The four rounded areas are gastric pouches, the gonads encircling their outer margins. The complexly branched canal system, and the notched margin, are characteristics of the Scyphozoa. (After A. G. Mayer, in the Medusae of the World, used by permission of the Carnegie Institution of Washington). B. Side view of *Aurelia aurita.* (After C. W. Hargitt, in Bulletin U. S. Bureau of Fisheries, 1904). C. Side view of *Metridium,* a common sea-anemone. The cylindrical body form, and numerous tentacles on an oral disk, are characteristics of the Anthozoa. (Copyright by General Biological Supply House, Chicago, used by permission). All figures about half natural size.

diameter; its margin possesses eight notches, the number most frequently found in Scyphozoa. (Fig. 28). In size, jelly-fishes range up to several feet in diameter. If a polyp stage in the life history occurs it is subordinate. Reproduction of the polyp is asexual, the process being *strobilation* (terminal budding); repro-

duction of the medusa is sexual. The nematocysts of some jelly-
fishes are quite poisonous to man, producing severe local irritation
or injury to sea bathers.

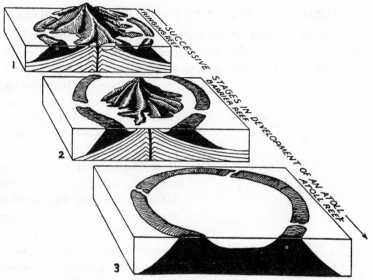

Fig. 29. Origin and evolution of an atoll according to the subsidence theory.[1]

Class Anthozoa. The sea-anemones (Fig. 28) and coral
animals are polyp-like in form, and have no medusa stage. They
are sessile, and may be enclosed within a calcareous external skeleton called "coral." Tentacles are numerous, being in several rows
around the elongated mouth. The latter opens into a tube, the
gullet or *stomodaeum,* which extends some distance into the
gastrovascular cavity. Surrounding the stomodaeum, the gastrovascular cavity is divided into several compartments by vertical
partitions, the *mesenteries.* Reproduction may be asexual or sexual
(the gonads lying along the internal margins of the mesenteries).
Reef-forming corals are limited for their activity to water, in the
warmer seas, of depths less than about 150 feet. Consequently,
there is a problem in explaining the existence of reefs extending
to much greater depths. A theory of coral-reef formation should

1 Reprinted by permission from *An Outline of the Principles of Geology,* by Richard
M. Field, published by Barnes and Noble, Inc.

also explain the existence of the three types of reefs, *fringing* and *barrier reefs* and *atolls*. The subsidence theory, proposed by Charles Darwin, is the most widely accepted theory today. (Fig. 29).

CHARACTERISTICS OF THE PHYLUM CTENOPHORA

The comb-jellies or sea-walnuts are, in most cases, walnut-shaped (i. e., biradially symmetrical) animals which are nearly transparent. A few species are, however, flattened in form. Externally there are eight rows of *paddle-plates*, each plate composed of a row of fused cilia. Each row, viewed from the edge, is a comb-like series of plates, the plates, corresponding to the teeth of the comb. For this reason the animals are called comb-jellies. There are usually two trailing tentacles. The animals swim with the mouth (oral end) forward. Ctenophores possess a gastrovascular cavity, with a stomodaeum and canals, two of the latter with excretory openings. They reproduce sexually, and are hermaphroditic. There is some difference of opinion as to whether they are diploblastic or triploblastic. The cell layers are thin, with a considerable thickness of non-cellular mesogloea. Between the outer and inner layers occur mesenchyme cells which may, by some interpretations, be considered mesoderm. By such interpretation ctenophores are triploblastic. *Mnemiopsis* (Fig. 30), irregularly common on our Atlantic coast, is about two to three inches high, and is luminescent; it is one source of the "phosphorescence" of the sea — which has nothing to do with phosphorus, and is more properly called bioluminescence. Venus' girdle and *Beroë* are other examples of the Ctenophora.

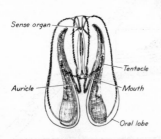

Fig. 30. *Mnemiopsis*, a common ctenophore of the Atlantic coast; side view. (After A. G. Mayer, in the Ctenophores of the Atlantic Coast of North America, used by permission of the Carnegie Institution of Washington).

REVIEW QUESTIONS

1. What are the characteristics of the Porifera? How do sponges differ in fundamental plan from other Metazoa?
2. Discuss the characteristics of Grantia, particularly its canal system. Illustrate the latter with a diagram.

3. Compare a polyp and a medusa.
4. Name and characterize the Classes of Coelenterata.
5. Describe in detail, and compare with each other, Hydra and Obelia.
6. Trace the life-history of Obelia.
7. What are corals? What is the subsidence theory of coral-reef formation?
8. By what criteria may we consider the Ctenophora more advanced than the Coelenterata?

CHAPTER IX

PLATYHELMINTHES, NEMATODA, ACANTHOCEPHALA, NEMATOMORPHA

Representatives of these phyla are elongated, bilaterally symmetrical animals of primitive structure. None are metameric. Many are parasites (see Chapter XXV). The Platyhelminthes are the flatworms. The Nematoda (Nematoidea), Acanthocephala, and Nematomorpha are round- or thread-worms.

(Note: One class of the Platyhelminthes, the Nemertea, is recognized by some zoologists as an independent phylum. In some schemes of classification in current use the Nematomorpha are combined with the Nematoda to form the Phylum Nemathelminthes; in a few classifications the Acanthocephala are also considered with the same group.)

CHARACTERISTICS OF THE PHYLUM PLATYHELMINTHES

The flatworms are triploblastic, but without a coelom. The digestive cavity (absent in tapeworms) is a gastrovascular cavity, except in the nemerteans. Although the simplest animals possessing bilateral symmetry, they have definite excretory, nervous, and reproductive systems. Hermaphroditism is the rule, except in nemerteans. The majority of the species are parasites, several being serious parasites of man and other animals. The phylum includes the planarians, common fresh-water animals; the flukes and tapeworms, all parasites — many with complicated life cycles involving several hosts; the nemerteans, chiefly marine, free-living ribbon-worms.

CLASSES OF THE PHYLUM PLATYHELMINTHES

Class Turbellaria. Fresh-water, marine, land (moist earth), or rarely parasitic flatworms. External epithelium ciliated, secreting mucous and possessing peculiar rod-like bodies, the rhabdites. (Example: *Dugesia*, formerly called *Planaria*.)

Class Trematoda. Flukes, all parasites — chiefly of vertebrates. External cilia absent, body covered by a cuticle. Suckers
usually present. Gastrovascular cavity present. Internal parasites
in this group have two or more alternate hosts. (Examples: sheep
liver-fluke, *Fasciola;* human liver-fluke, *Clonorchis.)*

Class Cestoda (Cestoidea). Tapeworms, all parasites, the
adults living in the digestive tracts of vertebrates. Body covering
a cuticle. Digestive cavity and mouth absent. Body usually a
ribbon-like chain of segments (proglottids) attached to the head
(scolex). (Example: pork tapeworm of man.)

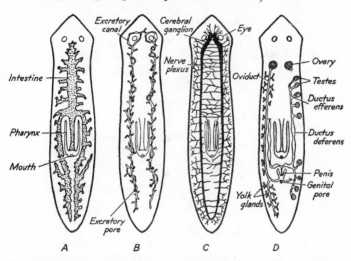

Fig. 31. Diagrams illustrating the internal morphology of *Planaria.* A, gastrovascular cavity; B, excretory system; C, nervous system; D, reproductive
system. (A,B,C, from specimens, and various authors; D, reprinted by permission from *Textbook of General Zoology,* by Curtis and Guthrie, published by
John Wiley & Sons, Inc.). About four times natural size.

Class Nemertea (Nemertinea). Ribbon-worms, mostly
marine; free-living. Body ciliated, usually flattened. Complete
digestive tract. Blood-vascular system. No coelom. May be considered separate phylum. (Example: *Cerebratulus.)*

EXAMPLES OF THE PHYLUM PLATYHELMINTHES

Class Turbellaria. *Dugesia.* (Figs. 31 - 33) is a genus of
small, fresh-water, free-living flatworms. The body surface is
ciliated. Two eye spots are present. From the mouth, on the ven-

tral surface near the center, a protrusible *pharynx (proboscis)* leads into the digestive cavity, an *intestine* of three main branches, one anterior and two posterior. Each main branch has many small lateral branches. Since an anus is absent, the digestive cavity is essentially a gastrovascular cavity—similar to that of coelenterates. The excretory system consists of two longitudinal *excretory tubes*

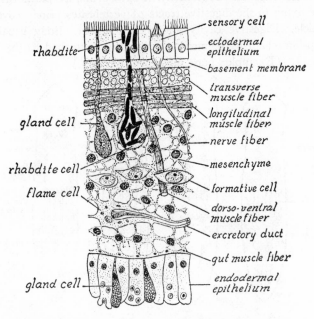

Fig. 32. Histology of a planarian; section of worm to show cellular structure; diagrammatic.[1]

leading from *flame cells,* with an anterior cross connection; the whole system opens to the outside through two dorsal *excretory pores.* The nervous system has two main longitudinal trunks with an anterior cross connection, and two anterior *ganglia* under the eye spots. The reproductive system is complex, the animal hermaphroditic. It may or may not be self-fertilizing. Some species reproduce by fragmentation. Some species possess marked powers of regeneration. Fragments from near the anterior end of the

1 Reprinted by permission from *Textbook of General Zoology,* by Curtis and Guthrie, published by John Wiley & Sons, Inc.

worm regenerate more rapidly than those more posterior in origin; this is an illustration of the theory of the *axial gradient of metabolism,* proposed by C. M. Child. (Fig. 33).

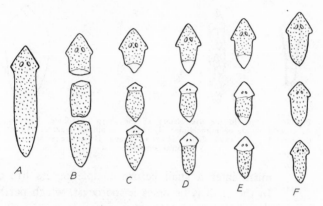

Fig. 33. Stages in the regeneration of a planarian cut transversely into three parts. The time intervals between the stages represented at B, C, D, E, and F average about three days. (Drawings by Marion I. Alexander, from living specimens).

Class Trematoda.

1. SHEEP LIVER-FLUKE, *Fasciola hepatica* (Linn).

   a. *Morphology.* (Fig. 34). The adult sheep liver-fluke lives in the bile ducts of the sheep (or occasionally other animals, including man). It is about an inch long and half as broad. The mouth is anterior, surrounded by a sucker. The single ventral sucker is a short distance behind it. The mouth opens into a pharynx and *oesophagus,* the latter branching into a double intestine, each portion having many small branches. This is a gastrovascular cavity. The excretory system (with flame-cells) drains into a single longitudinal excretory duct which opens at the posterior end. The nervous system is similar to that of *Planaria.*

   b. *Reproduction and Life History.* The adult reproduces sexually, and is hermaphroditic. The embryos develop in the uterus of the parent (a half-million may be produced by one worm), and leave the body of the sheep through the bile duct and intestine. If one encounters water of a moderately warm temperature it develops into a ciliated larva *(miracidium)* which

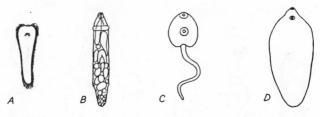

Fig. 34. Stages in the life history of the sheep liver-fluke, *Fasciola*. A, ciliated larva, or miracidium; B, redia, containing daughter rediae; C, cercaria; D, adult fluke. Stages C and D possess oral and ventral suckers.

must enter a snail before completing its life cycle. In the snail it becomes a sporocyst, which parthenogenetically produces *rediae*. A redia may reproduce daughter rediae for several generations, but eventually, still by parthenogenesis, will produce *cercariae*. A cercaria leaves the snail for the water, and may encyst on grass bordering the pond. If such a cyst is eaten by the sheep it develops into a young fluke which then invades the liver of the new host, thus completing the life cycle. (Fig. 34).

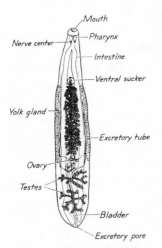

Fig. 35. *Clonorchis sinensis* (Cobbold), the human liver fluke of the Far East.

HUMAN LIVER-FLUKE, *Clonorchis sinensis* (Cobbold).

The adult lives in the bile ducts of man or other fish-eating mammals, and the species is Far Eastern in distribution. It is smaller and narrower than *Fasciola*, and the intestine divides into two lateral unbranched portions. Otherwise it is much like *Fasciola*. The developmental stages are passed in snails and fresh-water fishes; it is from the latter that the human infection is acquired. (Fig. 35).

Class Cestoda (Cestoidea).

HUMAN TAPEWORM FROM PORK (*Taenia solium Linn*).

a. *Morphology.* The adult is parasitic in the human intestine. It has no mouth or digestive cavity, but obtains food by absorption through its body wall. The adult tapeworm consists of a head *(scolex)* about a millimeter in diameter (containing hooks and four suckers for attachment), and a *neck,* followed by a chain of hundreds of segments *(proglottids)* which

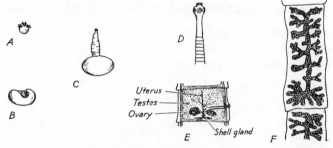

Fig. 36. The tapeworm, *Taenia,* and its life history. A, six-hooked embryo; B, bladder-worm or cysticercus, as it occurs in muscle tissue; C, bladder-worm with everted head or scolex; D, scolex, neck, and first (youngest) proglottids; E, proglottid with mature reproductive system; F, gravid proglottid, the uterus distended with embryos. (Redrawn after Leuckart).

bud from the neck and are progressively larger and more mature toward the posterior end. It is six to nine feet in length. Each proglottid is an independent individual from the standpoint of reproduction, and is hermaphroditic; the excretory and nervous systems, however, are continuous through the chain of proglottids. (Fig. 36).

b. *Reproduction and Life Cycle.* Mature proglottids, each containing a uterus filled with hundreds of fertilized eggs, break away from the posterior end and escape from the host in the feces. On the ground the proglottids may or may not disintegrate; further development depends upon the proglottid or the

scattered eggs containing embryos being eaten by a
secondary host. If they are eaten by a pig, the egg
shells are digested in the small intestine and the released embryos bore through the intestinal wall and
into the blood capillaries. They are then carried in
the circulation to the muscles, where they form *cysts*.
These develop scolex-like heads from the cyst wall.
The embryo is then a *bladder-worm* or *cysticercus*.
If inadequately cooked pork containing bladder-worms
is eaten by man, the heads are everted, attached to the
intestinal wall, and begin to bud proglottids — forming the mature tape-worm. (Fig. 36).

CHARACTERISTICS OF THE PHYLUM NEMATODA

The round- or thread-worms are widely distributed free-living
as well as parasitic animals. Many free-living species live in soil,
where they may be quite injurious to the roots of plants. All
species are elongated, cylindrical, covered with a tough cuticle;

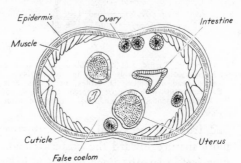

Fig. 37. Somewhat diagrammatic cross-section of
Ascaris, based, however, on a specimen. The fact that
mesoderm lines the outer wall of the body cavity
but does not cover the intestine is clearly shown;
hence the term false coelom.

and many species are pointed at both ends. A pseudocoel, similar
to a true coelom but lined by mesoderm only on the outer side
— and there by muscle rather than epithelial cells, is present.
(Fig. 37). Cilia are absent from all parts of the body. Free-living
forms may possess complex mouth-parts and several sense organs
— including eyespots. The parasitic forms are usually simpler in
structure. There is a complete digestive tract, differentiated into

various regions. The nervous system consists of an anterior ring, dorsal and ventral nerve cords, and smaller nerves. The excretory system consists of two lateral canals, opening together by a ventral anterior pore. The reproductive organs (most nematodes are dioecious) open posteriorly.

Animals with a pseudocoel are classified in this Outline in several different phyla. However, some authors combine these under the Phylum Aschelminthes. In the latter classification the phyla Nematoda, Acanthocephala, Nematomorpha, Rotatoria, and Gastrotricha are all considered Classes of the Phylum Aschelminthes.

EXAMPLES OF THE PHYLUM NEMATODA

Ascaris. This is a genus of parasites of the intestine of man and the larger domestic animals. *Ascaris lumbricoides* Linn., of man, varies in length from six to sixteen inches. Its morphology is typical of the phylum. (Fig. 37). It is dioecious, with internal fertilization and early development. (Ascaris is used a great deal in biological laboratories to illustrate the process of fertilization and early cleavage, as well as mitosis.) (See Fig. 6). The embryo, in the egg envelope, invades its new host by way of contaminated soil, food or water. After escaping from the egg envelope, in the intestine of the host, it migrates through the tissues into the air passages, is swallowed a second time from the pharynx, then develops in the intestine into the adult. The adult *Ascaris* feeds upon the food in the intestinal tract of its host.

Hook-worms. These are small intestinal parasites of man and other animals, the human parasites belonging to the genera Necator (Fig. 38) and Ancylostoma. The length averages under one-half inch. Prominent hooks are present in the genital bursa of the male, and smaller ones occur within the mouths of both sexes. Embryos, which occur in contaminated soil, invade the host through the skin of the feet, and migrate through blood vessels to the lungs; there they bore through the lung wall into the air passages, and from the pharynx are swallowed. In the intestine they become attached to the wall, where they live on blood from the host. The blood drainage in a heavy infection is sufficient to produce marked symtoms of anaemia.

Trichinella. The adults, which are less than one-eighth inch long, live along the mucous lining of the intestine of man

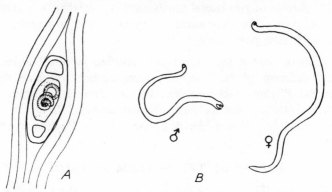

Fig. 38. A. *Trichinella,* in a cyst, in muscle fibers; B. *Necator,* a hook worm, male to the left, female to the right. The upper end is the anterior end in each case, the expanded posterior end of the male being the bursa.

and other animals. Larvae (rather than eggs) leave the body of the female. These invade the tissues of the body, commonly the muscles, and form cysts about themselves. If inadequately cooked flesh of an animal containing such larvae (*e. g.,* infected pork) is eaten, the larvae excyst and become adults. Infections tend to become very heavy, and often end fatally. (Fig. 38).

CHARACTERISTICS OF THE PHYLUM
ACANTHOCEPHALA

Acanthocephala are round-worms which have for attachment at the anterior end a proboscis covered with hooks. All are intestinal parasites of vertebrates, with usually a crustacean or insect as alternate host in young stages. A digestive cavity is absent. A pseudo-coelom is present, as well as an excretory system. The animals are dioecious. (Fig. 39).

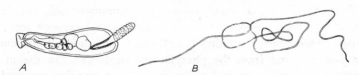

Fig. 39. A. One of the Acanthocephala, *Echinorhynchus clavula* Duj. (After Lühe). B. *Gordius,* the so-called h o r s e - h a i r snake or worm of the Phylum Nematomorpha.

CHARACTERISTICS OF THE PHYLUM
NEMATOMORPHA

The hairworms (including *Gordius,* the common "horse-hair snake" or worm) belong in this group. They are very thin in proportion to their length. The larvae usually parasitize insects, whereas the adults are free-living. A part of the coelom of the female is lined with epithelium, otherwise the body cavity is a pseudo-coelom. Neither excretory nor circulatory system present; mouth usually absent. The sexes are separate. (Fig. 39).

REVIEW QUESTIONS

1. What structural advances over the Coelenterata and Ctenophora are shown by the Platyhelminthes?

2. In what ways are the Nematoda more advanced than the Platyhelminthes?

3. Name and characterize the Classes of Platyhelminthes.

4. Give structures and functions of Planaria in detail.

5. Trace the life history and describe the stages of the sheep liver-fluke, human tapeworm from pork, Ascaris, hook-worm, Trichinella.

6. What are Acanthocephala and Nematomorpha?

Chapter X

MISCELLANEOUS MINOR PHYLA

The phyla included in this chapter do not constitute a closely related group. They are all triploblastic. Some possess a pseudocoel, some a coelom, but they are all relatively primitive. The Rotatoria, Bryozoa, and Brachiopoda all have many species, their representatives either being abundant today or having been so in the past. The Rotatoria and Gastrotricha are sometimes combined with the Nematoda, Acanthocephala, and Nematomorpha to constitute the Phylum Aschelminthes. (See Chapter IX).

CHARACTERISTICS OF THE PHYLUM ROTATORIA

The rotifers or wheel-animalcules are common aquatic organisms particularly abundant in fresh-water, where they are free-swimming, or crawl about on plants and debris. They are of

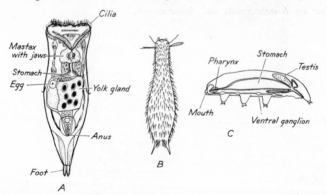

Fig. 40. A. *Epiphanes senta* (Müller), one of the Rotatoria (from Dieffenbach and Sachse, after Plate); B, *Chaetonotus schulzei* Metschn., one of the Gastrotricha (from Collin, after Zelinka); C, diagrammatic longitudinal section through a member of the Phylum Tardigrada (from Boaz, after Plate).

microscopic size, many species being smaller than the larger protozoa. The body, usually cylindrical, is enclosed in a cuticle. Prominent groups of cilia are present at the anterior end. The *foot,* at the posterior end, sometimes possesses adhesive glands. The digestive system consists of an anterior mouth opening into a *mastax,* a muscular pharynx provided with chitinous jaws which masticate the food. There is a glandular stomach, a short intestine, and an anus. Excretory and nervous systems are present, but a circulatory system is absent. The body cavity is a pseudocoel. (Fig. 40). The sexes are separate. There may be a complicated life history, in which during the summer several generations of females are reproduced parthenogenetically, followed by the production of both sexes in the fall, parthenogenetically. The fertilized egg, covered by a protective cyst, may remain dormant through the winter, hatching as a female capable of parthenogenetic reproduction the following spring. Adults may during slow drying acquire envelopes which resist dessication and protect the organisms against great extremes of temperature. By some authorities, rotifers are considered related to the probable ancestor of the Annelida. (Chapter XII).

CHARACTERISTICS OF THE PHYLUM GASTROTRICHA

The gastrotrichs constitute a small group of microscopic aquatic animals somewhat like the rotifers, but with a more flattened body. They live among debris and algae. They may be partly or entirely covered with plates, spines, or hooked bristles. Their locomotion is by means of two ventral bands of cilia. A digestive system, coiled excretory tubes, a muscular system, and a nervous system are present. Gastrotrichs are said to be hermaphroditic, but may be parthenogenetic females; if the latter is true, the males are unknown. (Fig. 40).

CHARACTERISTICS OF THE PHYLUM TARDIGRADA

The tardigrades or water-bears have been variously considered as primitive arthropods or as representatives of an independent group. They are very small animals which live in fresh or salt water or in damp soil, but most abundantly in mosses. The body seems to be segmented; the head is fairly distinct, and possesses a pharynx with a sucking or piercing *stylet.* A nervous system is present, consisting of supraoesophageal, suboesophageal, and four ventral ganglia. Respiratory and circulatory systems are absent. The body cavity is a coelom. The sexes are separate. There is marked resistance to dessication, as in rotifers. (Fig. 40).

CHARACTERISTICS OF THE PHYLUM CHAETOGNATHA

These small marine arrow-worms, typified by *Sagitta,* have well-developed digestive and sensory systems, and a true coelom. The mouth is bordered by prominent bristles. The species are hermaphroditic. (Fig. 41).

CHARACTERISTICS OF THE PHYLUM BRYOZOA

The bryozoa or moss animals are small aquatic organisms, mostly marine, which are usually colonial and sessile. Some species secrete a calcareous, coral-like deposit. The mouth is surrounded by a tentacle-bearing ridge, the *lophophore.* The digestive tract

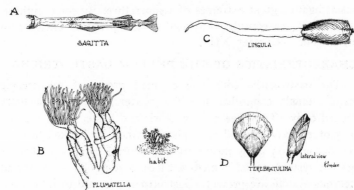

Fig. 41. A. *Sagitta,* of the Phylum Chaetognatha; B, *Plumatella,* a fresh-water member of the Bryozoa, two individuals at the left, a small colony at the right; C and D, *Lingula* and *Terebratulina,* of the Phylum Brachiopoda. (Copyright by General Biological Supply House, Chicago, reprinted by permission).

is U-shaped, the anus opening near the mouth. A nervous system is present. The animals are hermaphroditic, and fertilization and early development are internal. The larvae are ciliated and free-swimming. Fresh-water bryozoa commonly reproduce by internal buds, *statoblasts,* which survive the winter or other unfavorable period. (Fig. 41).

It is quite probable that animals included in this phylum should be placed in two separate groups of phylum rank. Some bryozoa have a pseudocoel; in these the anal opening is surrounded by the lophophore. These may be considered members of the Phylum Entoprocta. The other forms have a true coelom, and the anal opening is just outside the lophophore. These constitute the Phylum Ectoprocta or the Bryozoa in the strict sense.

CHARACTERISTICS OF THE PHYLUM BRACHIOPODA

The brachiopods or lamp-shells constitute a phylum of marine animals of ancient origin. Species were much more numerous and individuals more abundant during the Palaeozoic than now. The animal is enclosed within two calcareous shells, a dorsal and a ventral (in contrast to the right and left valves of a bivalve mollusk). It is sessile, and may be attached to the substrate by a stalk, the *peduncle*. Lateral to the mouth are the two ciliated arms of the horse-shoe-shaped lophophore. An anus may or may not be present. Excretory and nervous systems are present, as well as a contractile heart. A true coelom is present. The sexes are separate, fertilization is external, and the larvae are ciliated and free-swimming. (Fig. 41).

REVIEW QUESTIONS

1. Characterize the Phyla Rotatoria, Gastrotricha, Tardigrada, Chaetognatha, Bryozoa, Brachiopoda.

2. The Phyla Bryozoa and Brachiopoda have often been classified together. Why?

Chapter XI

ECHINODERMATA

CHARACTERISTICS OF THE PHYLUM ECHINODERMATA

These are all marine animals which are (at least superficially) radially symmetrical, the body usually on a plan of five radiating *antimeres,* with the mouth at the center. Calcareous plates are present in the skin, and the majority have dermal spines. A coelom is present. The digestive system is complete, although the anus may be non-functional. Locomotion (never very rapid) is by means of tube-feet, whose movements are regulated by a hydrostatic pressure system, the water-vascular system. A nervous system, consisting of an oral ring and radiating nerve cords, is present. There is also a haemal or blood system present, consisting of a circular vessel and five radiating vessels; the liquid in these does not circulate. Separately specialized respiratory and excretory systems are absent. The functions of these systems are provided by dermal projections, the branchiae or papulae, between the calcareous plates of the skin. The sexes are nearly always separate; fertilization takes place in the sea-water, and the larvae are bilaterally symmetrical and free-swimming.

Similarity in developmental stages, combined with common precipitation reactions (the latter not positive evidence), suggest close evolutionary relationships between this phylum and the primitive members of the Phylum Chordata. In both phyla, the blastopore, which is the opening into the gastrocoel, becomes the anus. In both phyla, the coelom forms typically from pouches of the archenteron (gastrocoel). These embryonic traits do not characterize the invertebrate evolutionary line that includes the Annelida, Mollusca, and Arthropoda; in these, the mouth is formed from the blastopore, and the coelom is typically formed by a splitting of the mesoderm. The fact that adult echinoderms are radially symmetrical while chordates are bilaterally symmetrical is not a serious objection to the theory that these are related. The radial symmetry of echinoderms is secondarily acquired; the larvae are bilaterally symmetrical.

MAJOR CLASSES OF THE PHYLUM ECHINODERMATA

(Note: Classes known only from fossils are omitted.)

Class Crinoidea. Usually sessile, attached by a stalk

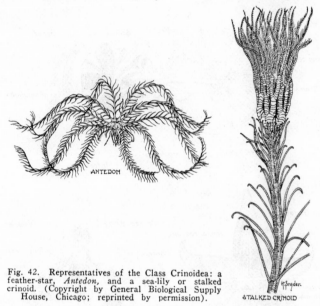

Fig. 42. Representatives of the Class Crinoidea: a feather-star, *Antedon,* and a sea-lily or stalked crinoid. (Copyright by General Biological Supply House, Chicago; reprinted by permission).

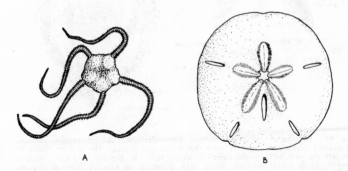

Fig. 43. A. Brittle-star, Class Ophiuroidea. B. Key-hole sand-dollar, Class Echinoidea.

from the aboral surface; though some are free-swimming. Much more abundant in species and individuals during the Palaeozoic. (Examples: sea-lily, feather-star). (Fig. 42).

Class Asteroidea. Possess a central disk and broad rays which are hollow and contain branches of the coelom. Tube-feet in a groove along oral side of ray. (Example: star-fish). (Fig. 44).

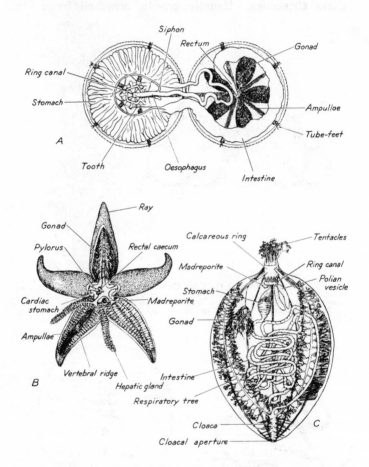

Fig. 44. Morphology of representative Echinodermata. A. Sea-urchin, *Arbacia punctulata* (Lamarck), opened by a horizontal cut through the test or shell; to the left the oral half, to the right the aboral half. B. Starfish, *Asterias vulgaris* Verrill, from aboral surface, three rays dissected to exposed internal organs. C. Sea-cucumber, *Thyone briareus* (Leseur), the body opened on one side. (After W. R. Coe, Echinoderms of Connecticut, by permission of the author).

Class Ophiuroidea. With the disk distinctly marked off from the five, thin, flexible rays. The latter are branched in the basket-stars. (Examples: serpent-stars, brittle-stars (Fig. 43), basket-stars.)

Class Echinoidea. The body is compact, a flattened globe or disk without free rays; covered with calcareous plates, often with prominent spines. (Examples: sea-urchin (Fig. 44), sand-dollar (Fig. 43), sea-biscuit.)

Class Holothurioidea. Elongated cylindrical body, flexible and soft, the skeletal elements of the skin being reduced. (Example: sea-cucumber). (Fig. 44).

EXAMPLES OF THE PHYLUM ECHINODERMATA

Starfish (Class Asteroidea).

1. EXTERNAL CHARACTERISTICS. Five broad *rays* extend outward from the central *disk*. The mouth is in the center of the lower surface of the disk (the lower side of the animal being therefore called the *oral side*). A prominent colored plate, the *madreporite,* is on the *aboral side* of the disk near the intersection of two rays. The body surface is covered with *spines* except in the broad, deep *ambulacral grooves* which extend along the oral surfaces of the rays. The *tube-feet,* locomotor organs, are present in definite rows (four in *Asterias*) and great numbers in the ambulacral grooves. (Fig. 45). Small sac-like protrusions of the coelomic wall, the *branchiae* or *papulae,* extend out between the calcareous plates into the surrounding sea-water, functioning as respiratory and excretory organs. Minute forceps-like appendages, the *pedicellariae,* occur over the body surface; these function in the removal of foreign particles from the surface.

2. MORPHOLOGY AND PHYSIOLOGY OF ORGAN SYSTEMS. (Fig. 44).

   a. *Digestive System.* The mouth leads through a short oesophagus into the large, lobed, *cardiac portion* of the *stomach;* this is separated by a constriction from the *pyloric portion,* somewhat smaller, which receives ducts from five pairs of large *hepatic glands* or *caeca* (digestive); from the pylorus extends a short intestine, bearing two rectal caeca, to the anus, a small opening on the aboral surface near the center of the disk. The cardiac portion of the stomach is everted through the mouth in feeding, and folded about the food, the latter being digested before the stomach is retracted. Hence the intestine and anus are practically non-functional. The food consists chiefly of mollusks and crustacea; damage to oyster beds, through destruction of oysters, is enormous.

b. *Water-vascular System.* (Fig. 45). The tube-feet are hollow, communicating with *radial canals* in the roof of the ambulacral groove, these in turn joining a *circular canal* in the disk, which communicates with the outside through the *stone canal* and madreporic

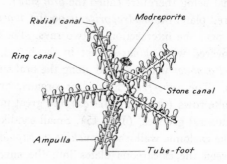

Fig. 45. Diagram of the water-vascular system of a starfish. (After W. R. Coe, Echinoderms of Connecticut, by permission of the author).

plate. At the base of each tube-foot is a bulb-like expansion of the system, an *ampulla,* whose constriction results in the extension of the tube-foot. The latter has a suction disk at its distal surface.

c. *Nervous System.* There is a *nerve ring* in the disk, with a ventral, radial *nerve* in each ray. These have many fine branches, and each radial nerve terminates in an eye-spot at the tip of the ray.

3. REPRODUCTION AND DEVELOPMENT. The sexes are separate. Paired gonads are present in each ray, these opening to the outside by pores on the aboral surface near the base of the rays. The eggs and sperm cells are shed at the same season, and fertilization takes place in the seawater. During development, starfish pass through free-swimming, bilaterally symmetrical larval stages. (Fig. 46).

Sea-Urchin (Class Echinoidea).

1. EXTERNAL CHARACTERISTICS. The body is a flattened globe, with a spine-covered external shell or *test*. The test consists of twenty radiating rows of closely fitting calcareous plates. The mouth, provided with five teeth, is in the center of the oral surface, and is surrounded by a broad membranous area free from spines, the *peristome*. Five pairs of branched *dermal branchiae* or "gills" occur around the margin of the peristome. The spines are movable at the base. There are five rows of long thin tube-feet, those on the oral surface being used in locomotion, but the others in respiration. The anus opens in the center

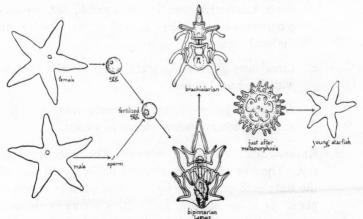

Fig. 46. Diagram of the life history of a starfish, showing the larval stages. (Copyright by General Biological Supply House, Chicago, reprinted by permission).

of the aboral surface, within a central group of plates, the *periproct*. This is surrounded by the five *genital plates,* of which one (which is the madreporite also) is larger and is finely perforated. The plates perforated for tube-feet are the *ambulacral plates;* the intermediate rows, which terminate in the genital plates, are *interambulacral plates.* Three-pronged *pedicellariae* are present.

2. MORPHOLOGY AND PHYSIOLOGY OF ORGAN SYSTEMS. (Fig. 44).

   a. *Digestive System.* The mouth has five teeth set in a calcareous framework operated by muscles, the "Aristotle's lantern." There is a short esophagus; a broad, lobed, coiled stomach; a broad intestine coiled in the direction opposite to that of the stomach; a short rectum. From the esophagus to the posterior end of the stomach there leads a tube embedded in the stomach wall, the *siphon.* The food consists chiefly of sea-weeds, but small organisms and dead animal matter may be eaten.

   b. *Water-vascular System.* There is a circular vessel, five radiating vessels, tube-feet with ampullae — the system similar to that of the starfish. Locomotion is much less active than in the starfish, but involves movements of the spines as well as the tube-feet on the oral side.

   c. *Circulatory System.* An oral circular vessel is present, with five radial vessels.

   d. *Nervous System.* There is a nerve ring, with five radial branches; a nerve plexus is present.

3. REPRODUCTION AND DEVELOPMENT. The sexes are separate. The five gonads are attached to the aboral wall of the test; each one opens by a *genital pore* in a genital plate. As in the starfish, fertilization occurs in the sea-water, and there is a bilaterally-symmetrical, free-swimming larva, in this case called a *pluteus.*

Sea-Cucumber (Class Holothurioidea).

1. EXTERNAL CHARACTERISTICS. Sea-cucumbers have a soft, sac-like, elongated body with small calcareous plates in the skin. The mouth is at one end, surrounded by branched tentacles. The tentacles are hollow, and extended by water pressure — being connected with the water-vascular system. Locomotion is usually on the side — the three rows of tube-feet on the ventral surface being broad and used for locomotion, while the two rows on the dorsal side are thin and elongated, and used for respiration. The *cloacal aperture* (anus) is at the posterior (aboral) end.

2. MORPHOLOGY AND PHYSIOLOGY OF ORGAN SYSTEMS. (Fig. 44).

    a. *Digestive System.* The mouth is surrounded by a calcareous ring. It leads through a short oesophagus into a muscular stomach, which narrows into the very long, convoluted intestine. This expands into the short muscular cloaca, which opens at the posterior end. Two long, branched "respiratory trees" join the cloaca; their functions may be respiratory and excretory, but they are probably also hydrostatic regulators of the internal pressure. The food consists of very small animals and plants, in mud and sand, conveyed to the mouth by the tentacles.

    b. *Water-vascular System.* The madreporite is inside the coelom. There may be one or two large *Polian vesicles* attached to the ring canal (hence they are not radially arranged). Otherwise the water-vascular system is like that of other echinoderms.

    c. *Circulatory System.* There is a ring vessel, with radial vessels.

    d. *Nervous System.* A nerve ring is present, and radial nerves. Sea-cucumbers respond quickly and vigorously to stimulation.

3. REPRODUCTION AND DEVELOPMENT. The sexes are usually separate, although hermaphroditism occurs (with eggs and sperm cells not developing simultaneously). The free-swimming, bilaterally-symmetrical, larval stage is called the *auricularia*.

REVIEW QUESTIONS

1. What are the characteristics of the Phylum Echinodermata, and the Classes with existing representatives?

2. Describe the water-vascular system.

3. Compare starfish, sea-urchin, and sea-cucumber with reference to both external and internal characteristics.

4. Discuss the process of development in echinoderms.

5. Why may the Echinodermata be considered more advanced than certain other phyla which may be characterized by bilateral symmetry?

Chapter XII

ANNELIDA

CHARACTERISTICS OF THE PHYLUM ANNELIDA

The Annelida (sometimes called Annulata) are segmented worms found in fresh-water, marine, and terrestrial habitats. A few even are parasites. A coelom is present, typically divided into compartments by transverse septa. Complex digestive, nervous, excretory, and reproductive systems are present, these being usually metameric either wholly or in part. The muscular system is ordinarily segmentally arranged. There is, in most but not all annelids, a system of blood vessels containing circulating blood. The animals may be dioecious or hermaphroditic; asexual reproduction occurs in some species. Most annelids possess a characteristic, ciliated, larval stage, the *trochophore.*

CLASSES OF THE PHYLUM ANNELIDA

Class Archiannelida. Small marine worms of simple structure, without setae or parapodia. Dioecious or hermaphroditic. Trochophore larva. (Example: *Polygordius.)*

Class Polychaeta. Practically all marine, with numerous setae present on lateral appendages, the parapodia. A distinct head usually present. Dioecious; trochophore larva. (Example: *Nereis.)* (Fig. 47).

Class Myzostoma. Parasites of echinoderms. Mostly disk-shaped, without evident segmentation. Parapodia present. No blood-vascular system. Mostly hermaphroditic; all with a trochophore larva. (Example: *Myzostoma.)*

Class Oligochaeta. Mostly fresh-water or terrestrial worms, without parapodia, and with few setae. No distinct head. Hermaphroditic; without trochophore larvae. (Example: earthworm.) (Figs. 48, 49).

99

Class Hirudinea. Fresh-water, marine, or terrestrial worms, with a flattened body with more external segments than internal ones. Neither setae nor parapodia. Anterior and posterior suckers present. Coelom largely filled with connective tissue. Hermaphroditic; without a typical trochophore larva. (Example: leech.) (Fig. 50).

Class Echiurida. Marine worms, unsegmented in adults. No parapodia, but a few setae usually present. A non-retractile proboscis overhangs the mouth. Dioecious; the larva a trocho-phore. (Example: *Echiurus.*)

Class Gephyrea (sometimes considered a separate phylum). Marine worms possessing an introvert, an anterior structure surrounding the mouth, which may be everted. Parapodia and setae absent. Segmentation absent in adults (a partial external segmentation in some species). Dioecious; in those species whose development is known there is a trochophore larva. (Example: *Phascolosoma.*)

EXAMPLES OF THE PHYLUM ANNELIDA

Clam-Worm or Sand-Worm, Nereis (Class Polychaeta).

1. EXTERNAL CHARACTERISTICS. (Fig. 47). These are elongated, cylindrical (slightly flattened dorso-ventrally) worms, with very pronounced segmentation. In length they may exceed one foot. They inhabit burrows in sand and rocks of the inter-tidal zone; and are active chiefly at night. There is a distinct head, containing a protrusible pharynx provided with *jaws,* surrounded by the *peristomium* and roofed over by the *prostomium.* The latter bears four *simple eyes* dorsally, and two short tentacles and two *palps;* the former, four long tentacles. Behind the head each segment (except the last) has prominent lateral appendages, the *parapodia,* each bearing numerous *setae* — these probably involved in movement in the burrows in which the animal lives. The last segment bears two long *cirri.*

2. MORPHOLOGY AND PHYSIOLOGY OF ORGAN SYSTEMS.

a. *Digestive System.* A straight tube through the body, the pharynx leads into an esophagus and the latter into the intestine (stomach-intestine). Two glandular pouches open into the sides of the esophagus. The intestine is regularly constricted in each segment. A typhlosole (see Earthworm) is absent.

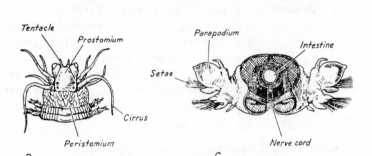

Fig. 47. *Nereis.* A. Dorsal view of entire animal, about one-third natural size. (Copyright by General Biological Supply House, Chicago, reprinted by permission). B. Dorsal view of anterior end. C. Diagram of a cross section of a typical segment. (B and C after Snodgrass).

b. *Respiratory and Circulatory Systems.* Respiration takes place through the skin, chiefly in the parapodia. The blood (which contains the red pigment hemoglobin) is contained in contractile vessels, a *dorsal longitudinal vessel* in which the blood flows anteriorly, a *ventral vessel* in which it flows posteriorly, and a pair of connecting loops in each segment which give off branches to the internal organs.

c. *Excretory System.* In each segment except first and last is a pair of coiled *nephridia,* which drain the coelomic segment anterior to the one in which it is contained.

d. *Nervous and Sensory Systems.* The "brain," *supraesophageal* or *cerebral ganglion* is in the dorsal part of the head; it joins the *subesophageal ganglion* by

two *circumesophageal connectives*. A *ventral nerve
cord* extends the length of the worm from the subesophageal ganglion, with a swelling or *segmental
ganglion* in each metamer. The four simple eyes, the
palps, and the tentacles, all of which are sense organs,
receive nerves from the supra-esophageal ganglion.
Lateral, branching *nerves* are given off by the ventral
cord. The eyes contain structures which may be interpreted as *cornea, lens,* and *retina,* and are analogous
with those of vertebrates.

3. REPRODUCTION AND DEVELOPMENT. *Nereis* is dioecious,
with the testes or ovaries arising from the coelomic walls.
Both gonads are segmentally arranged in a few to many
segments. The mature gametes escape through the temporarily ruptured body wall; fertilization is in the sea-
water; in development they pass through a trochophore
stage. The reproductive system is less complex and more
metameric than in the earthworm.

Earthworm, Lumbricus (Class Oligochaeta).

1. EXTERNAL CHARACTERISTICS. Earthworms are elongate,
cylindrical worms, in which segmentation is visible externally as infoldings in the *cuticle.* Over one hundred
metameres are present in the commonly studied species.
The mouth is a slit at the anterior end, under a dorsal
projection, the prostomium. The anus is at the posterior
end. In sexually mature worms, a smooth swelling, the
clitellum, occupies six or seven segments from about the
thirty-second, back. On each segment, except the first
and last, are four pairs of short bristles or setae. Internally, the coelom is divided into compartments by transverse partitions which lie under the external infoldings.
(Fig. 48).

2. MORPHOLOGY AND PHYSIOLOGY OF ORGAN SYSTEMS.
(Fig. 48, 49).

   a. *Digestive System.* The digestive tract is a straight
   tube consisting of, in order: mouth, stout swollen
   pharynx (segments two to six), elongate narrow
   esophagus (six to fourteen), thin-walled *crop* (fif-

teen, sixteen), muscular *gizzard* (seventeen, eighteen), intestine (segments nineteen to end of body), and anus. The intestine has a dorsal internal fold,

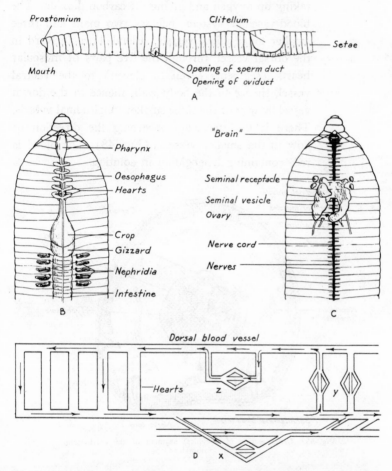

Fig. 48. The earthworm. A. Side view of anterior third of body. B and C. Dorsal views of dissections, with body-wall spread out. B. Digestive, circulatory, and excretory organs—the nephridia shown in only five segments, however. C. Nervous and reproductive systems; the four testes lie under the spots marked T. D. Diagram illustrating the direction of blood-flow; the capillary systems marked x, y, and z are alternative routes; there is not general agreement concerning the direction of flow in the smaller vessels.

the *typhlosole* (Fig. 49), running its length. The oesophagus has three pairs of *calciferous glands* along its sides. (Fig. 48).

b. *Respiratory and Circulatory Systems.* The earthworm breathes through the moist cuticle covering the entire surface, blood capillaries in the body wall taking up oxygen and giving off carbon dioxide. The blood-vascular system includes two main and three smaller longitudinal vessels. Blood flows forward in the dorsal vessel, through the five pairs of muscular hearts (segments seven to eleven) to the ventral vessel, thence to the body wall, thence to the dorsal vessel by way of the three smaller longitudinal vessels. There is disagreement concerning the direction of flow in the smaller vessels. (Fig. 48). The blood is red, containing hemoglobin in solution.

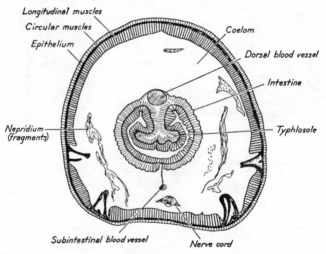

Fig. 49. Cross section of a typical segment of the earthworm, diagrammatic.

c. *Excretory System.* Paired nephridia occur in every segment except the first three and last one. Each nephridium drains material from the coelomic cavity anterior to it through its nephrostome and coiled tubule out through a ventral excretory pore. It also receives material by diffusion from blood capillaries surrounding the tubule. (Fig. 48).

d. *Nervous and Sensory Systems.* There are sense organs in the skin sensitive to contact and light. The nervous system is a ventral chain of ganglia, one in each segment beginning with the fourth, and an anterior suprapharyngeal ganglion, the "brain," in segment three. Nerve cords around the pharynx connect the "brain" with the first ventral ganglion. Three pairs of nerves in each metamer extend outward from the ventral nerve cord. (Fig. 48).

3. REPRODUCTION AND DEVELOPMENT. Earthworms are hermaphroditic but not self-fertilizing. Two pairs of testes are present (segments ten and eleven), enclosed within *seminal vesicles,* of which there are three pairs (segments nine to eleven). Spermatozoa from the vesicles pass into two pairs of *vasa efferentia,* which join to form the paired *vasa deferentia* beginning in segment twelve and opening to the outside in segment fifteen. *Seminal receptacles,* paired, occur in segments nine and ten, opening externally between nine and ten, and ten and eleven. One pair of ovaries in segment thirteen contains the eggs, which pass to the outside through *oviducts* opening in segment fourteen. During copulation, spermatozoa from each worm are transferred to the receptacles of the mate. After separation, a *cocoon* formed about the clitellum slips forward over the worm (by movements of the worm), receiving the eggs at segment fourteen and the stored spermatozoa from the receptacles. After the worm has backed out of the cocoon the ends of the latter close, enclosing the zygotes. These develop into small worms in the cocoon.

Leech, Hirudo (Class Hirudinea).

1. EXTERNAL CHARACTERISTICS. The body is two to three inches long, flattened dorso-ventrally. There are twenty-six metamers (in the medicinal leech), but with two to five external annulation in each. Setae and parapodia are absent. There is a small anterior, oral sucker and a large posterior one, these being for attachment to the host whose blood furnishes food for the leech. The mouth contains three chitinous jaws, arranged in a triangle, each

covered with minute serrations. Segments nine to eleven function as a clitellum. (Fig. 50).

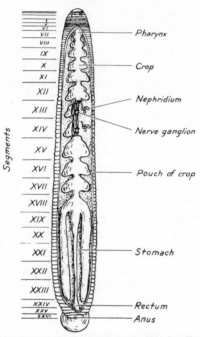

Fig. 50. Morphology of a leech, *Hirudo;* diagrammatic representation of a dissection from the dorsal side.

2. MORPHOLOGY AND PHYSIOLOGY OF ORGAN SYSTEMS. (Fig. 50).

a. *Digestive System.* The mouth leads into a muscular pharynx (segments four to eight) surrounded by salivary glands which secrete a substance which prevents blood coagulation. A large crop, with eleven pairs of lateral pouches, extends to segment eighteen, merging into a small tubular stomach. The latter, with an internal spiral fold, digests the blood which is gradually fed to it from the crop in which it has been stored. The fully distended crop may contain three times the leech's weight in blood, and require months for digestion. The stomach leads into the intestine and short rectum, the latter opening at the posterior end as the anus.

b. *Respiratory and Circulatory Systems.* Respiration takes place through the skin. Blood containing hemoglobin in solution is contained in longitudinal, lateral muscular vessels. There are also dorsal and ventral thin walled sinuses, which communicate indirectly with the muscular vessels and with other spaces in the reduced coelom. The blood vessels and sinuses are probably reduced portions of the coelom.

c. *Excretory System.* Paired nephridia occur in segments seven to twenty-three, each with an expansion, the bladder-like vesicle, near its outlet.

d. *Nervous and Sensory Systems.* The nervous system is similar to that of the earthworm, with the ventral ganglia more distinct, and the cerebral ganglion rather small. Five pairs of eyes occur on the first five segments, and somewhat similar segmental sense-organs on the succeeding segments.

3. REPRODUCTION AND DEVELOPMENT. The leech is hermaphroditic, with several pairs of testes and one pair of ovaries. Cross-fertilization is required; agglutinated masses of sperm cells *(spermatophores)* are passed by one individual through a *penis* into the *vagina* of the other worm. Development takes place inside a cocoon similar to that of the earthworm, and the larva does not pass through a trochophore stage.

REVIEW QUESTIONS

1. Characterize the Phylum Annelida and the Classes Polychaeta, Oligochaeta, and Hirudinea.

2. What advances do annelids show over other worm-like animals?

3. Describe the morphology and physiology of the earthworm, Nereis, the leech.

4. Discuss reproduction and development in the earthworm.

Chapter XIII

ONYCHOPHORA AND ARTHROPODA

The Onychophora are, in practically all textbooks, treated as a class, or at most a subphylum, of the Phylum Arthropoda; but good reasons exist for recognition of this group as a separate phylum, and it is here so treated. The Onychophora differ more from the Arthropoda than any arthropods from each other. Careful students of the group are generally agreed that they may be accorded phylum rank.

CHARACTERISTICS OF THE PHYLUM ONYCHOPHORA

Members of this group, commonly referred to by the name Peripatus (the name of a genus in the phylum), are relatively few in species and individuals; and, although widespread, they are today practically confined to tropical and subtropical regions. They are terrestrial in habitat, nocturnal in activity. In capturing their prey it is secured by a sticky slime secreted by and ejected from glands opening on the oral papillae (see below). The body, cylindrical and some two inches long, is covered with a flexible rough skin containing chitin (not in chitinous plates, however). Walking appendages of a lobe-type are the only external evidence of metamerism; the animal walks on these, hence they are not homologous with parapodia. They are also, however, quite unlike arthropod appendages. The head (which is not distinct) bears a pair of tentacles, a pair of simple eyes, the mouth with one pair of jaws, and an oral papilla at each side of the mouth. Nephridia (similar to those of annelids) constitute the excretory system. Cilia (absent in arthropods but present in annelids) occur in the sperm ducts. The nervous system is unique, consisting of a large dorsal ganglion or "brain" and two ventral nerve cords extending to the posterior end; the latter communicate by transverse commissures. Respiration is by tracheae (similar to those of terrestrial arthropods), air tubes which are commmonly unbranched, and which open to the outside in groups of pores irregularly arranged. There is a dorsal heart, and the blood circulates in a haemocoel (arthropod characters). The digestive tract consists of a buccal cavity (receiving a pair of salivary glands), a short oesophagus, a long stomach-intestine, and a short rectum opening at the anus at the posterior end. The coelom is greatly reduced. The sexes are separate; fertilization is internal—and development also, usually; hence most Onychophora are ovoviviparous. (Fig. 51).

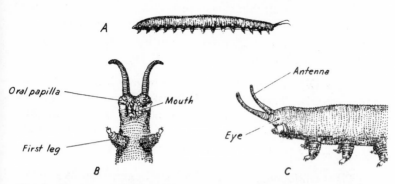

Fig. 51. Peripatus. A. Side view of entire animal. (Copyright by General Biological Supply House, Chicago, used by permission). B and C. Ventral and left lateral views of anterior portion (after Snodgrass).

CHARACTERISTICS OF THE PHYLUM ARTHROPODA

The arthropods are segmented animals with a chitinous exoskeleton and segmental appendages. The chitin is in articulating plates, on body and appendages, and with its associated muscles provides for a great variety of specialized movements. Segmentation is evident externally. This phylum is the largest in numbers of both species and individuals, the number of species exceeding all other animals combined. Marine, fresh-water, and terrestrial habitats are occupied by arthropods, although the insects — the largest group of all — are practically absent from marine habitats. The coelom is reduced. The haemocoel is part of the circulatory system, of which the pulsating portion is the dorsal heart. The excretory systems are not uniform, but do not consist of paired nephridia (as in annelids and Onychophora). Respiration is typically by gills or tracheae; if by the latter, the tracheal pores are typically one pair to a segment. The ventral nerve cord is median but sometimes shows its double origin. More than one pair of "jaws" are present. The sexes are separate, although parthenogenetic reproduction is characteristic of certain species.

MAJOR CLASSES OF THE PHYLUM ARTHROPODA

(Note: Classes not commonly treated in textbooks of college zoology are summarized in the section immediately following this.)

Class Crustacea. The great majority aquatic, and gill-breathers. Exoskeleton hard, limy chitin. Two pairs of antennae. Appendages typically biramous (see page 116). Head of fused segments, often joined with thorax to form cephalothorax. (Examples: crayfish, crab, lobster, barnacle, sow-bug, water-flea, *Cyclops*). (Fig. 52A).

Class Diplopoda. Terrestrial, slow-moving, mostly vegetarian animals. The body is cylindrical, with evident segmentation, two pairs of legs on most segments, the legs ventral. One pair of short antennae. Eyes two, each a group of ocelli, Respiration by tracheae. (Example: millipede.) (Fig. 52B).

Class Chilopoda. Terrestrial, active carnivorous animals. The body is flattened dorso-ventrally; segmentation is pronounced. One pair of legs on each body segment, lateral in position. One pair of long antennae; eyes, two groups of ocelli. Poison fangs on first body segment. Respiration by tracheae. (Example: centipede). (Fig. 52C).

Class Insecta (outlined in detail in Chapter XIV). Terrestrial and aquatic (rarely marine) animals of minute to moderately large size. Body of adults divided into distinct head, thorax, and abdomen — the latter of six to eleven segments. The thorax, of three segments, usually has three pairs of legs, and usually two pairs of wings (second and third segments). One pair of antennae present; usually two compound eyes and three ocelli. Respiration by tracheae. (Examples: cockroach, dragonfly, grasshopper, termite, louse, butterfly, fly, flea, bug, bee, beetle.) (Figs. 52D, 58, 59).

Class Arachnida. Terrestrial (some aquatic) animals of very small to moderate size. Body divided into cephalothorax and abdomen, the former with six pairs of appendages, the first pair

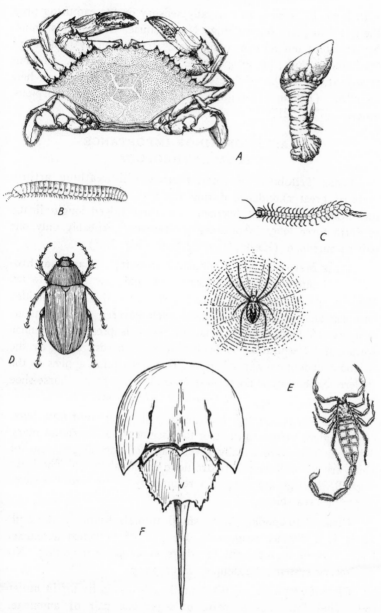

Fig. 52. Representatives of six classes of Arthropoda. A, Crustacea (crab and barnacle); B, Diplopoda (millipede); C, Chilopoda (centipede); D, Insecta (beetle); E, Arachnida (spider and scorpion); F, Merostomata (horse-shoe crab). (A-E, copyright by General Biological Supply House, Chicago, used by permission).

with jaws, the second pair usually sensory or for capturing prey, the last four pairs for walking. No antennae. Simple eyes (number variable) but no compound eyes. Respiration by book-lungs, tracheae, or both; or no specialized respiratory organs. In some classifications the horse-shoe crab (Class Merostomata) are here included. (Examples: spiders, ticks, daddy-long-legs, scorpions, mites.) (Fig. 52E).

CLASSES OF MINOR IMPORTANCE
PHYLUM ARTHROPODA

Class Trilobita. Extinct, marine, gill-breathing arthropods of great abundance during the Palaeozoic. Body divided into head, thorax, and abdomen; and these ridged longitudinally to form three lobes. Appendages biramous. Probably only one pair of antennae. (Example: trilobite.) (Fig. 52F).

Class Merostomata (Xiphosura, in part). Marine arthropods of limited geographic distribution and few species today. Modern species up to about two feet in length. Body divided into cephalothorax and abdomen, each covered by continuous carapace. A long, spear-like tail or telson is present. Antennae are absent. Respiration by book-gills, the "leaves" borne by the biramous abdominal appendages. (This description applies to the modern Xiphosura — horse-shoe crabs.) [Examples: horse-shoe crab (modern), eurypterid (extinct).] (Fig. 52F).

Class Pycnogonida. Marine animals with eight long legs, a head region, a trunk of three or four segments, and a rudimentary abdomen. There are usually seven pairs of appendages, four of which are for walking; there are none on the abdomen. The body is small, the legs are long. No respiratory or excretory system. (Example: sea-spider.)

Class Pauropoda. Very small animals living in the soil. There is a distinct head, with one pair of branched antennae. Nine pairs of legs present in adults, three pairs in young. No respiratory system. (Example: *Pauropus.*)

Class Symphyla. Quite small arthropods living in moist soil. They have twelve pairs of legs; one pair of antennae. Tracheae present, opening by one pair of spiracles on head. (Example: *Scolopendrella.*)

EXAMPLES OF THE PHYLUM ARTHROPODA
Spider (Class Arachnida).

1. EXTERNAL CHARACTERISTICS. The body is in two divisions, an oval *cephalothorax* which is truncate anteriorly, and a rounded *abdomen,* its attachment to the cephalothorax constricted. The cephalothorax bears six pairs of appendages. The first is the *chelicerae* or jaws, containing *poison glands;* the second is the *palps,* leg-like in females but shorter and terminating in a bulbous enlargement in males; the remaining four pairs are the eight walking legs typical of spiders. The eyes are on the anterior, dorsal surface of the cephalothorax; there are, in most common spiders, eight simple eyes. The genital opening, and openings of the *book-lungs,* are on the anterior ventral surface of the abdomen. At its posterior end, ventral to the anus, the *silk glands* (within the abdomen) open through a group of flexible tubes, the *spinnerets.* (Fig. 53).

2. MORPHOLOGY AND PHYSIOLOGY OF ORGAN SYSTEMS.

   a. *Digestive System.* The food (body juices of other animals) is drawn through the mouth and esophagus by a *sucking stomach,* which leads into a stomach with five pairs of lateral pouches or caeca. This narrows as it passes into the abdomen, then expands where it receives the ducts of the hepatic gland or "liver." The rectum, which possesses a dorsal *cloacal sac,* leads to the anus.

   b. *Respiratory and Circulatory Systems.* The *book-lungs* consist of folded lamellae inside the respiratory chambers, each lamella enclosing a blood *sinus.* Tracheae may supplement these, or replace them. The *heart* is in the dorsal part of the abdomen, lying in a *pericardial cavity* from which it receives blood through paired *ostia.* Blood is pumped out through vessels which empty into body sinuses. The large *ventral sinus* communicates with the sinuses of the book-lungs.

c. *Excretory System.* A pair of *Malphighian tubules* empties into the cloacal sac. These are similar in function to those of insects, but not structurally homologous — having a different embryonic origin.

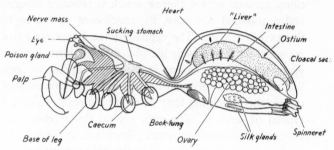

Fig. 53.   Diagram illustrating the morphology of a spider.
(Redrawn after Boaz).

d. *Nervous and Sensory Systems.* The ventral ganglia are united with the dorsal ganglion ("brain") to form one large nerve mass perforated by the oesophagus and sending out numerous branches. The principal sense organs are the *simple eyes,* of which eight, the maximum number, are usually present.

3. REPRODUCTION AND DEVELOPMENT. The sexes are separate. The gonads are contained in the ventral part of the abdomen, opening to the outside near the anterior end of the abdomen on the ventral surface. In copulation, the sperm cells of the male are transferred to the female by the modified palps. Fertilization is internal. The eggs are laid in silk cocoons, which, in some cases, are carried about by the females until the young spiders hatch.

Crayfish (Class Crustacea). The following account applies equally well to *Cambarus,* the genus of crayfishes of the eastern United States, *Astacus,* the genus found in Europe and the Pacific coast section of North America, and the lobster, *Homarus.*

1. EXTERNAL CHARACTERISTICS. (Figs. 54, 55).

a. *Divisions of the Body.* The major divisions are the *cephalothorax* and *abdomen.* The former is covered

by a hard shield, the *carapace,* which projects forward between the eyes as the *rostrum.* The first
thirteen pairs of appendages, and the eyes, are at-

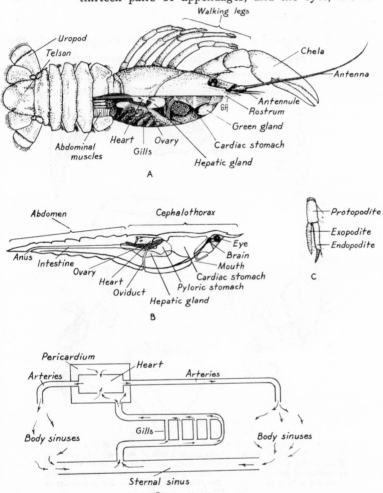

Fig. 54. The crayfish, *Astacus.* A. External features,—part of the carapace removed
to expose the internal organs in place. B. Diagrammatic longitudinal section, showing
internal organs in relative positions. C. The fourth swimmeret, an appendage showing
the primitive biramous condition (see Fig. 55). D. Diagram illustrating the direction
of blood flow.

tached to the cephalothorax; the remaining six are
attached to the abdomen, which terminates in a horizontal fin, the *telson.* The abdomen is divided into

segments, each protected dorsally and laterally by an arched skeleton. This consists of the dorsal *tergite* and two lateral *pleurae*. The ventral plates are known as *sternites*.

b. *Appendages*. Each appendage, except possibly the eye, is modified from the *biramous* type, which is ancestral and embryonic. It consists of the proximal *protopodite* and two distal branches, the *endopodite*

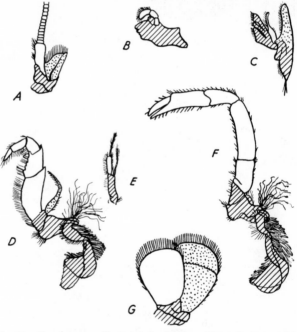

Fig. 55. Homology, as illustrated in the appendages of the crayfish, *Astacus*. Typical appendages from the left side of the body. A, antenna; B, mandible; C, second maxilla; D, third maxilliped; E, third abdominal appendage of female; F, second walking leg; G, uropod. The protopodite is shaded with parallel lines; the exopodite, with dots; the endopodite is unmarked. (Modified after Huxley).

(inner) and *exopodite* (outer). These are variously modified and reduced, as suggested in Table II, but are essentially alike in origin and structure. They illustrate well what is meant by homologous structures. (Figs. 54C, 55).

TABLE II. HOMOLOGIES OF THE APPENDAGES OF THE CRAYFISH

Number of Appendage	Name of Appendage	Modifications from Primitive Biramous Condition (Protopodite Always Present)
1	Antennule	Ex- and endopodites both elongated sensory filaments.
2	Antenna	Endopodite a long sensory filament, exopodite a short basal blade.
3	Mandible	Exopodite absent; remainder a strong food-crushing organ with a palp.
4	1st Maxilla	Exopodite absent. A thin organ lying just behind the mandible.
5	2nd Maxilla	Exopodite constitutes "bailer" of gill chamber.
6 7 8	1st Maxilliped 2nd Maxilliped 3rd Maxilliped	All parts present. Modified for manipulation of food.
9	Cheliped or 1st Walking Leg	Exopodite absent. Endopodite forms heavy pincher.
10 11	2nd Walking Leg 3rd Walking Leg	Endopodite forms small pincher. Exopodite absent
12 13	4th Walking Leg 5th Walking Leg	No pincher on endopodite. Exopodite absent
14	1st Swimmeret	In female very small or absent; in male modified for transfer of sperm.
15	2nd Swimmeret	In male modified for transfer of sperm; in female like next three appendages.
16 17 18	3rd Swimmeret 4th Swimmeret 5th Swimmeret	All parts present, — most nearly approach primitive form. Used in swimming and, in females, for egg attachment.
19	Uropod	All parts present, but broadened for swimming. Together with telson, constitutes tail fin.

2. MORPHOLOGY AND PHYSIOLOGY OF ORGAN SYSTEMS.

   a. *Body Cavity.* The coelom is present, but is largely encroached upon by organs. It is a *haemocoel*—constituting part of the blood system.

   b. *Digestive System.* Crayfish feed chiefly on small aquatic animals, but may eat decaying organic matter. The mouth, surrounded by several pairs of appendages — the "mouth-parts" — is followed by the esophagus, stomach (with *cardiac* and *pyloric chambers*), intestine, and anus. The cardiac stomach contains grinding organs. Digestive glands *(hepatic glands)* pour enzymatic secretions into the pyloric chamber of the stomach.

   c. *Respiratory System.* Feathery gills are attached to the basal segments of the second and third maxillipeds (Table II) and the first four walking legs. Second and (in *Astacus*) third rows of gills are attached under the outer row. These are bathed by water in the *gill chamber* (the space under each side of the carapace); they contain blood vessels. The current of water through the gill chamber is maintained by the *"bailer,"* a branch of the second maxilla.

   d. *Circulatory System.* (Fig. 54, D). The *heart* is dorsal, in a *pericardium.* Blood enters the heart through three pairs of *ostia,* valvular openings. It is pumped out through seven *arteries,* which empty into open spaces, the *sinuses.* These sinuses drain into the capillaries of the gills, from which the blood enters the heart through the pericardium.

   e. *Excretory System.* The two *green glands,* nephridial structures, open at the bases of the antennae.

   f. *Nervous System.* There is a dorsal "brain," with two circumesophageal connectives, and a ventral chain of ganglia. The first ventral ganglion is large, corresponding to several fused ganglia. Nerves branch from the brain and ventral cord.

g. *Sensory System.* The sense of touch and the chemical senses (taste and smell) are highly developed on anterior appendages. There are two *compound eyes* (consisting of many optical units, the *ommatidia),* each eye on the end of a stalk. Organs of equilibration, *statocysts,* are present at the bases of the antennules.

3. REPRODUCTION AND DEVELOPMENT. The sexes are separate (dioecious). Both testis and ovary are bilobed. The testis empties by *sperm ducts* through pores at the base of the fifth pair of walking legs; the *oviducts* convey eggs from the ovary to openings at the base of the third pair of walking legs. (Fig. 54, B). The early embryonic stages are completed while the eggs remain attached to the swimmerets of the female, and even the larvae, after hatching, remain attached for some time.

Class Insecta (See Chapter XIV, pages 129 and 133).

REVIEW QUESTIONS

1. Compare and contrast the Onychophora and Annelida.
2. What are the characteristics of the phylum Arthropoda?
3. Name and characterize the major classes of the phylum Arthropoda.
4. Describe the morphology of a spider.
5. Explain the principle of homologous structure as illustrated in the crayfish.
6. Describe the relations between respiratory and circulatory systems in the crayfish.

CHAPTER XIV

INSECTA

The insects may be distinguished from other arthropods by the presence of three pairs of legs, one pair on each of the three thoracic segments. Most insects have two pairs of wings also, borne on the second and third thoracic segments. The wings are variously modified in texture, shape, size, and complexity of venation; in two orders the hind wings may be absent, replaced by vestigial organs termed *halteres*. Head, thorax, and abdomen are distinct body regions, the last externally showing segmentation into six to eleven metameres. One pair of antennae is present,

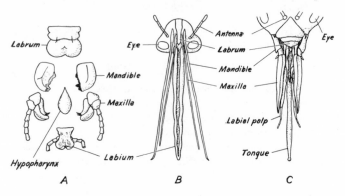

Fig. 56. Homology of the mouth-parts of insects. A. Biting mouth-parts of a grasshopper. B. Sucking mouth-parts of a bug. C. Lapping mouth-parts of a bee. (B and C redrawn after Henneguy).

and three pairs of primitively jaw-like mouthparts. The mouthparts may be mandibulate (true biting jaws), or they may be modified to form sucking mouth-parts. (Fig. 56). In general, the former are typical of the more primitive orders, or larval stages of more complex orders. Respiration in adults is by branching tracheae which open through paired spiracles on the sides of the body. Aquatic larvae may breathe by tracheal gills.

Development in primitive forms is *direct,* the young animals being only miniatures of the adults; in others there is an *incomplete metamorphosis,* the young being somewhat different from the adults and being active in all stages; in the more advanced types of insects there is *complete metamorphosis,* involving an active *larval stage,* an inactive *pupal stage,* and the active adult or *imago.* (Fig. 57).

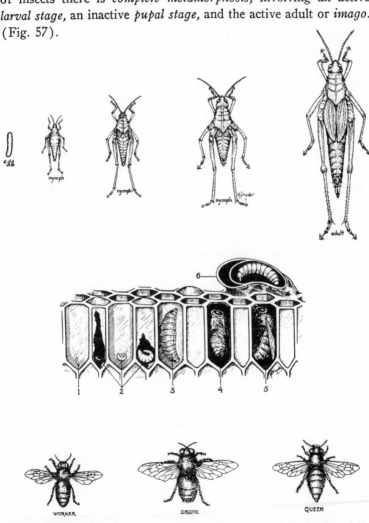

Fig. 57. Life histories of an insect with incomplete metamorphosis (southern lubber grasshopper, upper row of drawings), and one having complete metamorphosis (honey bee, middle and lower rows). All nymphal instars of the grasshopper are not shown. In the section of comb: 1, egg; 2-3, larvae; 4, pupa; 5, adult; 6, queen cell containing larva. (Drawings, except that of lubber grasshopper egg, copyright by General Biological Supply House, Chicago, used by permission).

Estimates of the number of species in the Class run as high
as several million. Over a half million have already been described
in published literature. In other words, there are more kinds of
insects than of all other animals combined. These are distributed
in terrestrial habitats from the equator to the arctic and from
sea-level to the snow-fields of the highest mountains; they have
even been collected in large numbers by nets carried by aeroplanes
or kites several thousand feet above the earth's surface. Many
live in fresh-water, particularly during early stages of development, although only a very few species are marine. The Orders
containing the greatest numbers of species are the Coleoptera
(200,000 described species), Lepidoptera (95,000), Hymenoptera
(70,000), Diptera (52,000).

In the following account all orders of insects recognized by
Brues and Melander (see References) are included. Inasmuch as
this list is much longer than the list of orders recognized in most
current textbooks it must be used with discretion, and in intelligent
comparison with other sources of information, textbook and lecture, available to the student. The characteristics given are believed
to be, in most cases, those of major value in recognition of representatives of the orders. Orders marked with an asterisk (*) are
those of major interest for the general zoology student. Descriptions in small type are of orders of relatively little importance to
the general student, either because the representatives are rare or
few in number or because they have a very limited geographic
distribution. Hence, three different categories of importance are
indicated by the printing. This should enable the student to use
the list wisely. At the same time, all the recognized orders are
named for the benefit of those needing the complete list.

Only two insect examples have been considered in detail,
these, the grasshopper and the honey-bee, being the types most
frequently studied in general zoology as representative of the Class.

ORDERS OF THE CLASS INSECTA

Order Protura. Very small, terrestrial, wingless; no eyes; antennae reduced or absent; sucking mouthparts; legs short, one-jointed
tarsus. Larvae with nine, adults with eleven abdominal segments. No
common names. (Sometimes separated from the insects as the Class
Mirientomata or Class Protura.)

Order Thysanura. Small, terrestrial, wingless; antennae long; legs with two- or three-jointed tarsus; three long terminal appendages of abdomen, the median one similar in form to the two lateral *cerci*. No metamorphosis. Bristle-tails and silver-fish. (Fig. 59A).

Order Entotrophi. Small, terrestrial, wingless; no eyes; antennae long; legs with one-jointed tarsus; prominent cerci. No metamorphosis. No common names.

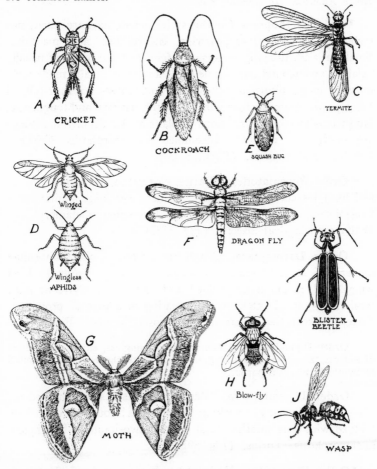

Fig. 58. Representatives of insect orders. Those illustrated in this figure are of major importance, each being marked with an asterisk in the text descriptions. A, Orthoptera; B, Blattariae; C, Isoptera; D, Homoptera; E, Hemiptera; F, Odonata; G, Lepidoptera; H, Diptera; I, Coleoptera; J, Hymenoptera. (B-J, copyright by General Biological Supply House, Chicago, used by permission).

Order Collembola. Small, wingless; moderately long antennae; legs with one-jointed tarsus; a median abdominal leaping (or springing) appendage. No metamorphosis. Spring-tails. (Fig. 59B).

Order Grylloblattodea. Wingless, terrestrial insects about an inch long; body depressed, head rather prominent; antennae long; legs moderately long, adapted for running; tarsi five-jointed; cerci long. Little metamorphosis. Limited geographically to N. E. Asia and N. W. North America. No common names.

*Order Orthoptera (in the strict sense, as here used, not including walking-sticks, earwigs, cockroaches, and mantids). Small to large jumping insects, the femur of the hind leg usually enlarged; compound and simple eyes; antennae usually moderately to very long; biting mouth-parts; tarsi three- to four-jointed (rarely two-jointed); fore-wings straight, narrow, and toughened; hind wings membranous, folded in plaits at rest (sometimes wings are vestigial or absent). Incomplete metamorphosis. Crickets, katydids, grasshoppers. (Figs. 58, 60).

Order Phasmatodea. Large, elongated, stick-like (rarely leaf-like) insects; antennae long, slender; legs long, similar, tarsi five-jointed; wings usually absent. Incomplete metamorphosis. Walking-sticks, leaf-insects. (Fig. 59C).

Order Dermaptera. Small to moderate size; antennae moderately long, slender; fore-wings hardened *(elytra);* hind wings oval, membranous, folded and covered by elytra at rest; tarsi three-jointed; abdomen terminating in a pair of prominent forceps (cerci). Incomplete metamorphosis. Earwigs. (Fig. 59D).

Order Diploglossata. Moderate-sized, wingless, external parasites of rodents. Short antennae; long, thin cerci; tarsi three-jointed. Limited to South Africa. Viviparous.

Order Thysanoptera. Very small insects which feed on plant juices (usually); sucking mouth-parts; four narrow wings fringed with long bristles; tarsi one- or two-jointed. Incomplete metamorphosis. Thrips. (Fig. 59E).

*Order Blattariae. Moderate to large size, oval, flattened, running insects; head nearly covered by pronotum; prothorax broad, movable; wings when present overlapping on abdomen, fore-wings tougher than hind wings; tarsi five-jointed; cerci prominent. Incomplete metamorphosis. Cockroaches. (Fig. 58.)

Order Mantodea. Moderate to large sized predatory insects, the front legs thick and heavily spined; head freely movable, with prominent eyes and antennae; body elongate, sometimes with abdomen expanded; wings usually short (may be absent), over-lapping when closed; tarsi usually five-jointed. Incomplete metamorphosis. Praying mantids. (Fig. 59F).

Order Embiodea. Small to moderate size, elongated; head prominent; elongated thorax; four similar wings (hind wings not fan-like); tarsi three-jointed. Incomplete metamorphosis. Few species, limited to tropics and subtropics. No common names.

*Order Isoptera. Small to moderate sized, soft-bodied insects (the large head may be heavily chitinized), living in large colonies and having pronounced polymorphism; large, prominent jaws; wings four, similar, long and narrow, lost at maturity; tarsi usually four-jointed. Incomplete metamorphosis. Termites, "white ants." (Fig. 58).

Order Corrodentia. Small, soft-bodied, usually with wings which when present are relatively large, the fore-wings larger than the hind wings; short body; tarsi two- or three-jointed, the first joint long. Incomplete metamorphosis. Book-lice, bark-lice. (Fig. 59G).

Order Zoraptera. Very small social insects, with winged and wingless forms of both sexes; fore-wings larger than hind; tarsi two-jointed, the first joint short. Incomplete metamorphosis. No common names.

Order Mallophaga. Small, wingless, external parasites of birds (rarely mammals); body flattened, usually broad; biting mouth-parts; short legs, not particularly stout. Incomplete metamorphosis. Bird lice. (Fig. 59H).

Order Anoplura. Small, wingless, external parasites of mammals, body usually somewhat flattened, mouth a fleshy beak (sucking mouth-parts); legs stout. True lice. (Fig. 59I).

*Order Homoptera. A variable group of small to moderately-large insects which feed on plant juices; with sucking mouth-parts (inserted at the posterior margin of head); four wings, never with basal portion hardened, when folded sloping over sides

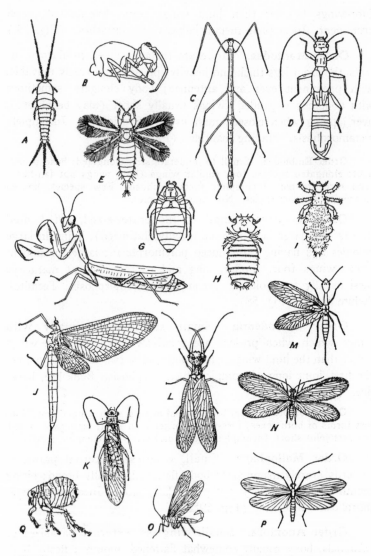

Fig. 59. Representatives of insect orders whose descriptions in the text are in large type but not marked with asterisks. A, Thysanura; B, Collembola; C, Phasmatodea; D, Dermaptera; E, Thysanoptera; F, Mantodea; G, Corrodentia; H, Mallophaga; I, Anoplura; J, Plectoptera; K, Plecoptera; L, Megaloptera; M, Raphidiodea; N, Neuroptera; O, Mecoptera; P, Trichoptera; Q, Siphonaptera. (A, B, D, E, G-J, M, O-Q, after Schröder, and after Schröder, from others, some modified; C, after Bolivar and Ferrière; F, redrawn from a photograph; K, redrawn from Needham and Claassen; L, after Berlese; N, redrawn after Froggatt).

of body. Typically with incomplete metamorphosis. (In scale insects, females are wingless, and males have only the fore-wings). Cicadas, leaf-hoppers, tree-hoppers, spittle insects, aphids or plant lice, mealy-bugs. (Fig. 58).

*Order Hemiptera (perhaps more frequently called Heteroptera). Very small to large terrestrial and aquatic insects which feed on plant or animal juices; with sucking mouth-parts (inserted usually toward front of head) ; large, free prothorax; wings overlap on abdomen, the basal portion of the fore-wings thickened — distal portion membranous. Incomplete metamorphosis. True bugs, water-striders, back-swimmers. (Fig. 58).

*Order Odonata. Large predatory insects with elongated body (particularly the abdomen) ; head freely movable, with large eyes; wings four, similar, elongate and moderately narrow (not folded), membranous throughout, with numerous longitudinal and transverse veins; legs moderately small, tarsi three-jointed. Incomplete metamorphosis, nymphal stage aquatic, the arrangement of tracheal gills variable. Damsel-flies, dragon-flies. (Fig. 58).

Order Plectoptera. Slender, delicate insects, head not freely movable; four wings of complex venation, the fore-wings much larger than the hind ones; legs weak, tarsi usually five- or four-jointed. Incomplete metamorphosis, nymphal stage aquatic with three caudal filaments, and abdominal tracheal gills; life of adults very brief (hence the genus name *Ephemera)*. May flies. (Fig. 59J).

Order Plecoptera. Moderate to large-sized insects; four wings of complex venation, the hind wings larger and folded at rest; antennae long, thin; cerci long; legs strong, three-jointed tarsus. Incomplete metamorphosis; nymphal stage aquatic, breathing by thoracic or abdominal tracheal gills or without visible gills. Stone-flies. (Fig. 59K).

Order Megaloptera. Moderate to large sized predatory insects; four wings of relatively complex venation, similar in size, though hind wings are folded at rest; prothorax squarish. Complete metamorphosis (pupal stage present) ; the larva aquatic, with lateral abdominal tracheal gills. Hellgramite. (Fig. 59L).

Order Raphidiodea. Moderate-sized, slender, predatory insects; head large; antennae long, thin; prothorax elongate; four membranous wings, similar, numerous branched veins; tarsi five-jointed. Complete metamorphosis, larva terrestrial. Snake-flies. (Fig. 59M).

Order Neuroptera. Small to large, slender, predatory insects; head and prothorax free; eyes large; abdomen long, narrow; wings large, membranous, alike. Complete metamorphosis, larvae usually terrestrial, feeding on body juices of insects; pupae in cocoons. Green lace-wings, ant-lions, or doodle-bugs (larvae). (Fig. 59N).

Order Mecoptera. Small to medium sized; head usually prolonged downward, eyes large; four wings usually present, long, narrow, alike; antennae long, slender; legs long, slender for running, tarsi five-jointed. Complete metamorphosis, larva caterpillar-like. Scorpion-flies. (Fig. 59O).

Order Trichoptera. Small to medium-sized; head free, eyes prominent; hind wings usually with moderately broad anal area; wings membranous, covered with hairs; legs alike, tarsi five-jointed. Complete metamorphosis, aquatic larva usually living in a case constructed of foreign objects. Caddis-flies, caddis worms (larvae). (Fig. 59P).

*Order Lepidoptera. Small to very large insects with large wings covered with scales—which form color pattern (absent in certain areas occasionally); antennae long, variously modified, *e. g.,* clubbed, feathered; sucking mouth-parts, coiled under head; legs similar, ordinarily with five-jointed tarsus. Complete metamorphosis, larva a caterpillar with biting mouth-parts. Moths, skippers, butterflies. (Fig. 58).

*Order Diptera. Very small to medium-sized insects with but one pair of wings (on mesothorax), wings of metathorax replaced by knobbed *halteres;* antennae variable; sucking, piercing, and lapping mouth-parts; legs usually alike, five-jointed tarsus. Complete metamorphosis, larvae usually legless maggots. Flies, gnats, mosquitoes. (Fig. 58).

Order Siphonaptera. Small, wingless, jumping insects; rather small head and thorax, large abdomen, body with bristles; antennae short, thick; piercing, sucking mouth-parts; legs stout, large. Complete metamorphosis; larva worm-like, free-living; pupa in cocoon. Fleas. (Fig. 59Q).

*Order Coleoptera. Minute to very large, hard-bodied insects; head and prothorax free; antennae usually ten- or eleven-jointed, variously modified; mandibulate mouth-parts; fore-wings (elytra) hard, hind wings membranous, usually folded at rest; tarsi usually four- or five-jointed. Complete metamorphosis. Beetles, weevils. (Fig. 58).

Order Strepsiptera. Small parasites of other insects, males winged and free-living; females worm-like, wingless, legless parasites; fore-wings of male reduced to small stubs; hind wings large, without cross veins. Complete metamorphosis of males. "Twisted-winged insects."

*Order Hymenoptera. Small to medium-sized insects with four membranous wings, the fore-wings larger; head free, mandibulate mouth-parts adapted for lapping; antennae variable; eyes usually large; prothorax not free; tarsi usually five-jointed; abdomen with six or seven visible segments; ovipositor usually sting-like. Complete metamorphosis. Bees, ants, wasps. (Figs. 58, 61).

EXAMPLES OF THE CLASS INSECTA
Grasshopper (Order Orthoptera).

1. EXTERNAL CHARACTERISTICS. (Figs. 56, 57, 60).

   a. *Divisions of the Body.* Bodies of all insects have three major divisions — *head, thorax,* and *abdomen.* Each division consists embryonically of several segments. In the adult, three divisions of the thorax are visible — *prothorax, mesothorax,* and *metathorax.* In the grasshopper the dorsal part of the prothorax is a saddle-like covering, the *pronotum.* The abdomen is divided into numerous segments, all distinct except the last few, which are fused and modified to form the *external genitalia.* About nine abdominal segments are clearly evident.

b. *Appendages.*

(1) *Antennae.* One moderately long pair, consisting of numerous segments, is present on the head.

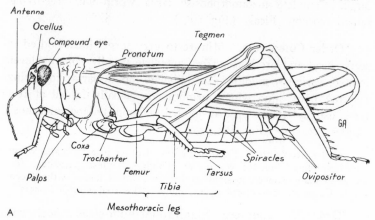

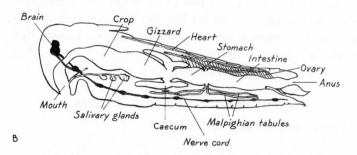

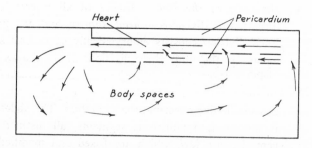

Fig. 60. The grasshopper, *Arphia pseudonietana* (Thomas). A. External features—the segments of a typical insect leg illustrated in the labels of the mesothoracic leg. B. Diagrammatic longitudinal section, showing the organs in their relative positions. C. Diagram illustrating the direction of blood flow.

(2) *Mouth-Parts*. (Fig. 56). The *labrum* (upper lip) is suspended from the *clypeus*. Immediately under it are the two *mandibles*, heavy chewing jaws. Under these are the two *maxillae*, each bearing a jointed palp. Between the basal parts of the maxillae lies the pear-shaped *hypoglossus*. The divided lower lip, *labium*, bears a pair of jointed palps. The *maxillary* and *labial palps* are sensory; the remaining parts function in food manipulation and mastication.

(3) *Legs*. There are three pairs, one each on prothorax, mesothorax, and metathorax. Those of the third pair are strong and elongated, adapted for leaping. Each leg is divided into segments, from proximal to distal end: *coxa, trochanter, femur, tibia, tarsus,* — the latter having three segments in grasshoppers. (Fig. 60). The tarsus terminates in a pad *(pulvillus)* and two *claws*.

(4) *Wings*. Grasshoppers usually have two pairs, one each on meso- and metathorax; but they may be absent or reduced. The anterior two, the *tegmina* (sing. *tegmen*), are hard, leathery, and more or less opaque. The posterior two are enlarged, membranous, transparent except when bearing color pattern or bands, and folded when at rest. Numerous veins are present in the wings.

(5) *External Genitalia*. In males, the posterior tip of the abdomen is rounded below. Copulatory apparatus is present, including characteristic lateral projections, the *cerci,* which are used as diagnostic characters of species. In the female, the posterior end of the abdomen consists of the dorsal and ventral *valves* of the *ovipositor,* an organ by which a hole is made in the ground for the deposition of a packet of eggs.

2. MORPHOLOGY AND PHYSIOLOGY OF ORGAN SYSTEMS. (Fig. 60).

a. *Body Cavity.* The coelom is a haemocoel, which is reduced in volume to limited spaces between the organs.

b. *Digestive System.* This consists of the mouth, a narrow oesophagus, a thin-walled crop merging directly into a thick-walled gizzard, followed by a thin-walled stomach, and the narrow intestine leading to the anus. These regions differ more in texture and thickness of walls than in internal diameter. A salivary duct, formed by the union of two ducts from the paired *salivary glands*, opens into the mouth. **Six** double *caeca* (blind sacs) surround gizzard and stomach, emptying into the anterior end of the stomach.

c. *Respiratory System. Tracheal tubes* and *air-sacs* extend throughout the body. These open to the outside through ten lateral openings, the *spiracles,* two on the thorax and eight on the abdomen. Air is carried to cells as air, not as oxygen in solution. CO_2 is partly excreted through other organs, however.

d. *Circulatory System.* There is a dorsal heart, blood entering it through five pairs of ostia from the pericardial sinus in which it is enclosed. The pericardial sinus receives blood from all parts of the body — from the sinuses through which the blood flows after being pumped from the anterior end of the heart. (Fig. 60C).

e. *Excretory System.* Numerous fine *Malpighian tubules* empty into the intestine at the point where stomach and intestine meet. These tubules, closed at their upper ends, drain excretory materials which diffuse from the haemocoel, into the intestine.

f. *Nervous System.* There is a dorsal, bilobed cerebral ganglion or "brain," joining the ventral cord by two circumesophageal connectives. In the ventral cord are three thoracic and five abdominal ganglia. Branching nerves extend out from the central system.

g. *Sensory System.* The antennae and palps probably contain organs of touch, taste, and smell. A *tympanic membrane* occurs on the surface of the first abdominal segment. This is involved in sound detection. (Sound producing organs on wings or legs are often present.) There are two large compound eyes, made up of many ommatidia; and three ocelli, or simple eyes.

3. REPRODUCTION AND DEVELOPMENT. The sexes are separate. Two testes or two ovaries are present, in the dorsal part of the body-cavity. Sperm-ducts extend from the testis, oviducts from the ovary, both types opening ventral to anus. Fertilization is internal. The fertilized eggs are deposited in the ground (by most species of grasshoppers) in packets, the female excavating a burrow with her ovipositor for the packet or *egg pod*. In most of our species, embryonic development begins during the same season but undergoes a dormant period, *diapause*, during the succeeding winter. Diapause is broken during the following growing season, and the young grasshopper hatches without wings but otherwise similar in appearance to the adult. Juvenile grasshoppers are called *nymphs*. In most species, there are five successive juvenile stages or *instars*, each terminated by a molt, before the mature form is attained some weeks after hatching. The process of molting is controlled by a series of hormones produced by structures in the neighborhood of the cerebral ganglia. Adult grasshoppers live only during the season in which they hatched. (Fig. 57).

Honey Bee (Order Hymenoptera).

1. KINDS OF INDIVIDUALS. Polymorphism (page 30) is evidenced in the occurrence of three *castes:* fertile males, *drones;* fertile females, *queens;* sterile females, *workers.* Pollen baskets (see below) are present only in workers. A drone has a broad abdomen; a queen, a somewhat narrow long abdomen. (Fig. 57).

2. EXTERNAL CHARACTERISTICS.

    a. *Divisions of the Body.* The head, thorax, and abdomen are quite distinct. The thorax shows typical division into prothorax, mesothorax, and metathorax. There are six visible segments in the abdomen.

    b. *Appendages.*

        (1) *Antennae.* There is one pair on the head, each antenna consisting of twelve segments in the male, thirteen in the female.

        (2) *Mouth-Parts.* (Fig. 56). The labrum is broad and short. A fleshy *epipharynx* projects beneath it. Two mandibles, horny jaws, are lateral to the labrum, and extend beyond it. The two maxillae extend much beyond the mandibles; they are covered with stiff hairs. Small maxillary palps are present. The labium is modified into a much elongated central portion, the *tongue,* and has a large palp on each side.

        (3) *Legs.* Each one of the three pairs of legs, pro-, meso-, and metathoracic, consists of coxa, trochanter, femur, tibia, and a five-jointed tarsus. The tarsus terminates in a pulvillus and lateral claws. The legs are covered with bristles, and have other structures used in collecting and carrying pollen, and in cleaning pollen from the body. An *antennae cleaner* and an *eye-brush* are present on the prothoracic legs. In the workers occurs the *pollen basket,* a concavity in the surface of the tibia of the metathoracic leg; and there is a spur on the mesothoracic leg used to pry pollen from the basket.

        (4) *Wings.* There are two pairs, meso- and metathoracic, both membranous. Veins divide each wing into "cells."

        (5) *External Genitalia.* The *sting,* present in queens and workers, is a modified ovipositor. In the male, a copulatory apparatus is present.

3. MORPHOLOGY AND PHYSIOLOGY OF ORGAN SYSTEMS. (Fig. 61).

    a. *Body Cavity.* The coelom is a haemocoel.

    b. *Digestive System.* The digestive tract consists of the mouth; opening into an elongated, thin esophagus; this joining a globular organ, the *honey sac;* which empties into a large, long stomach; followed by a narrow intestine, and an expanded *rectum,* which opens at the anus. Digestive glands are present in the wall of the stomach.

    c. *Respiratory System.* Oxygen is not transported in blood but as air in tracheae. Seven pairs of lateral spiracles, two on the thorax and five on the abdomen, admit air into the tracheae and air-sacs, branches of which convey it to all parts of the body.

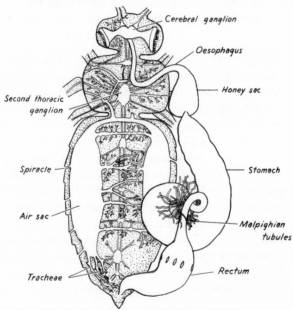

Fig. 61. Internal morphology of the honey bee, respiratory system partly eliminated on the right. (Redrawn from Henneguy, after Leuckart).

    d. *Circulatory System.* The dorsal heart lies in a peri-

cardial sinus, receiving blood through five pairs of
ostia. The blood is pumped anteriorly; after leaving
the anterior end of the heart it diffuses through the
haemocoel into the pericardial sinus.

e. *Excretory System.* Malpighian tubules drain into the
intestine at its anterior end.

f. *Nervous System.* The dorsal cerebral ganglion or
"brain" communicates with the ventral cord by two
commissures around the esophagus. The ventral
cord is double, and contains seven ganglia, some of
these representing fusions of several ganglia of the
embryo.

g. *Sensory System.* The antennae probably bear end-
organs of smell, hearing, and touch. Taste organs
are located near the mouth and on the tongue. There
are two large compound eyes, and three ocelli, the
latter on the dorsal surface of the head.

4. REPRODUCTION AND DEVELOPMENT. The queen bee is
impregnated by the male or drone but once during her
life time, during the nuptial flight, at which time the
spermatozoa are received in an organ, the *spermatotheca,*
in which they may live for many years. Fertilized eggs
give rise to workers or queens, the latter type of individual developing solely because of a different diet — the
"royal jelly." Drones develop from unfertilized eggs,
parthenogenetically, and are haploid as to chromosome
number. In sperm cell formation there is no meiosis,
whereas in oogenesis it does occur — the cells of females
being diploid. Each sex possesses two gonads, the ducts
from the two joining before reaching the genital opening.
Development is in the hive, through larval and pupal
stages — hence by complete metamorphosis.

REVIEW QUESTIONS

1. What are the general characteristics of insects?
2. What types of metamorphosis are illustrated by insects?

3. Compare the following orders of insects with reference to types of metamorphosis, kinds of mouthparts, and nature of wings: Thysanura, Orthoptera, Blattariae, Isoptera, Homoptera, Hemiptera, Odonata, Lepidoptera, Diptera, Coleoptera, Hymenoptera.

4. Describe and draw a typical insect leg.

5. Describe the organ systems of the grasshopper.

6. Describe the organ systems of the bee.

7. Compare respiratory and circulatory systems of insect, spider, and crayfish.

8. Explain the differences between the different castes of bees.

CHAPTER XV

MOLLUSCA

CHARACTERISTICS OF THE PHYLUM MOLLUSCA

The mollusks are soft-bodied, non-metameric, fundamentally bilaterally symmetrical animals which are usually enclosed within a calcareous shell of their own secretion. They are widely distributed in marine, fresh-water, and terrestrial habitats, but are most abundant in the ocean. They uniformly possess an enclosing envelope, the mantle, which forms the outer boundary of the mantle cavity. This is bounded internally by the main portion of the body. There is also always present a muscular mass, the foot, the form and function varying in the different classes. Mollusks have complex digestive, respiratory, excretory, and reproductive systems. Some of them have trochophore larvae, similar to those of annelids. The circulatory system consists of a chambered heart and a system of closed vessels involving special capillary systems in the excretory and respiratory organs; it is the most complex of invertebrate circulatory systems. In some mollusks the nervous and sensory systems are quite elaborate, the eyes in particular being similar to those of vertebrates. The mollusks are the most highly developed non-metameric animals, but recently discovered, segmented mollusks suggest an annelid ancestry.

CLASSES OF THE PHYLUM MOLLUSCA

Class Amphineura. Clearly bilaterally symmetrical animals; ventral elongated foot (no typical foot in one aberrant group); mantle cavity containing many gills lateral to it; dorsal surface covered with limy spicules or (more typically) eight calcareous plates. All marine. Dioecious or hermaphroditic. (Example: chiton.) (Fig. 62.)

Class Gastropoda. Commonly with spiral, single shell; foot a creeping organ; well-defined head, with tentacles and eyes;

a tooth-bearing ribbon (radula) in buccal cavity; respiration by gills, "lungs," or both. Marine, fresh-water, and terrestrial. Sexes separate, or hermaphroditic; oviparous or ovoviviparous; development typically involving trochophore and veliger larval stages. (Examples: snail, whelk, limpet, slug.) (Fig. 62.)

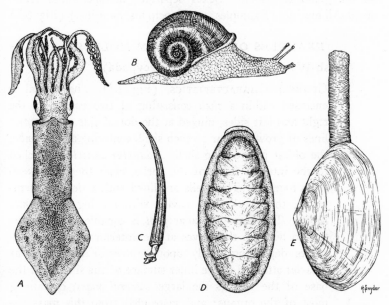

Fig. 62. Representatives of the classes of mollusks. A, Cephalopoda (squid); B, Gastropoda (land snail); C, Scaphopoda (*Dentalium*); D, Amphineura (chiton); E, Pelecypoda (clam). (Copyright by General Biological Supply House, Chicago, used by permission).

Class Scaphopoda. Mollusks living within a shell, open at both ends, shaped like an elephant's tusk; body elongated dorsoventrally; head rudimentary; foot pointed, lobed, for burrowing. Exclusively marine. Sexes separate; development through trochophore and veliger stages. (Example: *Dentalium*, "toothshell.") (Fig. 62.)

Class Pelecypoda. Bivalve mollusks, the body enclosed between right and left shells, hinged dorsally; body laterally compressed; no distinct head; muscular, ventral, laterally-compressed foot, for burrowing. Sexes separate, or hermaphroditic; development involves specialized larval stage. Marine or freshwater. (Examples: clam, mussel, oyster, scallop, ship-worm.) (Figs. 62-64).

Class Cephalopoda. Mollusks in which a clearly-defined head, with large eyes, is surrounded by part of the foot which is modified to form tentacles; part of foot modified to form funnel opening out from mantle cavity; very complex organ systems; shell present or absent, internal or external; in most cephalopods an ink gland is present. Sexes separate; no specialized larval stage. All marine. (Examples: squid, octopus, nautilus.) (Fig. 62.)

EXAMPLES OF THE PHYLUM MOLLUSCA

Fresh-Water Mussel (Class Pelecypoda).

1. GENERAL CHARACTERISTICS. (Fig. 63). The animal is enclosed within a *shell* consisting of two *valves,* on the right and left sides, hinged at the dorsal side. Concentric lines of growth occur on each shell, centering at the *umbo,* the oldest part of the shell. *Adductor muscles,* attached to the internal faces of the shells, close them and keep them together. The shells are lined with a delicate membrane, the *mantle,* the cavity within being the *mantle cavity.* The large muscular *foot* is capable of being extended between the valves at the anterior end, its movements depending partly upon *protractor* and *retractor muscles* attached to the inner surface of the shells. At the base of the foot is the large *visceral mass,* containing most of the organs; and suspended from this mass are four, sheet-like, parallel *gill-plates.* At the posterior end, leading into and from the mantle cavity are an *incurrent* (ventral) and an *excurrent* (dorsal) *siphon.* Water passes into the mantle cavity through the former and out through the latter.

2. MORPHOLOGY AND PHYSIOLOGY OF ORGAN SYSTEMS. (Figs. 63, 64).

   a. *Digestive System.* The mouth is at the anterior end of the visceral mass, opening from the mantle cavity. There is a short oesophagus, followed by a stomach; a long intestine, coiled partly within the foot, opening at the anus, which is near the excurrent siphon. The digestive gland, or *liver,* is a two-lobed organ, one lobe on each side of the stomach.

b. *Respiratory System.* Oxygen in solution is taken up by the *gills* from water in the mantle cavity; carbon

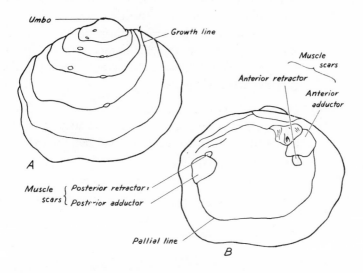

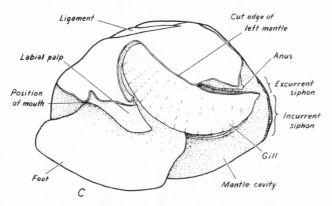

Fig. 63. Fresh-water mussel. A, outer surface of right valve; B, inner surface of left valve of *Quadrula lachrymosa* (Lea) (from drawings by Marion I. Alexander). C, exposed viscera of *Symphynota complanata* (Barnes) after removal of the left valve and mantle (redrawn from Coker *et al*, after Lefevre and Curtis).

dioxide is given off similarly. The gill filaments contain blood capillaries, and the gases are transported in the blood stream.

c. *Circulatory System.* (Fig. 64). Blood from the gills passes to the *heart,* through one of the two *auricles* and into the *ventricle.* The heart is enclosed in a pericardium. From the ventricle, blood is pumped both anteriorly and posteriorly through two *aortae* to various parts of the body. It is then collected in the *vena cava,* carried through the kidneys, thence to the gills and back to the heart.

d. *Excretory System.* The *kidneys* or *nephridia* drain, through *excretory pores,* into the dorsal part of the mantle cavity; wastes being carried out through the dorsal or excurrent siphon.

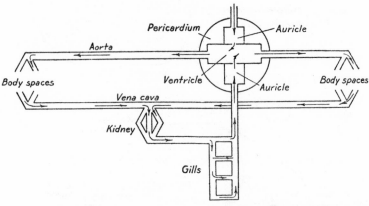

Fig. 64. Diagram illustrating the direction of blood flow in the fresh-water mussel. The gill circulation is represented on only one side of the body.

e. *Nervous System.* Three pairs of ganglia are present, one pair near the oesophagus, one in the foot, the other near the posterior end of the visceral mass. These are connected by longitudinal fibers, the two anterior ones being also connected transversely.

f. *Sensory System.* Sensory cells, probably sensitive to touch and light, occur along the margin of the mantle; an organ for detecting disturbance in equilibrium is present. Sense organs are, however, less well developed in mussels than in many other mollusks.

3. REPRODUCTION AND DEVELOPMENT. Mussels are typically dioecious. Spermatozoa are carried from the mantle cavity of the male through the excurrent siphon and into the mantle cavity of the female through its incurrent siphon. Fertilization occurs in the mantle cavity of the female, where development may continue in *brood-pouches*. The larva, a *glochidium*, is discharged through the excurrent siphon. It develops only as a parasite on gills or fins of fish, which it leaves when sufficiently mature.

Land Snail (Class Gastropoda). (Fig. 62). The shell is a somewhat flattened, coiled spiral. The snail, fundamentally showing bilateral symmetry, is considerably modified to conform to the coiled shell. A well-defined *head* is present, bearing two pairs of *tentacles,* the longer pair with *eyes* at their tips. A peculiar rasping organ, the *radula,* is present inside the mouth. The snail is air-breathing, respiration involving the "lung," the vascular wall of the mantle cavity, air entering through a small opening, the *pulmonary aperture.* Land snails are hermaphroditic, but not self-fertilizing.

REVIEW QUESTIONS

1. Why are mollusks considered the most advanced of non-metameric animals?
2. Name and characterize the classes of the phylum Mollusca.
3. Discuss the morphology and physiology of the fresh-water mussel.
4. Compare the circulatory, respiratory, and excretory systems of Mollusca, Insecta, and Annelida.

Chapter XVI

CHORDATA

CHARACTERISTICS OF THE PHYLUM CHORDATA

The chordates, with all their superficial differences, have in common the following three fundamental characteristics: (a) the notochord, a dorsal, gelatinous, stiffening rod, present during some stage in development; (b) a tubular nerve cord, situated dorsal to the notochord; (c) pharyngeal gill slits. Their best known and most numerous representatives are the vertebrates, exceeded in numbers of species only by arthropods and mollusks, and widely distributed in all types of habitats. The other chordates, the Acraniata or Prochordata, are limited to marine environments. A coelom is usually well developed, and metamerism is evident. Great complexities in animal organ systems occur within the phylum. The nearest relatives of the Chordata are the Echinodermata, though the relationship is not evident when we compare adults from these two phyla. Adult differences are, however, overshadowed by the similarity in the pattern of embryonic development and in the method of formation of the embryonic coelom.

(The present chapter summarizes the classification within the phylum and the special characteristics of the Acraniata. The five chapters next following deal with the major groups of Vertebrata or Craniata.)

CLASSIFICATION OF THE PHYLUM CHORDATA

Subphylum Enteropneusta (Hemichorda). Typically elongated, worm-like animals with three body divisions, proboscis, collar, trunk; a short, hollow atypical notochord, which is an anterior projection from the alimentary canal into the proboscis; numerous lateral gill slits; diffuse nervous system with dorsal and ventral trunks; dorsal and ventral blood vessels, tissue sinuses, anterior dorsal heart. Sexes separate; fertilization external; development in some through a tornaria larval stage similar to larvae of echinoderms. Marine, burrowing near shore, or living in deep sea; some are colonial. A widely accepted and quite logical interpretation of this group today is that it should be considered a distinct phylum, the Phylum Hemichordata. (Example: *Dolichoglossus*, "balanoglossus.") (Fig. 65.)

Subphylum Tunicata (Urochorda). Typically short, thick-bodied in adult condition, with a leathery covering *(tunic* or test) ; often attached as adults, but some are free-living. The tadpole-like larva has well-developed notochord and nerve cord in tail; with metamorphosis into adult these are lost. Typical adults

Fig. 65.   A. *Dolichoglossus.*   B. *Molgula,* a sea-squirt.

have incurrent (oral) and excurrent (atrial) openings, the former bringing water into the pharyngeal cavity, whose numerous gill slits open into the surrounding atrial chamber; water escapes to outside through atrial opening. Anus opens into atrial cavity. Circulatory system with heart which periodically reverses the direction of blood flow. Hermaphroditic; and reproduction may occur asexually by budding. All marine; free-swimming or attached (the best-known examples are attached, many of them living in colonies). (Examples: sea-squirt, sea-pork.) (Fig. 65.)

Subphylum Cephalochorda (Leptocardii). Small, elongated, compressed, with body shaped like a fish, but without paired fins or distinct head; well-developed notochord and nerve cord, extending length of body; pharynx with numerous gill slits, in an atrial cavity which opens ventrally just posterior to middle of body; direction of blood flow, forward on ventral side, backward on dorsal side (as in vertebrates), but distinct heart absent. Sexes separate; fertilization external. (Example: *Amphioxus* or *Branchiostoma.)* (Fig. 66.)

Subphylum Vertebrata (Craniata). Small to very large; marked development of a head, containing brain enclosed in cranium; notochord replaced in part or wholly by chain of cartilages or bones, the vertebrae; gill slits, in embryos only of higher vertebrates, and never so numerous as in Acraniata; jaws present in all but Class Agnatha (Cyclostomata); usually two pairs of paired appendages, never more; well developed heart divided into chambers; blood containing respiratory pigment (hemoglobin) in cells (erythrocytes or red corpuscles); paired eyes and ears in most. Sexes separate, or hermaphroditic; fertilization external or internal; oviparous, ovoviviparous, or viviparous. (Examples: lamprey, shark, trout, frog, snake, sparrow, rabbit, man.)

The Subphylum Vertebrata is subdivided as follows:

Superclass Pisces — fishes
    Class Agnatha (Cyclostomata) — hagfishes, lampreys
    Class Chondrichthyes — sharks, rays, chimaeras
    Class Osteichthyes—ganoids, bony-fishes, lung-fishes

Superclass Tetrapoda — amphibious and terrestrial vertebrates
    Class Amphibia — salamanders, frogs
    Class Reptilia — lizards, snakes, turtles, crocodiles
    Class Aves — birds
    Class Mammalia — mammals: moles, dogs, bats, whales, man

(Details of the above groups are included in Chapters XVII to XXI, inclusive.)

EXAMPLE OF THE ACRANIATA

Amphioxus (Branchiostoma) (Subphylum Cephalochorda or Leptocardii).

1. EXTERNAL CHARACTERISTICS. The body is two to three inches long, elongated, compressed, pointed at both ends; numerous muscle segments or *myotomes* are externally visible; a *dorsal* median *fin, caudal fin, ventral* median *fin,* and two ventral ridges anterior to the latter — the *metapleural folds* are present; the mouth is surrounded by a fringe of *cirri;* an *atrial pore* occurs about two-thirds

of the distance back from the anterior end; the *anus* is on the left side of the ventral fin, nine-tenths of the distance back from the anterior end. (Fig. 66).

2. MORPHOLOGY AND PHYSIOLOGY OF ORGAN SYSTEMS.

   a. *Skeletal System.* The *notochord*, extending the length of the body, serves as the axial skeleton. Other skeletal structures are poorly developed.

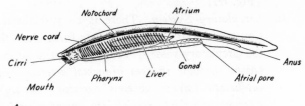

A

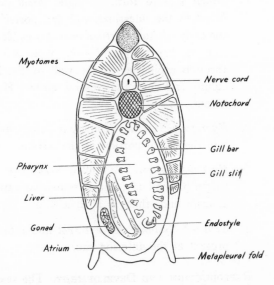

B

Fig. 66. *Amphioxus (Branchiostoma)*. A. Diagrammatic sketch of the right half, as exposed by sectioning in the sagittal plane (redrawn after Krause). B. Diagrammatic sketch of a cross-section through the posterior part of the pharynx.

   b. *Digestive System.* The mouth opens into an elongated *pharynx,* leading into the *intestine;* the *pharynx* has a ventral ciliated groove, the *endostyle;* the *liver* is an anterior diverticulum of the intestine.

c. *Respiratory System.* The walls of the pharynx are perforated by many *gill slits,* separated by *gill bars* containing the branchial capillaries involved in respiratory exchange. Water from the pharynx passes through the atrium and outside through the *atriopore.* (Fig. 66).

d. *Circulatory System.* There is no specialized heart. Contractions of the *ventral aorta* force blood through the circulatory vessels. From the ventral aorta, blood passes through *afferent branchial arteries, branchial capillaries* (where gaseous exchange occurs), and *efferent branchial arteries* into paired *dorsal aortae,* which join to form a single *dorsal aorta* carrying blood to the intestinal wall and posterior region of the body. A *subintestinal vein* carries blood anteriorly into an *hepatic portal vein,* from which it passes through capillaries in the wall of the liver diverticulum and into the ventral aorta. Hemoglobin is absent.

e. *Excretory System.* Numerous paired *nephridia* open into the dorsal portion of the atrium.

f. *Nervous System.* A tubular *nerve cord* extends the length of the body, and is somewhat expanded at the anterior end; there is no true brain.

g. *Sensory System.* An *eye-spot* and *olfactory pit* are present at the anterior end.

3. REPRODUCTION AND DEVELOPMENT. The sexes are separate; numerous pairs of gonads are present in the lateral portions of the atrium. Mature gametes are discharged into the atrium and escape through the atriopore. Fertilization occurs in the water. Cleavage is total, with the cells approximately equal; gastrulation occurs by invagi-

nation; the coelom is formed from *mesodermal pouches* which develop from the walls of the archenteron. Development is completed without metamorphosis.

REVIEW QUESTIONS

1. What are the fundamental characteristics of the phylum Chordata?
2. Name, characterize, and compare the subphyla of the phylum Chordata.
3. Describe Amphioxus in detail.

CHAPTER XVII

SUPERCLASS PISCES—FISHES

CHARACTERISTICS OF THE SUPERCLASS PISCES

The fishes are aquatic, gill-breathing vertebrates. (Breathing through a modified swim-bladder supplements gill-breathing in some species.) A brain, enlarged and divided into regions, is present; it is enclosed within a cartilaginous or bony cranium. Paired eyes are present. The ear is represented only by the semicircular canals, an organ of equilibrium. A well developed heart is present, and circulation involves flow of all the blood from the heart through the gills and thence to the rest of the body. Kidneys of the pronephric and mesonephric types occur.

CLASSES OF THE SUPERCLASS PISCES

Class Agnatha (Cyclostomata). Jawless fishes with anterior round mouth; smooth slimy skin; paired fins absent; a single dorsal nasal opening; pharynx with seven or more gill slits opening indirectly to the outside; notochord persistent, supplemented by incomplete cartilaginous vertebrae; brain of five divisions (telencephalon, diencephalon, mesencephalon, metencephalon, myelencephalon), less distinct than in higher vertebrates; ten cranial nerves; pronephros (kidney) in hagfishes, mesonephros in lampreys; no renal portal system. Sexes separate, or hermaphroditic. Living upon body fluids or organs of fishes, sucked through round mouth after it has rasped an opening in fish's body. Marine and fresh-water. (Examples: hagfish, lamprey.) (Fig. 67).

Class Chondrichthyes. Fishes with ventral mouth, provided with jaws (jaws present in all subsequently discussed classes of vertebrates), and possessing cartilaginous skeleton; skin typically covered with placoid scales (of combined ectodermal and mesodermal origin); two pairs of paired fins; caudal fin heterocercal (dorsal lobe the larger) in most; paired nasal cavities;

pharynx with five to seven gill slits (covered by a single operculum in the chimaeras); notochord partially replaced, complete vertebrae; brain of five divisions, with ten cranial nerves; mesonephros in adults; renal portal system present; spiral valve in intestine. Sexes separate; fertilization external or internal; oviparous or ovoviviparous. Practically all marine. (Examples: shark, ray, chimaera.) (Figs. 67-68.)

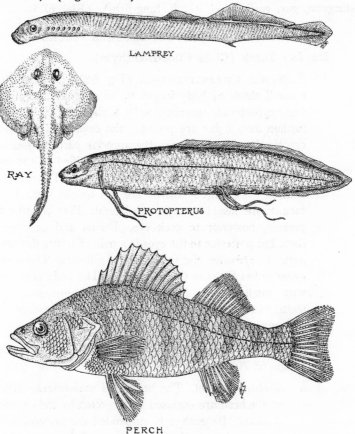

LAMPREY

RAY

PROTOPTERUS

PERCH

Fig. 67. Representatives of the Superclass Pisces. Lamprey (Class **Agnatha** or Cyclostomata). Ray (Class Chondrichthyes). *Protopterus*, a lung-fish; and perch (Class Osteichthyes). (Copyright by General Biological Supply House, Chicago, used by permission).

Class Osteichthyes. Fishes with jaw-mouths, and possessing a skeleton in part or wholly of bone; dermal bones supplement chondrocranium (cartilage cranium) to form complex skull;

scales ganoid, cycloid, or ctenoid (all of mesodermal origin) or absent; gills (embryologically six gill-slits, but usually four gills only in adults) covered by operculum; swim-bladder usually present, connected with pharynx or not; notochord mostly replaced by bony vertebrae; brain of five divisions, with ten cranial nerves; mesonephros in adults; renal portal system present; spiral valve in intestine of more primitive kinds. (Examples: *Polypterus,* sturgeon, gar, catfish, eel, perch, lung-fish.) (Fig. 67.)

EXAMPLE OF THE SUPERCLASS PISCES
Dogfish Shark (Class Chondrichthyes).

1. EXTERNAL CHARACTERISTICS. (Fig. 68). The dogfish is a small shark of body length up to approximately three feet, cylindrical, tapering, with a flattened head. Two median *dorsal fins* are present; the *caudal fin* is *hetero-cercal;* the paired fins are the anterior *pectoral fins* and posterior *pelvic fins;* the latter are modified in the male along their inner margins to form *claspers.* The mouth is ventral. The paired *nostrils* are pits on the ventral sur-face of the head; the *eyes* are lateral. Five *gill-slits* are present, posterior to each eye. Dorsal and anterior to these but posterior to the eyes is a pair of triangular open-ings, the *spiracles,* the vestigial first gill-slits. The *cloacal opening* lies between the pelvic fins. The body is covered with small *placoid scales;* these are homologous with teeth, consisting of dentine inside (of mesodermal origin) and enamel outside (of ectodermal origin).

2. MORPHOLOGY AND PHYSIOLOGY OF ORGAN SYSTEMS. (Figs. 68-70).

   a. *Skeletal System.* The brain and major sense organs of the head are enclosed or protected by the *chondro-cranium.* Beneath it is suspended the *visceral skele-ton,* consisting of the skeleton of lower jaw and *gill-arches. Vertebrae* of two kinds, *trunk* and *caudal* occur, both possessing *neural arches* but only the latter type with the *haemal arch.* The fins are supported by rays of cartilage proximally, and strengthened by rays of keratin distally. The *pectoral*

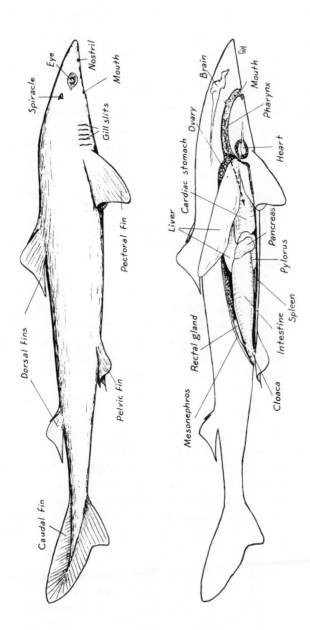

Fig. 68. Dogfish shark. Above: external features. Below: lateral view of a dissection in which the relative positions of the organs are shown (one liver lobe has been moved to expose certain organs otherwise concealed by it).

and *pelvic girdles* support pectoral and pelvic fins, respectively, and connect them with the axial skeleton.

b. *Muscular System.* Regularly metameric muscle segments or *myotomes* occur through the body. These are considerably modified in the head, and somewhat modified in the appendages.

c. *Digestive System.* The mouth possesses jaws covered with *teeth,* these being, as stated above, homologous with placoid scales. The *pharynx* opens laterally into five pairs of gill-slits (-*pouches*), and the *esophagus* posteriorly. The esophagus merges, without constriction, into the *cardiac portion* of the stomach, then the *pyloric portion* — which bends anteriorly in a U. This joins the *duodenum,* first division of the intestine, at a constriction, the *pylorus;* the duodenum expands into a portion of the intestine containing a *spiral valve,* followed by the rectum and the *cloaca* (the latter being a common drainage channel for digestive, excretory, and reproductive systems). A *pancreas* and *liver* are present, their ducts *(pancreatic* and *bile)* emptying separately into the duodenum. An elongated *gall bladder* is embedded in the liver. A large *rectal gland* is present.

d. *Respiratory System.* The last of the five gill slits bears a half-gill *(demibranch)* only, on its anterior wall, all the others having demibranchs on both anterior and posterior walls; hence there are nine demibranches on each side of the pharynx. In addition, a vestigial gill *(pseudobranch)* is present in each spiracle, this pair of organs being morphologically the first of the six embryonic gill-slits. Water enters the mouth, passes into the pharynx, and escapes through the gill-slits.

e. *Circulatory System.* The *heart* possesses a single dorsal *atrium (auricle)* which receives blood from the *sinus venosus,* and a single ventral *ventricle,* which pumps blood out through the *conus arteriosus.* The latter continues as the *ventral aorta,* which sends five *afferent branchial arteries* into the gills. Four *efferent branchial arteries* of each side, draining the gill capillaries, unite to form the *dorsal aorta,* through which blood reaches the entire body. Venous blood is returned to the sinus venosus primarily through the two

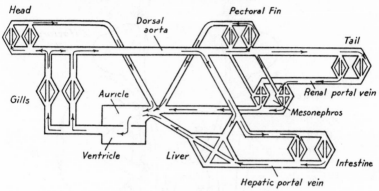

Fig. 69.   Diagram illustrating the direction of blood-flow in the dogfish shark. Typical of fishes in general.

lateral *ducts of Cuvier (common cardinal veins),* into which open *anterior cardinal veins* and *posterior cardinal veins.* In the *hepatic portal vein* blood flows from the capillaries in the walls of the digestive organs into the liver capillaries, and thence into the sinus venosus through two *hepatic sinuses.* The *renal portal veins* carry blood from the posterior end of the body into the mesonephric capillaries, from which it passes into the posterior cardinal veins. (Fig. 69).

f. *Excretory System.* The kidneys are two long, narrow mesonephroi, which drain into the cloaca through the *Wolffian* or *mesonephric ducts.* The mesonephroi are in the dorsal wall of the coelom just beneath the vertebral column.

g. *Nervous System.* The *brain* is of five divisions, with ten pairs of *cranial nerves* (Fig. 70, Table III). The spinal cord gives off segmentally arranged *spinal nerves.* An *autonomic nervous system* is present.

h. *Sensory System.* Except for shape, proportions, and absence of lids, the eyes are fundamentally like that in Fig. 87. The nostrils (*nasal pits*) open only externally, having no connection with the pharynx. They are lined with the *olfactory membrane,* from

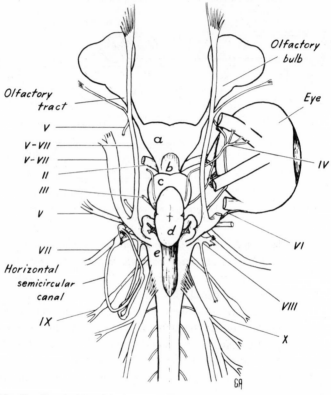

Fig. 70. Dorsal view of brain, cranial nerves, eye, and semicircular canals of dogfish shark. Cranial nerves are indicated by Roman numerals (See Table III); a, telencephalon (cerebral hemispheres); b, diencephalon: c, mesencephalon (optic lobes); d, metencephalon (cerebellum); e, myelencephalon (medulla oblongata). Nerve trunks common to the trigeminal and facial are labelled V-VII.

which nerve fibers pass to the *olfactory lobes* of the brain. *Lateral line canals,* and *ampullae of Lorenzini,* constitute cutaneous systems of sense organs which probably detect vibrations in the water. The *semicircular canals,* communicating with the *utriculus* of the *inner ear,* are (1) *anterior vertical,* (2) *posterior*

TABLE III. DIVISIONS OF BRAIN AND THEIR RELATIONS TO CRANIAL NERVES

Divisions of Brain		Cranial Nerves	
In Early Embryo	*In Late Embryo or Adult*	*Number and Name*	*Peripheral Distribution and Function*
PROSENCEPHALON	Telencephalon (Cerebrum)	I. Olfactory	Olfactory membrane; sensory.
	Diencephalon	II. Optic	Retina of eye; sensory.
MESENCEPHALON	Mesencephalon (Mid-brain)	III. Oculo-motor	Four eye muscles; motor.
		IV. Trochlear	One eye muscle; motor.
RHOMBENCEPHALON	Metencephalon (Cerebellum)		
	Myelencephalon (Medulla oblongata)	V. Trigeminal	Muscles and skin of face; mainly sensory.
		VI. Abducens	One eye muscle; motor.
		VII. Facial	Chiefly motor, to muscles of face.
		VIII. Auditory	Cochlea and semicircular canals; sensory.
		IX. Glossopharyngeal	Pharyngeal or gill region; sensory and motor.
		X. Vagus	Heart, lungs, digestive tract; sensory and motor.

vertical, (3) *horizontal*. These detect disturbances in equilibrium. Ventrally the utriculus communicates with the *sacculus*. The inner ear communicates with the exterior by paired *endolymphatic ducts*, extending dorsally from the utriculus.

3. REPRODUCTION AND DEVELOPMENT. Fertilization is internal — the male having copulatory organs, the *claspers*. The female has two *ovaries* near the anterior end of the abdominal cavity. Mature eggs escape through the surface membrane of the ovary into the coelom, whence they are drawn into the single funnel-like *ostium* which communicates with the two *oviducts*. The lower end of each oviduct is enlarged into the *uterus*, in which the developing embryo is retained until it is a small fish able to swim. The male has two *testes*, from which the sperm cells reach the Wolffian duct (which functions as the *vas deferens)* through numerous *vasa efferentia*.

REVIEW QUESTIONS

1. What advances do the Pisces show over more primitive chordates?
2. Name, characterize, and give examples of the classes of Pisces.
3. Describe the dogfish shark.
4. Trace the course of the blood through the circulatory system of the shark.
5. Name and locate the five divisions of the brain and the ten cranial nerves of the shark.

CHAPTER XVIII

SUPERCLASS TETRAPODA AND CLASS AMPHIBIA

CHARACTERISTICS OF THE SUPERCLASS TETRAPODA

These are vertebrates with typically two pairs of paired loco-motor appendages on a five-digit plan, a skull reduced by fusions and loss of elements from the complex fish type, and an ear which is an organ of hearing as well as equilibration. The brain is in five-divisions; either ten or twelve pairs of cranial nerves are present. Lungs are typically present. The heart is three- or four-chambered. Mesonephric or metanephric type kidneys are present in the adults. The sexes are separate.

CHARACTERISTICS OF THE CLASS AMPHIBIA

The Amphibia are vertebrates which typically are able to live both in fresh-water (none is marine) and on land, the majority undergoing a metamorphosis from an aquatic gill-breathing tad-pole to a lung-breathing adult—although some retain gills through-out life. External scales are absent from existing kinds, the skin being usually thin and moist. The skull is broad and depressed, with a small brain case; there are two occipital condyles; the pectoral and pelvic girdles provide some support of the body by limbs; the vertebral column is beginning to show differentiation into cervical, trunk, sacral, and caudal regions; the fore-limbs commonly have four digits; the hind limbs, five. The middle ear, when present, contains an auditory ossicle which really consists of two elements, stapes and columella; there is no external ear. The brain is of five divisions, with ten cranial nerves. Respiration may occur through gills, lungs, skin, pharyngeal and cloacal membranes, and various combinations of these. The heart possesses two atria and one ventricle, the pulmonary and systemic blood being mixed.

A renal portal system is present, connecting with the hepatic portal system through the ventral abdominal vein. The eggs are enclosed in gelatinous envelopes, and are usually laid in water.

ORDERS OF THE CLASS AMPHIBIA

Order Caudata (Urodela). Amphibia with tail in adult condition, lizard-shaped bodies; gills retained by adults of some species, lost in others; skeletal girdles providing poor support for limbs. (Example: salamander.) (Fig. 71.)

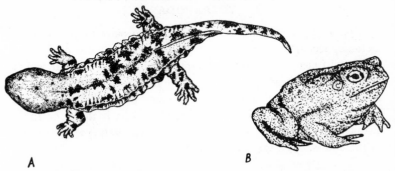

A   **B**

Fig. 71. Typical amphibia. A, *Cryptobranchus*, a salamander (Order Caudata or Urodela); B, *Bufo*, a toad (Order Salientia or Anura). (Figure A copyright by General Biological Supply House, Chicago, used by permission).

Order Salientia (Anura). Jumping amphibia without tail in adult stage; adult respiration through lungs; well developed limb and girdle skeletons. (Examples: frog, toad.) (Fig. 71.)

Order Apoda (Gymnophiona). Worm-like, legless, burrowing amphibia; eyes vestigial or absent; dermal scales (of mesodermal origin) embedded in skin. Oviparous or ovoviviparous. Tropical regions only. (Example: coecilian.)

EXAMPLE OF THE CLASS AMPHIBIA

Frog (Order Salientia or Anura).

1. EXTERNAL CHARACTERISTICS. The body is divided into a head and trunk (a neck is hardly evident). Of the two pairs of locomotor appendages, the hind pair is much elongated. The skin is smooth, moist, scaleless. The nostrils are anterior dorsal, the eyes dorsal, the *tympanic membranes* dorsal — just behind the eyes. The mouth is

very broad. Each hand bears four fingers and a rudiment of a fifth; each foot bears five toes, webbed.

2. MORPHOLOGY AND PHYSIOLOGY OF ORGAN SYSTEMS. (Figs. 72-74). (The coelom consists of two compartments, as in fishes, a pericardial and an abdominal cavity. The lungs are contained in the latter.)

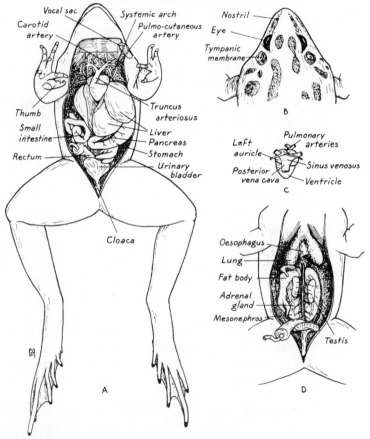

Fig. 72. The frog. A. Ventral view, with abdominal wall removed to expose organs in place. B. Dorsal surface of head. C. Dorsal side of heart. D, Ventral view, abdominal wall and some organs removed to expose organs of the dorsal part of the abdominal cavity.

a. *Skeletal System.* The *skull* consists of a small cylindrical *cranium,* and a broad, depressed *face.* The *orbits* are very large, and the *jaws* very broad. The

vertebral column consists of ten elements, the first
being the *atlas,* the ninth the *sacrum,* and the tenth
(greatly elongated) the *urostyle.* All vertebrae except first, ninth, and tenth bear elongated *transverse
processes* — so-called ribs. A *sternum* is present,
connected with the pectoral girdle, the latter consisting of *clavicle, coracoid, scapula,* and *suprascapula*
(cartilage). The pelvic girdle consists of *ilium,
ischium,* and *pubis.* The fore-limb skeleton consists
of, in order: *humerus, radio-ulna, carpals, metacarpals, phalanges;* the hind-limb skeleton, in order;
femur, tibio-fibula, tarsals, metatarsals, phalanges.

b. *Muscular System.* This is complexly differentiated
from the primitive myotomic arrangement, particularly in the appendages.

c. *Digestive System.* The mouth has numerous fine
teeth along the upper jaw, and *vomerine teeth* in the
roof of the mouth. The *tongue* is fleshy, bifurcate at
the tip, and attached anteriorly. The *esophagus* is
straight-walled, rather large, merging directly into the
stomach; the latter is elongate, curved toward the
animal's left, and muscular. The intestine consists of
the long, coiled *small intestine,* and the *rectum,* the
latter merging into the *cloaca.* Both *liver* and *pancreas* have ducts emptying into the *duodenum,* first
portion of the intestine. A globular *gall bladder* is
present. In cross section, the intestine or stomach is
found to have, from the outside in, four layers:
peritoneum, muscular layer, submucosa, mucosa.

d. *Respiratory System. External* and (later) *internal
gills* are present in the tadpole stage. The adult frog
breaths through *lungs,* each a sac with numerous cavities in its walls. The lungs communicate with the
outside through the two *bronchi,* the *larynx* (voice-
box), containing *vocal cords,* the *pharynx,* and the
nasal passages. The opening from pharynx into
larynx is a longitudinal slit, the *glottis.* The inner

openings of the nasal passages are the *internal nares.*
Some gas exchange takes place through the skin.

e. *Circulatory System.* (Fig. 74). The heart has two
auricles and one *ventricle.* Into the right auricle
opens a *sinus venosus.* Blood leaves the ventricle
through the *truncus arteriosus,* which bifurcates an-

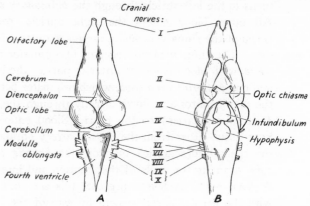

Fig. 73. Brain and cranial nerves of the frog; A, dorsal view;
B, ventral view. (Redrawn after Ecker).

terior to the heart, and then divides on each side into
three trunks, the *carotid, systemic, pulmocutaneous
arteries* (from anterior to posterior). Each carotid
divides into *internal* and *external carotids,* which pass
forward into the head; the pulmo-cutaneous sends
branches to lungs and skin; the two systemics (*sys-*

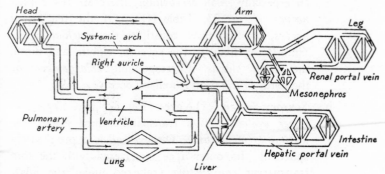

Fig. 74. Diagram illustrating the direction of blood-flow in a frog. Applies equally
well to toads, but not to salamanders.

temic arches) unite dorsally to form the *dorsal aorta*. Principal arteries branching from the dorsal aorta are, in approximate order: *coeliaco-mesenteric* (to stomach, liver, intestine), *segmental* (to muscles), *renal* (to mesonephroi), *genital* (to gonads), and the two *iliacs* (to the legs). Blood from the lungs returns to the left auricle through the *pulmonary veins*. All other blood enters the right auricle, passing through the sinus venosus, a large sac on the dorsal side. The sinus venosus receives two *anterior venae cavae*, with blood from the anterior part of the body, and one *posterior vena cava*, which originates between the mesonephroi and flows directly through the liver (not in capillaries) to the heart. Blood enters the liver tissue either from the *hepatic artery* (branch of the coeliaco-mesenteric) or from the *hepatic portal vein*, draining the walls of the stomach and intestine. A *renal portal system* is present; this communicates with the hepatic portal system by way of the *pelvic veins* and median *ventral abdominal vein*.

f. *Excretory System.* The "kidneys" are *mesonephroi*, and the kidney ducts are the *Wolffian* or *mesonephric ducts*. The latter empty directly into the cloaca, but a *urinary bladder* is present on the ventral side of the cloaca.

g. *Nervous System.* The brain is of five divisions, with an especially small *cerebellum;* there are ten *cranial nerves.* (Fig. 73, Table III). Of the ten *spinal nerves,* the first three constitute the *brachial plexus* (interlacing fibers); the seventh, eighth, and ninth, the *sciatic plexus.* Corresponding *enlargements* of the cord, *brachial* and *lumbar,* occur.

h. *Sensory System.* The eyes (Fig. 87) have *upper* and *lower eyelids,* and a transparent third eyelid, the *nictitating membrane.* The *eye-ball* is approximately spherical. Its outer face is covered with the thin transparent *conjunctiva* (reflexed under the lids), and under it the transparent but thicker *cornea.* The cornea is continuous with the *sclera,* the outer opaque covering of the eye-ball. Under the sclera lies the *choroid,* which, in front, merges into a doughnut-shaped shelf not in contact with the cornea, the *iris.* The opening in the iris is the *pupil.* The *crystalline lens* fits against the back of the iris, closing the pupil. The inside of the eye-ball is lined with nerve tissue, the *retina,* directly continuous with the *optic nerve* (the second cranial nerve). The cavity in front of the lens and iris contains the *aqueous humor;* the cavity behind, the *vitreous humor.* The eye is moved by six muscles: *superior, inferior, internal,* and *external rectus muscles;* and *superior* and *inferior oblique muscles.* Cranial nerves three, four, and six innervate these muscles. (See Fig. 70).

The ear includes organs both for hearing and the sense of equilibrium, the latter in the three *semicircular canals:* (1) *anterior vertical,* (2) *posterior vertical,* and (3) *horizontal.* A *tympanic membrane* (but no external ear) conveys impulses set up by sound waves to the *columella,* a thin bone in the middle ear, which transmits impulses through the *stapes* to the *cochlea,* the organ of hearing. The *middle ear* communicates with the pharynx through the *Eustachian tube.*

i. *Endocrine Glands.* The *pituitary gland* ("hypophysis," Fig. 73), which lies under the brain, has three lobes, each producing hormones. The *anterior lobe* produces a growth- and metamorphosis-stimulating hormone and one that stimulates the gonads. (The gonad-stimulating hormone that appears in the urine of pregnant women has the same effect; this is the basis for the use of frogs in one test for human pregnancy.) The *intermediate lobe* hormone controls expansion of pigment cells, and consequent darkening of the skin. The *posterior lobe* produces hormones related to water balance and to contraction of smooth muscle. The *thyroid gland* consists of two separate lobes, each near the base of one of the internal carotid arteries. Its secretions probably stimulate general metabolic activity; we know definitely that it stimulates metamorphosis of the tadpole into the adult frog. The *islets of Langerhans*, in the pancreas, probably regulate the balance of carbohydrate between liver and blood. Each *adrenal gland* (Fig. 72, D) contains both types of tissues characteristic of the human gland (Chap. XXI) mixed within the gland. All adrenal effects are not known, but the gland is essential for life. Hormones produced by the *gonads* are related to secondary sexual characteristics; e.g., the swollen thumb of the male during the breeding season is produced by a secretion from the growing testis.

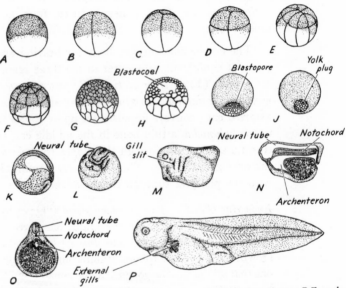

Fig. 75. Stages in the embryology of the frog; A, the uncleaved egg; B-F, early cleavage stages; G-H, blastula; I-K, gastrula; L-P, organ formation; N and O are, respectively, a longitudinal and a cross section of the embryo shown at M. (Adapted from figure copyright by General Biological Supply House, Chicago, used by permission).

3. REPRODUCTION AND DEVELOPMENT. Fertilization is external, but accompanies *clasping* (the male frog clasping the female and shedding sperm while the eggs are being discharged). The female has two ovaries, ventral to the

mesonephroi. Mature ova escape into the coelom, and are drawn into the two oviducts, which lead to the cloaca. Gelatinous envelopes are deposited around the eggs in the oviducts. Two testes are present in the male, communicating with the "kidney" by several vasa efferentia; sperm cells reach the cloaca through the Wolffian ducts. Development takes place in the water. Cleavage is total, but unequal — in the eight-cell stage the upper quartet of cells is distinctly smaller than the lower. Gastrulation is accomplished primarily by overgrowth of the smaller tween the two layers of mesoderm. In development, the frog passes through an aquatic, gill-breathing, larval stage, the tadpole, which metamorphoses into the frog. (Fig. 75).

REVIEW QUESTIONS

1. What are the Tetrapoda?
2. In what ways do the amphibia show advances over the fishes?
3. Name and characterize the orders of Amphibia.
4. Describe the skeleton of the frog.
5. Trace the course of the blood through the circulatory system of the frog.
6. Describe the typical vertebrate eye.
7. Explain how the structures of the ear are adapted in the frog for two different functions.
8. Discuss reproduction and development of the frog.

Chapter XIX

CLASS REPTILIA

CHARACTERISTICS OF THE CLASS REPTILIA

Reptiles are vertebrates with a dry skin covered with epidermal scales or plates. The skull is usually somewhat laterally compressed, and has a single occipital condyle; well developed girdles (except as they may be secondarily reduced or lost, *e. g.,* in snakes) are present; the vertebrae are differentiated into five regions—cervical, thoracic, lumbar, sacral, and caudal. The digits possess claws. An external auditory meatus is present or absent; the middle ear contains an auditory ossicle. The eyes have glands for keeping the surface moist. The brain has a cerebrum of increased size (over that of fishes and amphibians); and twelve cranial nerves are present in most reptiles. Respiration is by lungs which are more complex than in amphibians. The heart consists of two auricles and a ventricle, with the ventricle almost completely divided in some; the pulmonary arteries are separated from the systemic arteries; the functions of posterior cardinals are assumed by the median posterior vena cava. The kidney is a metanephros, and the renal portal system is reduced. Fertilization is internal; reptiles are oviparous or ovoviviparous; the oviparous types lay eggs with shells. Amnion and allantois are present in the reptilian embryo (as in birds and mammals).

MAJOR ORDERS OF THE CLASS REPTILIA

A great many reptilian orders, including those containing the dinosaurs and pterydactyls, are entirely extinct; and one order is represented today by a single living example, *Sphenodon,* of New Zealand, which shows traces of a pineal eye, and is therefore of considerable evolutionary interest (Order Rhynchocephalia). The best known existing reptiles belong to the following three orders, but in using this classification it should be remembered that these do not include all reptiles by any means:

Order Chelonia. Reptiles with skeleton partially modified to form dorsal and ventral shield-like coverings (carapace and plastron, respectively); jaws toothless, horny. Marine, fresh-water, and land. (Example: turtle.) (Fig. 76).

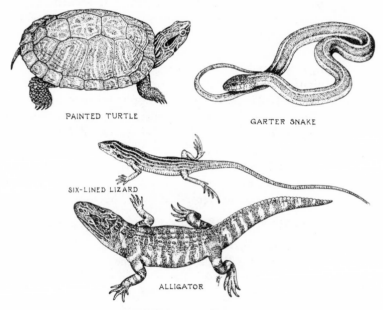

PAINTED TURTLE

GARTER SNAKE

SIX-LINED LIZARD

ALLIGATOR

Fig. 76. Typical reptiles. Turtle (Order Chelonia), snake and lizard (Order Squamata), alligator (Order Crocodilia). (Copyright by General Biological Supply House, Chicago, used by permission).

Order Squamata. Reptiles with body covered with small flexible scales; no abdominal ribs. Marine, fresh-water, and land. (Examples: lizard, Suborder Lacertilia; snake, Suborder Ophidia.) (Fig. 76).

Order Crocodilia. Large, thick-bodied reptiles; abdominal ribs present; ventricle of heart practically completely divided into right and left compartments. Marine or fresh-water. (Examples: alligator, crocodile). (Fig. 76).

EXAMPLE OF THE CLASS REPTILIA

Turtle (Order Chelonia).

1. EXTERNAL CHARACTERISTICS. Turtles are externally, and in skeletal relations, highly specialized, but internally of a generalized pattern which makes them nearest today to the reptilian ancestors of mammals. The body is enclosed between a dorsal arched shell of bony, scale-covered plates, the *carapace,* and a ventral flat shell of similar plates, the *plastron.* The plastron may be transversely hinged, but the shields permit very little freedom of movement. The head with its long neck, the tail, and the legs, protrude between the margins of carapace and plastron. The two nostrils are near the anterior end of the head. The lateral eyes are provided with upper and lower lids and nictitating membrane. There is no external ear, the tympanic membrane being covered with a layer of skin. The margin of the mouth is formed by horny jaws, and teeth are absent. The legs usually have five digits each, all provided with long *claws.* The cloacal opening is on the ventral side, at the base of the tail.

2. MORPHOLOGY AND PHYSIOLOGY OF ORGAN SYSTEMS.

   a. *Skeletal System.* The *ribs* and most of the vertebrae are fused with the carapace. The pectoral and pelvic girdles are both of the primitive three-bone arrangement; the former consists of *scapula* (fused to carapace) and ventral *procoracoid* and *coracoid;* the pelvic girdle consists of the *ilium* (fused to carapace), and the ventral *pubis* and *ischium.* The skull is a compact box, with heavy jaw musculature.

   b. *Digestive System.* There are no teeth. A broad, nonprotrusible tongue is present. The digestive tract consists of a distensible pharynx, thick-walled esophagus, stomach, small intestine, large intestine, and cloaca. Liver and pancreas are present, the former with a large gall bladder.

   c. *Respiratory System.* From the pharynx, through the glottis, the cartilage-ringed trachea leads to the two bronchi, which branch within the lungs, the latter somewhat divided into compartments. A cartilaginous larynx is present at the anterior end of the trachea.

d. *Circulatory System.* The blood system is not fundamentally very different from that of the frog except in the separation of pulmonary and aortic arterial trunks from the ventricle outward. The digestive tract is supplied with arterial blood from the left systemic arch, rather than from the dorsal aorta — as in the frog. The renal portal system is greatly reduced; it is connected with the hepatic portal system by the paired ventral abdominal veins.

e. *Excretory System.* The adult kidneys are *metanephroi;* the kidney ducts, *ureters.* These lead to the cloaca, not directly to the *urinary bladder;* the latter organ is a bilobed structure on the ventral side of the cloaca.

f. *Nervous System.* The *cerebral hemispheres* and *cerebellum* are both proportionally larger than in the fish or frog brain. Twelve cranial nerves are present, the *spinal accessory* and *hypoglossal nerves* being those not present in more primitive vertebrates.

g. *Sensory System.* Eyes, ears, and nostrils are moderately well developed sense organs. *Lachrymal glands* are present in the eye. An external auditory meatus is absent, the *tympanic membrane* lying directly under the skin, which is attached to it.

3. REPRODUCTION AND DEVELOPMENT. Fertilization is internal; a copulatory organ, a primitive, grooved *penis,* is formed from the cloacal wall in the male. The eggs, with leathery *shells,* are deposited on land, buried in sand. The developing embryo is enclosed in a membrane, the *amnion;* and it respires through a second specialized embryonic membrane, the *allantois.*

REVIEW QUESTIONS

1. What are the major characteristics of the class Reptilia?
2. What are the most important orders of existing reptiles?
3. Describe the morphology and physiology of the turtle.

Chapter XX

CLASS AVES

CHARACTERISTICS OF THE CLASS AVES

Birds are vertebrates with feathers; all of them have feathers, and no other animals do. They are flying vertebrates, possessing a wing in which the supporting elements are derived from middle and distal portions (not merely distal portions as in pterodactyls and bats). Skull characteristics include: pronounced fusion of bones; a horny beak, which, in existing birds, has no teeth; a large orbit; a single occipital condyle. Cervical vertebrae are numerous, and possess a heterocoelous (double saddle-joint) articulation. The body vertebrae have many fusions, and in most birds the terminal caudal vertebrae are fused to form the pygostyle. The sternum is deeply keeled in flying birds. The pectoral girdle of each side consists of scapula, clavicle, and coracoid, the latter being very large; the clavicles and single interclavicle are fused to form the furcula ("wish-bone"). Each anterior rib bears a posteriorly directed uncinate process. In the wing, the carpus and hand are reduced to vestiges of three digits. The tibia and part of the tarsus are fused together, as also is the remainder of the tarsus with the metatarsus; hence there is an intertarsal joint. The toes are two, three, or four in number. The middle ear contains an auditory ossicle; and an external auditory meatus is present. The eyes are well developed, with three eyelids; and possess a vascular structure, the pecten, in the cavity of the vitreous humor. In the brain, the cerebrum and, particularly, the optic lobes and cerebellum are greatly developed; there are twelve cranial nerves. Respiration is by lungs, which communicate with numerous accessory air sacs. The heart possesses two auricles and two ventricles, providing complete separation of pulmonary and systemic circulations; the single aortic arch is on the right side. A constant high body temperature is maintained. The digestive organs usually include a crop, glandular stomach, and muscular stomach (gizzard); two caeca are present at the beginning of the large intestine. The kidney is a metanephros, and renal portal veins do not break up into capillaries in the kidneys. Fertilization is internal; an intromittent organ in the male is present rarely; all birds are oviparous, laying hard-shelled eggs. Usually only one ovary, the left, is present.

MAJOR DIVISIONS OF THE CLASS AVES

So many orders of birds are recognized that in the following summary characteristics are given only for categories higher than orders. Extinct orders are named in parentheses.

Subclass Archaeornithes. Extinct toothed birds of the Jurassic; metacarpals separate; no pygostyle, caudal vertebrae individually bearing feathers attached in pairs.

(Order Archaeopterygiformes, *Archaeopteryx.*)

Subclass Neornithes. Extinct or modern, toothed or toothless; metacarpals fused; caudal vertebrae never individually bearing feathers in pairs, pygostyle present in most.

Superorder Odontognathae. Extinct, toothed birds of the Cretaceous.

(Order Hesperornithiformes, *Hesperornis.*)
(Order Ichthyornithiformes, *Ichthyornis.*)

Superorder Palaeognathae. Mostly flightless birds, with keelless sternum; all with the vomer forming a bridge in the palate.

Order Struthioniformes, ostrich.
Order Rheiformes, rhea.
Order Casuariiformes, cassowary, emu.
(Order Dinornithiformes, moa.)
(Order Aepyornithiformes, *Aepyornis.*)
Order Apterygiformes, kiwi.
Order Tinamiformes, tinamou.

Superorder Impennes. Penguins; wings vestigial, the feathers reduced to scale-like structures; metatarsals incompletely fused.

Order Sphenisciformes, penguin.

Superorder Neognathae. Most modern birds; keeled sternum; metatarsals fused; vomer always small, and not forming a bridge across the palate.

Order Gaviiformes, loon.

Order Colymbiformes, grebe.

Order Procellariiformes, albatross, fulmar, shearwater, petrel.

Order Pelecaniformes, pelican, cormorant, frigate-bird.

Order Ciconiiformes, heron, stork, ibis.

Order Anseriformes, duck, goose, swan.

Order Falconiformes, vulture, hawk, eagle.

Order Galliformes, chicken, turkey, pheasant, quail.

Order Gruiformes, rail, crane, coot.

(Order Diatrymiformes, *Diatryma*.)

Order Charadriiformes, sandpiper, plover, gull, auk.

Order Columbiformes, pigeo.

Order Psittaciformes, parrot, cockatoo.

Order Cuculiformes, cuckoko, road-runner.

Order Strigiformes, owl.

Order Caprimulgiformes, nighthawk, whip-poor-will.

Order Micropodiformes, swift, hummingbird.

Order Coliiformes, coly or mouse-bird.

Order Trogoniformes, trogon.

Order Coraciiformes, kingfisher, motmot, hornbill.

Order Piciformes, woodpecker, toucan.

Order Passeriformes, kingbird, crow, robin, sparrow, wren.

EXAMPLE OF THE CLASS AVES

Pigeon (Superorder Neognathae, Order Columbiformes).

(General characteristics of the Class not repeated).

1. EXTERNAL CHARACTERISTICS. The head is small in proportion to the body; the toes are three in front, one

behind. The *bill* has a fleshy swelling on the dorsal side of the base, the *cere*. *Feathers* are of three types (Fig. 77): (1) *contour,* possessing a *vane,* distributed in definite tracts, the *pterylae;* (2) *down,* without a vane, possessing *barbs* not interlocking with each other, generally

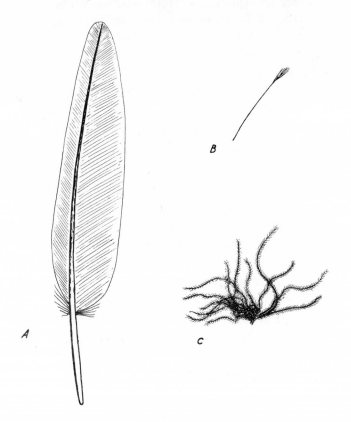

Fig. 77. Types of feathers. A, contour feather, in this case a flight feather; B, filoplume; C, down feather.

distributed over the body; (3) *filoplumes,* small, with a thread-like shaft terminating in a few barbs, developing around the base of contour feathers. Feathers are changed annually by a *molt* following the breeding season. There is only one cutaneous gland, the *uropygial gland,* in the rump.

2. Morphology and Physiology of Organ Systems.

a. *Skeletal and Muscular Systems.* (Fig. 78). The *quad-
rate* (of the skull) has two dorsal articular surfaces;
all *pelvic bones* are fused; a *pygostyle* is present; the

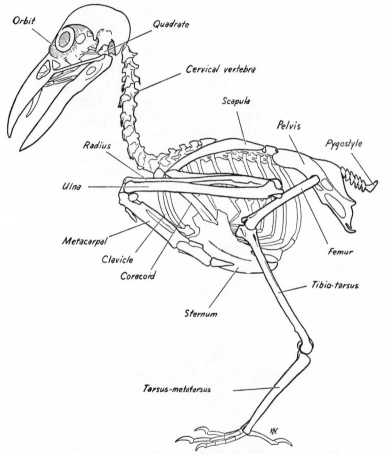

Fig. 78.   Skeleton of a crow, a typical flying bird, of the Order Passeriformes.
(Drawing by Kisa Noguchi).

sternum has four deep posterior notches. The *pectoralis major* muscle, originating on the *keel* of the
sternum, pulls the *humerus* (therefore, wing) down;
the *pectoralis minor,* operating over a pulley at the
shoulder, elevates the wing.

b. *Digestive System.* The tract consists of oesophagus, *proventriculus (glandular stomach), gizzard,* small and large intestines. A gall bladder is absent (but may be present in some birds). A *crop* opens into the oesophagus; the cells of its lining slough off to form the "pigeon's milk" with which the young birds are fed. Two *caeca* are present at the beginning of the large intestine.

c. *Respiratory System.* The trachea divides into two bronchi at the *syrinx* (voice-box). The lungs are supplemented by air sacs — four paired and one medial in position. The active phase of respiration is expiration; the passive phase, inhalation.

d. *Circulatory System.* This is typical of the Class; the direction of blood flow is as in the diagram for the mammal (Fig. 82), the only significant difference being that the single arterial arch is on the right rather than the left side (as in mammals).

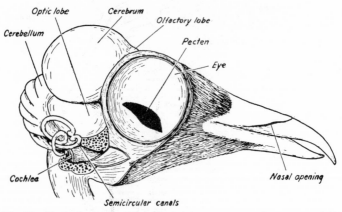

Fig. 79. Head of pigeon; with brain and inner ear exposed, and outer half of eye-ball removed. (Redrawn after Krause).

e. *Excretory System.* The kidneys are *metanephroi; ureters* empty directly into the cloaca; a urinary bladder is absent.

f. *Nervous and Sensory Systems.* Typical of the Class. (Fig. 79).

3. REPRODUCTION AND DEVELOPMENT. Fertilization is internal; no specialized copulatory organ exists. The ovary is single, left. Ova receive a covering of *albumen* and a *shell* during their passage through the oviduct. The incubation period is sixteen to eighteen days. The young hatch in a helpless condition (*altricial*, as opposed to the *precocial* condition of such birds as chicks and ducklings), with a scanty covering of down; the young fly about four weeks after hatching.

REVIEW QUESTIONS

1. Characterize the class Aves.
2. Why are birds said to be merely feathered reptiles?
3. What are the major subdivisions of the class Aves?
4. Discuss feather distribution and structure.
5. Describe the morphology and physiology of the pigeon.

Chapter XXI

CLASS MAMMALIA

CHARACTERISTICS OF THE CLASS MAMMALIA

Mammals are vertebrates with hair. They possess milk or mammary glands, well developed in the female. Mammals are variously modified for running, burrowing, swimming, and flight. Nails, claws, or hoofs are present on the digits; and there may be numerous sweat and oil glands in the skin. Teeth are commonly differentiated into four types: incisors, canines, premolars, molars. The number of bones in the skull is considerably reduced from the condition in other vertebrates. There are two occipital condyles. Seven cervical vertebrae is the usual number. In the pectoral girdle the coracoid bone is typically absent, and the clavicle sometimes vestigial or absent. (See Table IV for summary of skeletal elements.) Three auditory ossicles are present: malleus, incus, stapes; the cochlea (end organ for hearing) is a very complex structure, more or less coiled; there is an external auditory meatus and an external ear (pinna). The nictitating membrane of the eye may be vestigial. The cerebrum is proportionally much larger than in other vertebrates, and the cerebellum is also large; there are twelve cranial nerves. Respiration occurs through lungs containing many small subdivisions; each lung is in a pleural cavity; a muscular diaphragm is present. The heart is four-chambered, as in birds; a constant temperature is maintained—warm blood; the single aortic arch is on the left. Several pairs of salivary glands open into the mouth. One caecum, at junction of small intestine and colon (large intestine), is present. The kidney is a metanephros, with ureters emptying directly into the urinary bladder; no renal portal veins are present, even as vestiges. Genital and anal apertures are separate in practically all mammals, both male and female. Fertilization is internal, an intromittent organ, the penis, being present. Practically all mammals are viviparous, the embryo developing in the uterus, metabolic exchanges between embryo and mother taking place through the placenta.

MAJOR DIVISIONS OF THE CLASS MAMMALIA

In the following summary, characteristics of categories higher than orders are given briefly; orders containing existing mammals are listed, with examples; extinct orders are omitted.

Subclass Prototheria. Egg-laying mammals, of Australian region; possess cloaca.

Order Monotremata, duckbill.

Subclass Allotheria. Extinct mammals of primitive structure.

Subclass Theria. Structurally more complex mammals.

Superorder Pantotheria, extinct.

Superorder Metatheria. Pouched mammals, the young completing their development in a marsupium (pouch).

Order Marsupialia, opossum, kangaroo.

Superorder Eutheria. True placental mammals, early development completed in the uterus.

Order Insectivora, mole, shrew.

Order Dermoptera, flying lemur.

Order Chiroptera, bat, flying fox.

Order Primates, lemur, monkey, ape, man.

Order Edentata, sloth, ant-eater, armadillo.

Order Rodentia, rat, squirrel, beaver, porcupine, woodchuck.

Order Lagomorpha, rabbit, pika.

Order Carnivora, cat, dog, skunk, raccoon, bear, seal, walrus.

Order Cetacea, whale, dolphin.

Order Tubulidentata, aard-vark.

Order Proboscidea, elephant.

Order Hyracoidea, Procavia (the "coney" of the Bible).

Order Sirenia, manatee, dugong.

Order Perissodactyla, horse, tapir, rhinoceros.

Order Artiodactyla, pig, cow, deer, antelope, camel, hippopotamus.

EXAMPLES OF THE CLASS MAMMALIA

Rabbit (Subclass Theria, Order Lagomorpha).

(General characteristics of Class omitted.)

1. EXTERNAL CHARACTERISTICS.

    Large external ears (*pinnae*) are present; the eyes are large, with nictitating membrane; the *lips* are soft and flexible. Long hairs (*vibrissae*) occur on the sides of the muzzle. The front legs are smaller than the hind; the latter are elongated, adapted for leaping. The forelegs have five digits; the hind, only four. There is a short tail. The anus is below the tail, the *urogenital opening* anterior to the *anus*. Scent glands occur near the anus. There are four or five pairs of *mammary glands,* externally evident through *teats*.

2. BODY CAVITIES.

    The coelom is divided into four compartments: the *pericardial cavity,* containing the heart; the *peritoneal cavity,* containing the abdominal viscera; and the two *pleural cavities,* each enclosing one of the lungs.

3. MORPHOLOGY AND PHYSIOLOGY OF ORGAN SYSTEMS.

    a. *Skeletal System.* (See Table IV and Figure 80). On each side the teeth are: *incisors,* two above, one below; *canines* absent; *premolars,* three above, two below; *molars,* three above and below. Hence the *dental formula* is $\dfrac{2-0-3-3}{1-0-2-3}$.

    b. *Digestive System.* The tongue bears *taste papillae;* there are four pairs of *salivary glands*: *parotid, infraorbital, submaxillary, sublingual.* A *gall bladder* is present, and separate *bile* and *pancreatic ducts* open into the *duodenum.* The *caecum* is unusually large, thin-walled, about twenty inches long, bearing a finger-like *vermiform appendix* at the tip.

c. *Respiratory System.* The nasal passages contain coiled *turbinal bones,* which increase the olfactory surface. The *larynx* is roofed by an *epiglottis,* and contains *vocal cords.* The two lungs are contained

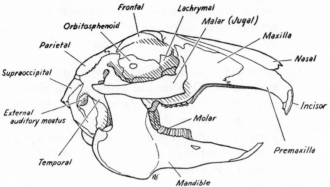

Fig. 80. Side view of skull of rabbit. (Drawing by Kisa Noguchi).

in separate pleural cavities. Inspiration is the active phase in breathing, accompanied by depression (flattening) of the *diaphragm* and elevation (with outward arching) of the ribs.

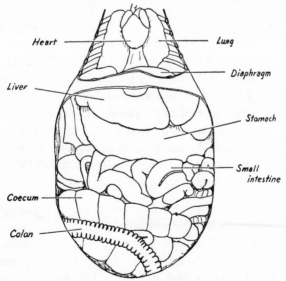

Fig. 81. Ventral view of thoracic and abdominal viscera of the rabbit. (Redrawn from Von Mojsvar after Foster).

d. *Circulatory System.* (See Figure 82). The most important special characteristics of the rabbit include: branches of the *aortic arch* are the *innominate artery* (dividing into *right subclavian* and *right* and *left carotid arteries*) and the *left subclavian artery.* Two *anterior vena cavae* are present, right and left, instead of one only — as in man.

e. *Excretory System.* The *kidneys* are compressed, bean-shaped. The median cavity of the kidney (*pelvis*) communicates with the *urinary bladder* through the *ureter.* From the bladder to the exterior, urine passes through the *urethra,* which joins the *genital sinus* of the female or the *vas deferens* of the male. A cloaca is absent.

f. *Nervous System.* The *cerebrum* of the brain is large in proportion to the total brain volume; the *cerebellum* is large, and possesses two lateral lobes. The optic lobes are four, each lateral portion being divided by a transverse groove into anterior and posterior lobes.

g. *Sensory System.* There is an *external ear,* and sound waves are transmitted through an *external auditory meatus* to the *tympanic membrane.* The *middle ear* contains the three ossicles, *malleus, incus,* and *stapes.* The *cochlea* is somewhat spirally coiled. The eye does not contain the pecten. The olfactory membrane is increased in area, and the sense of smell in effectiveness, by an increase in the size of the olfactory membrane; it follows the curvature of the scroll-like bony plates in the nasal cavities.

4. REPRODUCTION AND DEVELOPMENT. Fertilization is internal; an intromittent organ, the *penis,* is present. The testes are contained in *scrotal sacs.* Development takes place in the two *uteri;* the rabbit *placenta* is formed from fused *chorion* and *allantois.* The period of *gestation* (time from fertilization to birth) is thirty days. As many

as ten *foetuses* (uterine embryos) may develop simultaneously. Rabbits are sexually mature at about three months after birth.

Man (Subclass Theria, Order Primates).

1. EXTERNAL CHARACTERISTICS. The major body divisions are *head* and *neck, trunk,* and two pairs of appendages—the *arms* and *legs.* Hair is present on the head, axillae, and pubes, with a greater distribution in the male, including the face. The face is vertical; the head axis is at right angles to the main axis of the body, which is vertical. Five digits are present on each appendage.

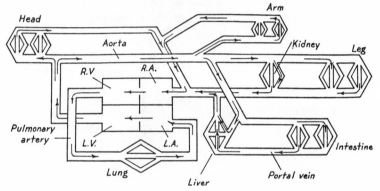

Fig. 82. Diagram illustrating the direction of blood-flow in man. Applies equally well to all mammals and (by substituting "wing" for "arm") to all birds. The aortic arch swings to the left in mammals, to the right in birds.

2. BODY CAVITIES. The coelom is divided into the *peritoneal cavity, pericardial cavity,* and two *pleural cavities.*

3. MORPHOLOGY AND PHYSIOLOGY OF ORGAN SYSTEMS.

   a. *Skeletal System.*

      (1) *Morphology.* Table IV lists the bones of the human body classified by location. See also Fig. 83.

         The *dental formula* of man is $\dfrac{2 - 1 - 2 - 3}{2 - 1 - 2 - 3}$

      (2) *Physiology.* The major functions of the skeleton are support, protection, and movement (supplying points of origin and insertion of muscles).

The normal formation of bone in a developing child depends upon the presence of a dietary element, vitamin D, contained plentifully in cod-liver oil and capable of being formed in one's body on exposure to sunlight. The ratio of calcium in blood and bone is regulated by the hor-

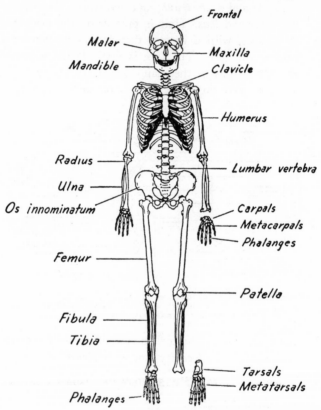

Fig. 83. The skeleton of man. (Adapted from figure copyright by General Biological Supply House, Chicago, used by permission).

mone secreted by the parathyroid glands. A growth regulating hormone from the anterior pituitary gland is involved in bone-growth; its excessive secretion may be associated with gigantism; inadequate secretion may be associated with dwarfishness.

TABLE IV. BONES OF THE HUMAN SKELETON

AXIAL SKELETON	Skull	Cranium	1 occipital, 2 parietals, 1 frontal, 2 temporals (each containing 3 ossicles of middle ear), 1 sphenoid, 1 ethmoid.
		Face	2 nasals, 1 vomer, 2 inferior turbinals, 2 lacrimals, 2 malars, 2 palatines, 2 maxillae, 1 mandible, 1 hyoid.
	Vertebral Column		Vertebrae: 7 cervical, 12 thoracic, 5 lumbar, 5 sacral (fused into 1), 1+coccygeal.
	Thoracic Basket		24 ribs, 1 sternum (of 3 elements).
APPENDICULAR SKELETON*	Pectoral Girdle		1 clavicle, 1 scapula.
	Pectoral Appendage		1 humerus, 1 radius, 1 ulna, 8 carpals, 5 metacarpals, 14 phalanges.
	Pelvic Girdle		1 os innominatum, consisting of ilium, ischium, and pubis.
	Pelvic Appendage		1 femur, 1 patella, 1 tibia, 1 fibula, 7 tarsals, 5 metatarsals, 14 phalanges.

* Bones of the appendicular skeleton are given from only one side; to arrive at the total number of bones each of these figures should be multiplied by two.

TABLE V. ORIGINS, INSERTIONS, AND ACTIONS OF
REPRESENTATIVE MUSCLES OF THE HUMAN BODY

Name of Muscle	Origin	Insertion	Action
MASSETER	Zygomatic arch; temporal and malar bones	Mandible, at angle of jaw	Closes jaws
BICEPS	Two points on scapula	Tubercle on radius	Flexes arm at elbow
TRICEPS	One point on scapula; two on back of humerus	Proximal end of ulna.	Extends arm at elbow
DELTOID	Clavicle and scapula	Outer surface of humerus	Raises arm outward from body
PECTORALIS MAJOR	Clavicle, sternum, cartilages of ribs	Ridge on outer surface of humerus	Pulls arm forward
GASTROCNEMIUS	Two spots on distal end of femur at back	Calcaneum,— the tarsal bone of the heel	Extends foot at ankle

b. *Muscular System.*

(1) *Morphology.* A skeletal muscle consists typically of a mass of striated muscle fibers extending across a joint of the skeleton. The end which moves least during contraction is the *origin*; the end moving most, the *insertion*. The movement accomplished constitutes the action. Table V gives origins, insertions, and actions of a few typical muscles.

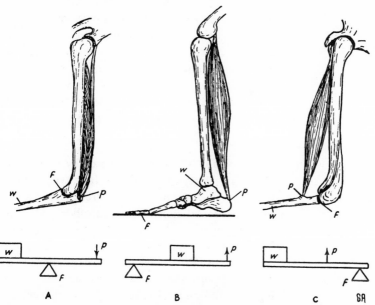

Fig. 84. Diagrams to suggest the relations between the three classes of levers and the actions of skeletal muscles. A. First class lever, illustrated by the triceps muscle extending the arm at the e'bow. B. Second class lever, illustrated by the gastrocnemius muscle raising the weight of the body on the toes. C. Third class lever, illustrated by the biceps muscle flexing the arm at the elbow. Abbreviations: F, fulcrum; P, power; W, weight.

(2) *Physiology.* Muscular contraction involves no change in total volume of tissue; the muscle thickens at the same time it shortens. The shortening takes place across a skeletal joint, resulting in movement at the joint. The movable part behaves like a mechanical lever, the joint being the fulcrum. All three lever types occur in the

human body, the types, with corresponding muscle-skeleton examples, being illustrated in Fig. 84. The chemical processes in muscle contraction involve a trigger reaction, in which stored energy from ATP is released suddenly. The state of internal stress which is disturbed on stimulation is restored by energy released in the decomposition of phosphocreatine, a muscle constituent. The phosphoric acid and creatine are then recombined, the energy for this coming from the oxidation of sugar or the formation of lactic acid from glycogen (the latter process non-oxidative). Most of the lactic acid may later be reconverted into glycogen. Only the recovery phase involves oxidation. A muscle becomes fatigued if contractions occur so frequently that the oxidative recovery cannot take place.

c. *Digestive System.*

(1) *Morphology.* The mouth is closed by fleshy lips. There are thirty-two teeth, of four types: eight *incisors*, four *canines*, eight *premolars*, twelve *molars* (dental formula given under Skeletal System, above). The tongue bears *taste-buds*. Three pairs of *salivary glands* empty into the mouth: *parotid*, *submaxillary*, and *sublingual*. The *esophagus* is a straight muscular tube opening into the *stomach*. The latter is curved, its *greater curvature* to the left. The upper end of the stomach is the *cardiac end;* the lower, the *pyloric*. The *small intestine* consists of three parts: *duodenum*, *jejunum*, and *ileum*; the *large intestine* or *colon* consists of *ascending*, *transverse*, and *descending portions;* the latter merges into the *sigmoid flexure* and *rectum*; the rectum opens to the outside through the *anus*. There is no cloaca. A *caecum* is present at the junction of colon and ileum, the *vermiform appendix* being a diverticulum of it. *Ducts* from

both *liver* and *pancreas* empty into the duodenum. Other digestive glands are present in the stomach walls and the lining of the intestine.

(2) *Physiology.* The food, after being masticated in the mouth and mixed with *saliva* is swallowed by voluntary movements. Its passage through the alimentary canal is, however, largely involuntary. Food is retained in the stomach until thoroughly acidified, and is passed through the *pyloric valve* a small amount at a time. Mechanical actions of the intestine involve forward movement of the contents by *peristalsis,* and a rhythmic segmentation, the latter process allowing for complete mixing with intestinal enzymes and complete absorption by the intestinal walls. Water is resorbed in the colon. *Defecation,* discharge of undigested or unabsorbed materials, is voluntary. As stated in Chapters II and III, digestion is accomplished by specific hydrolyzing enzymes. *Salivary diastase (ptyalin)* converts sugar into maltose; but its action is stopped by the high acidity of the stomach. In the stomach, *pepsin,* in the presence of hydrochloric acid, hydrolyzes proteins to peptones and proteoses— simple compounds of amino-acids. From the pancreas, three enzymes are derived: *pancreatic diastase,* with the same function as salivary diastase; *trypsin,* which completes digestion of proteins, proteoses, and peptones to amino-acids; and *lipase,* which hydrolyzes fats to glycerol and fatty acids. The double sugars, maltose, sucrose, and lactose, are acted upon by the corresponding enzymes *maltase, sucrase,* and *lactase* in the small intestine, yielding single sugars. An additional protein-splitting enzyme, *erepsin,* is also present in the small intestine.

(3) *Nutrition.* The diet must contain food to supply energy, provide specific compounds for growth, and to maintain nitrogen balance. It must also contain

water, minerals, and vitamins. Energy value of food is measured in *Calories* (kilocalories); the yield from carbohydrates and proteins is 4 Calories per gram, that from fats is 9 Calories per gram. To maintain *basal metabolism* (bodily activity necessary merely to maintain life) 1600 to 1800 Calories per day are required by the adult human being. Total metabolic requirements vary from 2500 to 5000 and are correlated with activity. Specific compounds needed for manufacture of new protoplasm include eight amino acids and three fatty acids. Proteins must always be in the diet to offset continuous excretion of nitrogen in the urine; they maintain nitrogen balance.

Vitamins are specific nutritional requirements that need be present only in small quantity. They are required in enzyme systems. When insufficient in the diet certain *deficiency diseases* appear. Among these are: beriberi, in the absence of adequate vitamin B_1 (thiamine); scurvy, associated with a shortage of C (ascorbic acid); and rickets, with a deficiency of D (calciferol). The water-soluble vitamins (the B and C vitamins) are involved in cellular metabolism and in erythrocyte formation. The fat-soluble vitamins are involved in the chemistry of vision (A), calcium and phosphorus metabolism (D), and blood clotting (K).

d. *Excretory System.*
   (1) *Morphology.* There are two *kidneys* (true kidneys or *metanephroi*), each with a duct, the *ureter,* which conveys urine to the *urinary bladder.* Urine escapes from the bladder through the *urethra.* The urinary and reproductive ducts have a common external opening. Excretion also takes place through the *sweat glands* in the skin, and through the *lungs;* and certain proteins discharged into the blood by the liver are excretory products. In the kidney, each kidney unit consists of a *Bowman's capsule,* the *proximal*

and *distal convoluted tubules,* with the *loop of Henle* intervening.

(2) *Physiology.* Bowman's capsule, which surrounds a knot of blood capillaries, the *glomerulus,* functions as a filter. The convoluted tubules have a more active function, in that they secrete additional materials into the cavity of the tubule, and remove others from the tubule. The sweat glands are of great importance in temperature regulation, the act of perspiring being important through the effect of evaporation, in reducing surface temperature. The rate of perspiration is determined by the blood supply of the sweat glands, which, in turn, is under autonomic nervous control.

e. *Respiratory System.*

(1) *Morphology.* The air passages in the nose are increased in surface area by *turbinal bones.* The passages open into the roof of the *pharynx* at the back of the *soft palate.* From the pharynx, the air passage leads into the *larynx* through an opening covered by a flap, the *epiglottis.* The larynx is at the upper end of the *trachea* or wind-pipe. The latter bifurcates, forming two *bronchi,* one entering each lung, where it repeatedly divides into the smaller *bronchial tubes;* these terminate in the thin-walled *alveoli,* which are surrounded by pulmonary capillaries. Each lung is covered by a membrane, the *visceral pleura,* which is reflexed back at its root to line the cavity in which the lung lies. The outer wall of the cavity is lined with *parietal pleura.* Each pleural cavity is separate, and neither communicates with any other portion of the coelom.

(2) *Physiology.* Since alveolar air normally contains more oxygen and less carbon dioxide than does the blood in the pulmonary capillaries, oxygen tends to diffuse into the blood and car-

bon dioxide from the blood into the alveoli. This is called *"external respiration."* The oxygen is carried in the blood chiefly in loose combination with *hemoglobin* — forming *oxy-hemoglobin.* In the capillaries in the systemic (non-pulmonary) portion of the blood system the concentration gradient is just the opposite of that in the lung walls, *viz.,* the oxygen will diffuse into the cells and carbon dioxide will diffuse out. This is called *"internal respiration."* The combustion which takes place within the cell is, properly speaking, *cell respiration.* The movements which involve air coming into and leaving the lungs properly constitute *"breathing,"* not "respiration." The mechanics of breathing involve movements of the floor and wall of the chest cavity. The floor is formed by the *diaphragm,* a transverse muscle separating chest and abdominal cavities; increase in height of the cavity results from contraction of this muscle. Increase in thickness of the cavity accompanies elevation of the *ribs,* by contraction of *intercostal muscles.* Since the parietal pleura is attached to the outer wall, increase in size of the chest is accompanied by withdrawal of the parietal pleura from the lungs. Decrease of air pressure in the pleural cavity then acts as a vacuum in drawing air into the lungs through the air passages.

f. *Circulatory System.*

(1) *Morphology.* The blood consists of a liquid substrate, the *plasma,* in which are contained *erythrocytes (red corpuscles), leucocytes (white corpuscles),* and *thrombocytes (blood platelets).* Its circulation is maintained by the rhythmic contraction of the heart, the rate of the heart beat being intrinsic but subject to modification

by autonomic nervous control. There are two *auricles* or *atria* in the heart, both thin-walled, and two *ventricles,* the latter with thick muscular walls. Blood to the lungs leaves from the *right ventricle* and passes through the two *pulmonary arteries.* It is returned to the *left auricle* of the heart through the *right* and *left pulmonary veins.* From the left auricle it enters the *left ventricle,* passing through the opening guarded by the *mitral valve.* The left ventricle pumps the blood into the *systemic circulation,* through the *aorta,* whose main arch is to the left. Branches from the arch of the aorta are: the *innominate artery,* dividing into *right subclavian* and *carotid arteries*; the *left carotid artery*; and the *left subclavian artery.* The carotids extend into the head; the subclavians, through the shoulder into the arm. The *descending aorta* gives off branches to muscles, lungs, and abdominal viscera, and divides in the lower portion of the abdominal cavity into the *common iliac arteries,* which carry the blood into the legs. The venous system consists of: a *portal vein,* carrying blood from the alimentary canal to the liver (a renal portal vein is absent); the *inferior vena cava,* a large vein draining the lower part of the body, and emptying into the right auricle; and the *superior vena cava,* formed by the union of *right* and *left innominate veins,* each of these formed by a *jugular* and *subclavian vein.* The jugulars drain the head, the subclavians the arms. Intercellular spaces are drained by a set of channels called *lymph vessels,* which empty into the subclavian veins near the heart; the lymph vessel on the left, the *thoracic duct,* drains all the lower portion of the body.

(2) *Physiology.* The course of the blood, outlined in the account of the Morphology, is diagram-

med in Fig. 82. Functions of the blood include: transport of food material and oxygen to the cells, and waste material away from the cells, temperature regulation, transport of hormones, and disease resistance. Blood capillaries in the walls of the intestine absorb end products of carbohydrate and protein digestion. These are conveyed to the lungs by the portal vein. Products of fat digestion are absorbed by the *lacteals,* through which they are conducted to the veins by way of the thoracic duct. The disease-resisting function is accomplished by the *antigen-antibody reactions* of the blood, a foreign protein (antigen) in the blood stimulating the formation of an antibody. The latter may precipitate the foreign protein if it is in solution, or agglutinate the foreign bodies if insoluble. In the latter case, *phagocytosis* (the engulfing of the foreign material by white corpuscles) is increased. A poison (*toxin*) produced by a foreign organism stimulates production of an *antitoxin,* a kind of antibody. The thrombocytes are functionally important in blood-clotting, whereas, the erythrocytes, which contain hemoglobin, are involved in carrying oxygen. Release of *thromboplastin* from disintegrating thrombocytes initiates blood clotting. This substance causes combination of calcium and *prothrombin*, both already in the blood plasma, to form *thrombin*. Thrombin is an enzyme that transforms *fibrinogen* (a plasma protein) into *fibrin*, the fibrous material that traps the erythrocytes in the clot. The liquid squeezed out by the contracting clot is *serum*.

g. *Nervous System.* (Figs. 85, 86).

(1) *Morphology.* The *cerebral hemispheres* (derived from the *telencephalon*) are so large in the human brain that the *diencephalon* and *midbrain* (*mesencephalon*) are completely concealed

by them. The *cerebellum* (*metencephalon*) is, however, relatively large. These, with the *medulla oblongata* (*myelencephalon*), constitute the five divisions of the brain. The medulla merges into the *spinal cord,* which has two enlarged regions, the *cervical* and *lumbar enlargements.* There are twelve *cranial nerves,* as in reptiles, birds, and other mammals, with essentially the same distribution. Man has thirty-one *spinal nerves*: eight *cervical,* twelve *thoracic,* five *lumbar,* five *sacral,* and one *coccygeal.* The spinal

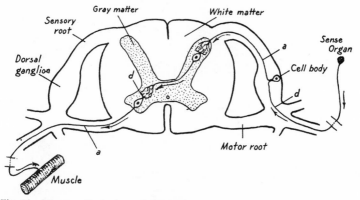

Fig. 85. Diagram illustrating relations between spinal cord and spinal nerves. Three neurons, constituting a simple reflex arc, are represented. The direction of the nerve impulse through these neurons is indicated by arrows. Abbreviations: a, axon; d, dendron.

nerves join to form *cervical, brachial, lumbar,* and *sacral plexuses* in man. The brain and spinal cord are surrounded by three membranes or *meninges,* the *pia mater,* next to the brain or cord; the *dura mater,* lining the cranium and neural canal of the vertebrae; and the loose *arachnoid membrane* between them. Each spinal nerve has two *roots,* a *dorsal* or sensory, bearing a ganglion, and a *ventral* or motor. The nerve branches into three *rami,* a *dorsal,* a *ventral,* and the *communicating ramus* (containing fibers of the autonomic nervous system). The *autonomic nervous system* is related structurally to the central nervous system but the actions it controls are independent of the will; it consists of two portions, the *sympathetic system,* arising in the thoracic region,

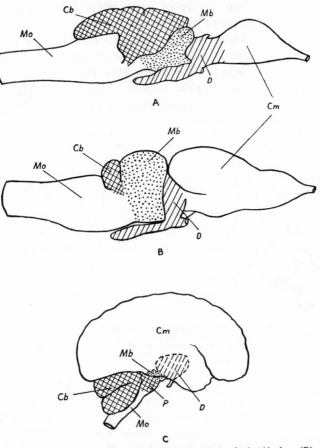

Fig. 86. Diagrammatic side views of the brains of the shark (A), frog (B), and man (C). From anterior to posterior (right to left) the five major divisions distinguished are: telencephalon, diencephalon, mesencephalon, metencephalon, myelencephalon. Abbreviations: Cb, cerebellum; Cm, cerebrum; D, diencephalon; Mb, mid-brain; Mo, medulla oblongata; P, pons.

and the *parasympathetic system,* arising in the cranial and sacral regions. These are functionally antagonistic.

(2) *Physiology*. The principle function of the nervous system is the conduction of *nerve impulses* from one part of the body to another. The cells involved are the highly specialized *neurons*, typically consisting of a *cell body*, and a *dendron* and an *axon*. Neurons are associated together in *nerve tracts* and *reflex arcs*. The nerve impulse may pass over a single neuron in either direction, but only from the axon of one neuron to the dendron of the next in an association tract or reflex arc. Such a connection is a *synapse*. A simple reflex arc involves at least: a *receptor* (sense organ), an *afferent neuron,* an *efferent neuron*, and an *effector* (motor organ). From a few to many *associating* or *internuncial neurons* are nearly always present between afferent and efferent neurons. The connections between neurons (synapses) are not intimate, probably; most of the delay in the passage of a nerve impulse through a reflex arc is due to the number of synapses over which it must pass rather than the total distance it travels. The nerve impulse travels at a measurable speed, about 120 meters per second in man. It is accompanied by a wave of negativity which may be detected by a galvanometer. The recovery of a nerve after excitation (in preparation for conducting the next impulse), which takes place in a small fraction of a second, involves the oxidation of food; it is a chemical as well as a physical process. Furthermore, chemical secretions called *neurohumors* are involved as intermediaries in the effects produced at terminals of the autonomic nervous system. One neurohumor, *acetylcholine*, appears to be the factor in transmission of nerve impulses across synapses.

h. *Sensory System*.

(1) *Eye*. (Fig. 87). The eye is best understood in

analogy with a camera. In a camera, light is refracted by a lens; the eye also has a *lens*, but in addition two liquid refractive media, the *aqueous* and *vitreous humors*. Whereas in a camera focussing is accomplished by moving the lens forward and backward, in the eye this is accomplished by changing the shape of the lens. An *iris* diaphragm, concentrating the rays of light in the center of the lens, is present in both eye and camera. In the *retina,* the human eye possesses a sensitive plate containing a light-sensitive chemical (*visual purple*). This analogy does not, of course, explain sight itself; a camera cannot see. The brain gives man the final interpretation of visual stimuli, after impulses set up in the retina are conducted to the brain over the *optic nerve.*

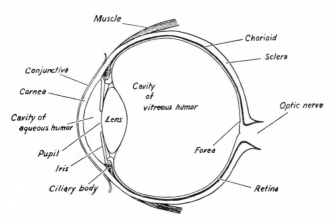

Fig. 87. Vertical section through the human eye. The relations, though not the proportions, are typical of vertebrates in general. (Modified from various authors).

(2) *Ear.* (See pages 156 and 165). The organ of equilibrium is associated with the organ of hearing, both being in the *inner ear.* The functioning of the former depends upon movements of the liquid in the *semicircular canals.* The organ of

hearing involves an *outer ear,* for collecting and concentrating sound waves, terminating in the *tympanic membrane.* Movements of this membrane are conducted by the chain of ossicles in the middle ear (*malleus, stapes,* and *incus,* in that order) to the inner ear, which contains the real end-organ of hearing, the *organ of Corti.* Ability to distinguish between sounds of different pitch involves, according to a widely held theory, response by sympathetic vibration to different frequencies at different levels along the organ of Corti.

(3) *Other Sense Organs.* In general, other sense organs involve relatively simple terminal nerve elements which do not occur in complexly differentiated organs. The senses of taste, smell, pain, pressure, temperature, and others are of this general type.

i. *Endocrine Glands.* Although not constituting an organ system, these organs may be summarized together. In all cases their secretory products are picked up and carried in the blood stream rather than in specialized ducts; hence they are called "ductless glands." The *pituitary gland,* at the base of the brain, consists of two main divisions, the *anterior* and *posterior lobes.* The former secretes *hormones* involved in growth, regulation of sex development, and the regulation of the activity of other endocrine glands. The posterior lobe secretes hormones which effect smooth muscle activity in various parts of the body. The *thyroid gland,* a bilobed structure in front of the trachea, secretes a hormone which regulates development and general metabolism. The *parathyroid glands,* four small bodies which may be embedded in the thyroid, secrete a hormone which regulates calcium balance between bones and blood. The *thymus,* ventral to the anterior end of the heart, secretes a hormone involved in early development and growth. The *pineal gland,* on the dorsal side of the diencephalon, secretes a hormone which is said to have a similar stimulating effect on development, but not growth. The *adrenal glands* lie above the kidneys. They secrete a hormone from the *medulla* which produces the same effects accomplished by stimulation of the sympathetic portion of the autonomic system. From the *cortex* is secreted a hormone involved in the regulation of metabolism. Hormones involved in the development of secondary sexual characters and in the regulation of menstruation, pregnancy, and lactation are secreted by cells in the *gonads.*

4. REPRODUCTION AND DEVELOPMENT.

   a. *Morphology of Reproductive Organs.* The two *ovaries* of the female lie in the lower part of the abdominal cavity near the open ends of the *oviducts* or *Fallopian tubules.* The two tubules join to form the *uterus,* which communicates with the *urogenital sinus* externally through the *vagina.* The opening of the urogenital sinus is bounded laterally by two pairs of folds, the inner *labia minora* and the outer *labia majora.* The *clitoris,* homologous with the penis of the male, lies at the anterior margin of the urogenital sinus. In the male the *testes* are contained in the *scrotum.* The numerous ducts of each testis, the *vasa efferentia,* empty into the single *vas deferens,* which, like the one from the other testis, receives a *seminal vesicle.* Secretions of various glands contribute to the *seminal fluid,* in which are contained the *spermatozoa* which have been formed in the testes. From the seminal vesicle a duct joins the *urethra,* which traverses the *penis,* the latter consisting of three columns of spongy, erectile tissue, rendered turgid by concentration of blood in its vascular spaces.

   b. *Physiology of Reproduction and Development.* The developing *ovum* is contained in a *follicle* in the ovary, which grows as the egg cell grows. When fully formed, the follicle ruptures, releasing the ovum. This is *ovulation*. The ovum is drawn into the Fallopian tubule, where fertilization (conception) may occur if motile sperm cells are present. (The sperm cells move through the uterus and up the Fallopian tubules following copulation, and fertilization normally occurs at the upper end of the Fallopian tubule.) If fertilization does not occur, the ovum is carried down the tubule, through the uterus, and leaves the body through the vagina. In that case the *corpus luteum,* formed at the surface of the ovary from the ruptured follicle gradually decreases in size; and in about two weeks after ovulation the lining of the uterus goes through a process of rapid disintegration, the process of *menstruation*. Ovulation and menstruation, two events in the *menstrual cycle* of approximately twenty-eight days, are normal aspects of the sex cycle of a woman between *puberty* and *menopause,* except when interrupted by *pregnancy*. If fertilization of the ovum occurs, development begins in the Fallopian tubule, and when the embryo reaches the uterus it is *implanted* in the wall of the uterus. In this case the corpus luteum persists and grows, forming an endocrine gland whose hormone provides for maintenance of the embryo in the uterus and inhibits the menstrual cycle. As the embryo (*foetus*) develops, part of its tissue becomes embedded in the maternal tissue lining the uterus, to form the *placenta,* an organ in which substances in maternal and foetal blood may diffuse back and forth through relatively few intervening membranes. There is no direct connection of blood stream, nervous system, or any other system between embryo and mother. At the end of the period of pregnancy, about ten lunar months after fertilization, *birth* or *parturition* occurs. Shortly thereafter, *lactation* or milk secretion begins. This is continued through stimulation occasioned by the drainage of the ducts of the *mammary glands.*

REVIEW QUESTIONS

1. Characterize the class Mammalia.
2. Give the major morphological characteristics of the rabbit.
3. What is a dental formula? Give examples.
4. Is man a typical mammal?
5. Name the bones of the human skeleton.
6. What are the relations between the skeletal and muscular systems?
7. Trace the path of food through the digestive tract. Name and locate the enzymes that act upon it, and state their specific effects.
8. How do the kidneys function?
9. Describe the respiratory system, and explain how oxygen from outside the body reaches the cells within the body.
10. Trace the course of the blood in the human body.
11. Compare the circulatory systems of a fish, an amphibian, and a mammal.
12. Discuss the functional relations between the circulatory, digestive, excretory, and respiratory systems.
13. Name and trace the twelve cranial nerves of the higher vertebrates.
14. Compare the brains of a series of typical vertebrates.
15. What is a reflex arc? Discuss the passage of a nerve impulse over a reflex arc.
16. Describe the sense organs of man.
17. Name the most important endocrine glands of man, and give the functions of their secretions.
18. Describe the male and female reproductive organs of man.
19. What are the physiological characteristics of the menstrual cycle?
20. Briefly discuss human embryonic development.

Part Three

BIOLOGICAL PRINCIPLES

———

CHAPTER XXII

GENETICS

DEFINITIONS OF HEREDITY AND GENETICS

Heredity is the transmission of traits physical or mental, from parents to offspring. The scientific study of this transmission is *genetics;* it may follow either statistical or experimental methods.

THE CONTINUITY OF THE GERM-PLASM

Some forty years ago, August Weismann suggested that all hereditary change must originate in the germ-plasm, inasmuch as *the germ-plasm constitutes the only organic continuity from one generation to the next.* The concept of the continuity of the germ-plasm is the basic principle in all studies of biological inheritance.

MENDELISM

Gregor Mendel. Working on garden peas, studying the effects of crossing peas of contrasting characteristics and their descendants, Gregor Mendel discovered in the early 1860's the principles now known as Mendel's Laws. Their true scientific value was not appreciated until 1900, after Mendel's death.

Mendel's Experiments. These involved seven pairs of contrasting characters of the garden pea. Mendel discovered that the progeny of a cross of unlike parents of pure lines were all alike, resembling one parent only. When the flowers of these (the F_1 generation) were permitted to be self-fertilizing, on the other hand, both of the original parental types were present in their progeny. These types were present in numbers approximating a 3:1 ratio—three like the F_1, to one like the parental type which did not appear in the F_1 generation. The latter type Mendel called *recessive;* the former, *dominant.* Seeds from plants showing the recessive trait produced plants all having the recessive trait; but seeds from a plant showing the dominant trait but having the recessive trait in its ancestry developed into both types of plants. (Fig. 88).

Interpretation of Mendel's Experiments. The importance of the gametes was realized by Mendel, who saw that to explain the ratios he obtained he had to assume that a given gamete could contain a determiner for one character but not its opposite or alternative. If the determiner for the dominant trait was derived from both parents *or from either one,* the offspring would show the dominant trait; the recessive trait appeared only when the gametes from *both parents* contained its determiner. Each trait appeared as if determined by a single factor in each gamete—the gametes being themselves "pure" for one of the two contrasting characters. This explanation coincided also with Mendel's observation that, regardless of the number of contrasting characters studied at one time, the hereditary behavior of each one was independent of the others.

Mendel's Laws. Aside from the idea of dominance, which is not universally true, Mendel's chief contributions were the concepts of (1) *segregation* and (2) *independent assortment.* A corollary of the former is the concept of the *purity of the gametes.* Independent assortment does not hold true of determiners showing linkage (see below). These two concepts are referred to as Laws of Mendelism.

Terminology of Mendelian Inheritance. Unit characters may be determined by single *factors* or *determiners,* now called *genes.* Alternative characters are *allelomorphic;* their determiners can not occur in the same gamete. A zygote containing two determiners for the same character is *homozygous;* one containing the genes for alternative characters is *heterozygous.* All organisms that look alike with reference to alternative characters belong to the same *phenotype;* all organisms of the same genetic behavior with reference to alternative characters belong to the same *genotype; e.g.,* heterozygous tall peas and homozygous tall peas are of the same phenotype but two different genotypes.

Examples of Mendelian Inheritance. While it is not true that all inheritance is so simple as in the cases of the characters Mendel studied, yet it is necessary to understand such simple situations in order to comprehend more complex ones.

1. EXAMPLES FROM THE GARDEN PEA. Two contrasting characters studied by Mendel had to do with length of stem, and color of seed. Mendel found that the tall stem condition was dominant over dwarf, and that yellow seed color was dominant over green. This means, of course, that when Mendel crossed homozygous tall and dwarf plants their progeny were all tall; and that when he crossed homozygous yellow and green their progeny were all yellow. When, in his experiments, he considered inheritance of two or more pairs of contrasting characters at the same time he found that they behaved entirely independently of each other. If tall plants with yellow seeds were crossed with dwarf plants having green seeds, the progeny proved to be all tall plants with yellow seeds. If these F_1 plants were permitted to be self-fertilized, however, their progeny were of four different phenotypes, in the ratio of approximately nine tall yellow: three tall green: three dwarf yellow: one dwarf green. The basis of this assortment is shown diagrammatically in Figure 88. The principle involved is the principle of independent assortment, one of the Mendelian Laws.

2. EXAMPLES FROM GUINEA-PIGS. Certain contrasting characters in the guinea-pig behave in inheritance much as the ones given from the garden pea. Black coat color is dominant over white; a rough coat shows dominance over a smooth one; short hair is dominant to the long-haired or angora condition. When homozygous black guinea-pigs are crossed with white ones, the progeny are all black; and when angor and homozygous short-haired. guinea-pigs are mated, their progeny are all short-haired. (N.B.—The whites and angoras, being recessive, are homozygous of necessity.) In the same fashion, if one

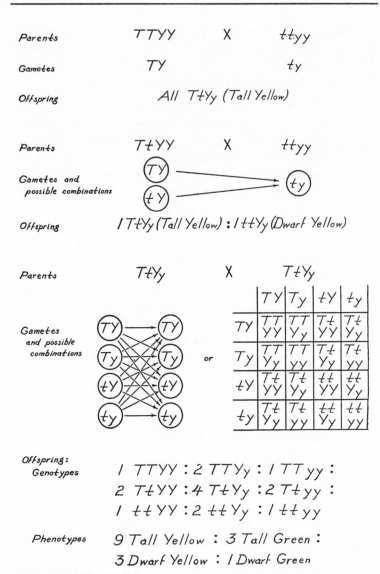

Fig. 88. Diagrams illustrating assortment of genetic factors for tall or dwarf plants, and yellow or green seeds, in three kinds of crosses of the garden pea. From top to bottom these are: Homozygous tall yellow, crossed with homozygous dwarf green; Heterozygous tall, homozygous yellow, crossed with homozygous dwarf green; Heterozygous tall yellow, crossed with heterozygous tall yellow. The latter cross is the so-called dihybrid cross. Since peas are normally self-fertilized, this illustrates the assortment expected in the progeny raised from the seeds of one such plant. Two graphical methods of representing all possible combinations of the gametes from the two parents are shown in the last example, under the heading "gametes and possible combinations."

parent is homozygous for all three dominant traits, and the other homozygous for all three recessives, the progeny will all show the three dominant traits but, of course, will be heterozygous for each. (Such animals are called tri-hybrids.) If we use B as the gene for black; b, for white; R, for rough; r, for smooth; S, for short hair; s, for long hair or angora; we find:

Parents	BBRRSS	X	bbrrss
Gametes	All BRS		All brs

Progeny (F$_1$)   All BbRrSs

Now if such a tri-hybrid is crossed with the triple recessive we find new combinations of characters appearing, again illustrating the law of independent assortment:

Parents	BbRrSs	X	bbrrss
Gametes	Eight different kinds:		All brs
	BRS, BRs, BrS, Brs,		
	bRS, bRs, brS, brs.		

Progeny (F$_1$)   Eight phenotypes, in equal numbers, as follows: 1 black rough short; 1 black rough long: 1 black smooth short: 1 black smooth long: 1 white rough short: 1 white rough long: 1 white smooth short: 1 white smooth long.

       Eight genotypes, in equal numbers, as follows: 1 BbRrSs: 1 BbRrss: 1 BbrrSs: 1 Bbrrss: 1 bbRrSs: 1 bbRrss: 1 bbrrSs: 1 bbrrss.

Problems in Mendelian Inheritance.

1. METHODS OF SOLVING MENDELIAN PROBLEMS. The two common methods of solving Mendelian problems are the Punnett-square method and the algebraic method.

a. **The Punnett-square or "checker-board" method** (includ-all pictorial or graphical methods) is too unwieldy for problems that cannot be solved by rapid inspection, but it illustrates well the chance combinations of gametes. First, one determines all possible gametes from each parent, following the law of segregation. Then, one determines all possible combinations of all types of gametes from one parent with all types of gametes from the other parent, duplicate zygotes being sorted out and grouped together after all combinations are made. The method is illustrated in Fig. 88.

b. **The Algebraic Method.** Inspection of the results of a cross between two heterozygous parents suggests the fundamental relationship between Mendelian crosses and the products of algebraic quantities. To illustrate: Bb becomes B + b after segregation in the gametes. Bb X Bb becomes, therefore, $(B + b) (B + b)$ or $(B + b)^2$. Just as $(a + b)^2 = a^2 + 2ab + b^2$, so $(B + b)^2 = B^2 + 2Bb + b^2$ (which is, of course, 1BB: 2Bb: 1bb). In a more complicated cross: Bbrr $\times$ BbRr becomes $[(B + b)r] [(B + b) (R + r)]$. Now there are only three possible results in a simple cross involving but one pair of characters: (1) the offspring are all alike if both parents are homozygous; (2) half the offspring are like one parent and half like the other if one parent is homozygous and the other heterozygous; and (3) there is one homozygous dominant to two heterozygous dominants to one homozygous recessive if both parents are heterozygous. The ratios to be expected in more complex crosses are all combinations of these three conditions, and may be analyzed by considering each pair of characters alone, in order. This does not, of course, require any laborious multiplication. One simply keeps in mind the three possible results in single-factor crosses and applies these ratios to other situations. Applying this method to the last named cross, we should analyze the inheritance of black-white first, then the rough-smooth. In a Bb X Bb cross we have two heterozygotes, yielding the ratio: 1BB: 2Bb:1bb. In the case of the other pair of characters, we have one heterozygous and one homozygous parent, rr x Rr, yielding: 1rr: 1Rr. We then combine the ratios, as in the following scheme in which all the factors of one ratio are multiplied by all the factors of the other:

1BB	$\begin{cases} 1rr \\ 1Rr \end{cases}$	1BBrr 1BBRr
2Bb	$\begin{cases} 1rr \\ 1Rr \end{cases}$	2Bbrr 2BbRr
1bb	$\begin{cases} 1rr \\ 1Rr \end{cases}$	1bbrr 1bbRr

The last column represents the expected genotypic ratio. Any number of characters can be handled similarly, for example:

AabbCCdd X AaBbccDd

$$
1AA
\begin{cases}
1bb \quad 1Cc \begin{cases} 1dd \\ 1Dd \end{cases} & \begin{matrix} 1AAbbCcdd \\ 1AAbbCcDd \end{matrix} \\[2ex]
1Bb \quad 1Cc \begin{cases} 1dd \\ 1Dd \end{cases} & \begin{matrix} 1AABbCcdd \\ 1AABbCcDd \end{matrix}
\end{cases}
$$

$$
2Aa
\begin{cases}
1bb \quad 1Cc \begin{cases} 1dd \\ 1Dd \end{cases} & \begin{matrix} 2AabbCcdd \\ 2AabbCcDd \end{matrix} \\[2ex]
1Bb \quad 1Cc \begin{cases} 1dd \\ 1Dd \end{cases} & \begin{matrix} 2AaBbCcdd \\ 2AaBbCcDd \end{matrix}
\end{cases}
$$

$$
1aa
\begin{cases}
1bb \quad 1Cc \begin{cases} 1dd \\ 1Dd \end{cases} & \begin{matrix} 1aabbCcdd \\ 1aabbCcDd \end{matrix} \\[2ex]
1Bb \quad 1Cc \begin{cases} \mathbf{1dd} \\ 1Dd \end{cases} & \begin{matrix} 1aaBbCcdd \\ 1aaBbCcDd \end{matrix}
\end{cases}
$$

The phenotypes, usually fewer in number than genotypes, may be found by this method, simply by combining phenotypic rather than genotypic ratios from single-factor crosses.

2. SAMPLE PROBLEMS IN MENDELIAN INHERITANCE.

a. *Problem*: What is the expected ratio of genotypes and phenotypes in a cross between a homozygous rough angora guinea-pig and one heterozygous for rough short hair?

Answer: Genotypes: 1RRss : 1RRSs : 1Rrss : 1RrSs
Phenotypes: 1 rough angora : 1 rough short

b. *Problem*: In a litter of six guinea-pigs, one has black rough hair, two have black smooth hair, two have white rough hair, and one has white smooth hair. The mother has white smooth hair. Describe the father, and give genotypes of both parents and all offspring.

Suggestions for solution: The female parent, showing both recessive characters is, of necessity, a double homozygote. The nearest Mendelian ratio which fits the observation of the litter is 1:1:1:1.

This means two 1:1 ratios combined; each such results from a heterozygous X homozygous cross. The same type of litter could result from either of the following type crosses: BbRr X bbrr or Bbrr X bbRr. The data given for the female eliminate the second as a possibility in this case.

Answer: The father had black rough hair, being heterozygous for both characters. The mother is homozygous white and smooth. All black and all rough offspring are heterozygous; all white and all smooth offspring are homozygous.

SEX DETERMINATION

The first clue to the structural basis for Mendelian inheritance came with the discovery that the chromosome constituents of cells differ between the two sexes. Most chromosome pairs are alike in both sexes, but one pair shows consistent differences. In most animals the members of this pair are alike in the female (the two X-chromosomes) whereas in the male only one X-chromosome is present, accompanied by a dissimilar one (the Y-chromosome) or not accompanied at all. The male may be represented by the letters XY (or XO), the female, XX. In segregation, half the gametes of the male contain the X-chromosome, the other half the Y-or no chromosome representative of that pair; all the gametes of the female contain the X-chromosome. It is really, therefore, a case in which the female is homozygous and the male heterozygous; and in every combination of sperm and egg cell the expected ratio of the two sexes should be 1:1—which is, of course, approximately the observed ratio. Other factors may change the ratio in mature individuals; this is merely the ratio of zygotes at fertilization. To illustrate:

Parents	XX (female)	X	XY (male)
Gametes	All X		½X, ½Y
Progeny	½XX (female)		½XY, (male)

The opposite condition, in which the female is heterozygous, occurs in birds and lepidoptera (moths and butterflies). In this case the gamete from the female determines the sex; but the ratio is, of course, not affected. (Various special cases and exceptions occur, *e.g.*, sex-reversal in fishes, amphibians, and birds, and the so-called intersexes and gynandromorphs.)

THE GENE THEORY OF HEREDITY

General Statement. It was but a step from the discovery of the chromosome basis of sex determination to the realization that pairs of determiners must exist, similarly, in homologous pairs of chromosomes.

The Gene Theory. The theory which recognizes the determiners (*genes*) as localized in the chromosomes is now solidly based on a huge number of statistical data—the most significant studies having been carried out by Morgan and his associates on the common fruit-fly of the genus *Drosophila*. Genes for allelomorphic characters cannot exist in the same gamete because their positions in the chromosomes are identical. Therefore, when the homologous chromosomes are segregated in gametogenesis, the genes for alternative characters are also separated. (Fig. 13). The evidence for the gene theory now includes the localization of particular genes in particular dark zones in the chromosomes of Drosophila, these chromosomes in the salivary glands being particularly large and susceptible to detailed study.

Interaction of Genes. A particular character may be the resultant of the interaction of two or more genes, rather than of one alone. These may interact to produce a *blending,* or they may be *complemental, i.e.* two or more genes may be necessary before a given trait becomes evident at all. In addition to these, *lethal genes* are known—their presence in the homozygous condition preventing development of the organism.

Linkage. It has been further discovered that not all unit characters are independently assorted. Certain traits tend to always accompany certain other traits. All these characters which occur together are said to be linked; their genes apparently occur in the same chromosome pair. As evidence for this, it has been found that the number of linkage groups coincides with the number of chromosome pairs and that one group is typically linked with sex. (In *Drosophila,* there are four linkage groups, and four pairs of chromosomes.)

Crossing-Over. During synapsis, in gametogenesis, the chromosomes of a homologous pair are in intimate contact. It is believed that during this contact allelomorphic genes may be translocated—genes for alternative characters in some way changing places. One explanation given involves the possible twisting of the chromosomes about each other during synapsis. The end result is that certain characters which have occurred together ("linked") may become occasionally separated. One assumes that the farther apart on a chromosome these linked genes occur the greater is the possibility of crossing-over. On that theory "chromosome maps" have been devised showing the probable position on each chromosome of each gene it is known to bear. The studies of Painter, Bridges, and others on the morphology of unusually large chromosomes are yielding a structural as well as theoretical basis for this mapping.

THE NATURE OF GENES

Gene Action. An individual gene affects a particular character through its influence on the process by which that character develops. The mechanism of this action appears to be the direct relationship between a gene and a particular protein, usually an enzyme, the gene providing the information or "recipe" by which the appropriate protein is synthesized.

Chemical Nature of the Gene. Recent evidence clearly relates the gene to the DNA molecule of the chromosome. The gene appears to be a segment of a DNA molecule in which the particular sequence of nucleotides (see Chap. II) provides the necessary information. The DNA segment constitutes a template by which a complementary RNA molecule is produced. The RNA thus produced, now called *messenger RNA*, moves from the nucleus into the cytoplasm, where it becomes attached to a ribosome (Fig. 5), and where it provides the pattern for the synthesis of a particular kind of protein molecule.

The Genetic Code. The characteristics of a particular protein depend upon the sequence and kinds of amino acids composing it. (There are twenty different kinds of amino acids in naturally occurring proteins.) The specific sequence is determined by a *code* carried by the messenger RNA molecule, this RNA constituting the intermediary between gene and protein. The clue to this code was found in 1961.

A particular sequence of three nitrogenous bases in the RNA molecule determines the particular amino acid introduced at a particular position in the protein molecule being synthesized. The amino acid appropriate to this position is apparently brought into position by a special type of RNA, *transfer RNA*, and the energy for this process is derived from ATP. Four types of nitrogenous bases occur in DNA or RNA. If we consider each a single letter, their sequences could provide a vocabulary of code words based on either one, two, three, or four letters. Since there are twenty amino acids involved, only three-letter or four-letter codes would provide a large enough vocabulary to distinguish the twenty. Recent evidence indicates that the code is determined by three-nucleotide sequences, in other words that it is a three-letter code. (Examples: the sequence adenine-cytosine-cytosine in RNA codes the amino acid histidine; guanine-guanine-uracil in RNA codes the amino acid tryptophan.)

THE ORIGIN OF VARIATIONS

The structural basis of heredity explains the persistence of traits, but not their modifications. Changes in the genetic constitution of an organism may be due to new combinations, to chromosome mutations, or to gene mutations. These are the raw materials of evolution.

New Combinations. The crossing of two heterozygous individuals may produce new combinations of characters not previously present; the combinations are new, not their individual elements.

Chromosome Mutations. Following synapsis in gametogenesis, the pairs of chromosomes do not always normally separate. In rare cases all or most may go into one germ-cell, leaving none or few in the other. Following fertilization, the chromosome number is abnormal: it may be *triploid* if one gamete contained the reduced or haploid number but the other was diploid; or it may be *tetraploid* if both gametes were diploid. Such organisms may show traits entirely different from those of either parent, yet heritable. Similarly, dislocation and translocation of parts of chromosomes may result in heritable variations. Polyploids, multiple chromosome mutants, have been recently produced artificially by treatment with colchicine.

Gene Mutations. Traits may disappear or entirely new ones appear in a given line of descent. If these changes are inherited, they may be due to the loss, gain, or modification of genes in particular chromosomes. Such mutations have been induced by Muller by treatment of *Drosophila* with X-rays; but no ordinary environmental conditions which will produce mutations are known, except possibly cosmic rays, which are known to increase the rate of "spontaneous" mutation, and therefore should be considered. From our present-knowledge of the chemical nature of the gene it is evident that gene mutations must involve changes in the sequence of nucleotides in the DNA molecule.

INHERITANCE OF ACQUIRED CHARACTERISTICS

In spite of the obvious adaptation of organisms for their environments, there is no positive evidence for the origin of species through direct action of the environment. The production of heritable changes (mutations) by X-rays, radium, and colchicine, have involved direct effects on the germ-cells. Somatic or body changes are not inherited—apparently because there is no mechanism by which they affect the germ-cells.

HUMAN HEREDITY

Galton's Laws. Galton enunciated two principles, from his statistical study of human inheritance: (1) the *law of ancestral inheritance, viz.,* each parent contributes on the average about one-fourth of the inherited traits, each grand-parent one-sixteenth, each great-grand-parent one sixty-fourth, etc.; (2) the *law of filial regression, viz.,* the offspring of unusual parents tend to be more nearly average than their parents.

Mendelian Inheritance. Although human heredity may involve multiple factors, sex-linkage, or other complications, data suggest simple Mendelian inheritance of certain traits. In general, brown eye color is dominant over blue, curly hair over straight, dark hair over light, average intellectual ability over very high or low intellectual ability. Certain abnormalities are inherited as dominants over the normal condition, *e.g.,* excessively short digits, extra digits, hereditary cataract. Others may be recessive to the normal, *e.g.,* albinism, hereditary epilepsy and "insanity," deaf-mutism. Certain abnormalities appear as sex-linked recessives, appearing in màles with a single factor, but in females only when there are two factors, *e.g.*, hemophilia, red-green color blindness.

IMPROVING MANKIND

Relations of Heredity and Environment. It is frequently true, although fortunately not always, that the biologist makes a fetish of heredity while the sociologist can think only of environment. The man who has a ready positive answer to the question, "Which is more important, heredity or environment?" cannot be a competent judge of their relative importance. Until the two viewpoints are fused, the contribution of neither biology nor sociology can reach its full value; heredity and environment are two sides of the same coin. It seems likely that the absolute limits of achievement, given an ideal environment, are set by heredity; but excellent hereditary possibilities may be limited or destroyed by an unfavorable environment. The heredity sets the *potential* limit of achievement, the environment sets the *actual* limit of achievement.

Eugenics. The improvement of mankind by improving his heredity is *eugenics*. This goal may be achieved, theoretically, by selection. We know that all men are not born equal. This difference at birth is the result primarily of differences in heredity. If future generations come from the best representatives of the present generation, then the average of human ability will be raised. The application of eugenics may be positive — encouraging reproduction of the most desirable; or it may be negative — reducing reproduction of the intellectually and physically unfit. Negative eugenics may be applied either by (1) spreading information on methods of birth-control or (2) sterilization by an operation which prevents reproduction. The former is a questionable solution, for the application of birth-control methods requires intelligent volition, something not to be expected of the intellectually inferior. Sterilization might reasonably be compulsory in cases where its application would clearly benefit human society.

There is no place in eugenics, however, for race prejudice. Human race differences are morphological; and individual differences within each race are greater than the average differences between races. There is no demonstrable superiority or inferiority of one race with reference to others. Consequently there is no biological basis for favoring one race over others.

Euthenics. The improvement of mankind by improving his environment is *euthenics*. This may be thought of as a temporary expedient, since improvement in an individual which is due to his environment is not inherited. However, many individuals of superior heredity are handicapped by unfavorable environment, and an improvement in the latter releases hidden potentialities. Even if heredity may be the more important factor in individual cases, environment is the factor most easily improved. Furthermore, the beneficial effects of an improved environment may be evident within one generation, and some of these benefits will persist.

REVIEW QUESTIONS

1. What is the significance of the principle of the "continuity of the germ-plasm" in heredity?
2. Who was Gregor Mendel, and what discoveries are associated with his name?
3. Define: heredity, segregation, gene, allelomorphic, homozygous, heterozygous, phenotype, genotype.
4. Devise and solve a problem illustrating the principles of Mendelism.
5. What is the chromosome mechanism of sex-determination?
6. Explain the relation between the segregation of genes and the reduction in chromosome number during maturation.
7. What is linkage? Explain its morphological basis.
8. How is the phenomenon of crossing-over made use of in the preparation of "chromosome maps"?
9. What is the modern theory of the nature and action of a gene?
10. Name and give the origins of the different types of inherited variations.
11. How do the principles of Mendelism apply to human heredity?
12. Discuss the relative roles of eugenics and euthenics in the improvement of mankind.

Chapter XXIII

TAXONOMY

DEFINITION OF TAXONOMY

Taxonomy is the science of animal and plant classification.

PURPOSE OF TAXONOMY

Classification of organisms is necessary for convenience—its first purpose. The grouping of animals according to similarities makes scientific biology possible. Of equal importance in modern biology is the attempt of the taxonomist to discover and indicate genetic relationships, similarities due to common ancestry in the course of evolution.

THE CONCEPT OF SPECIES

The working unit of the taxonomist is the *species,* usually thought of as having a real objective existence. No absolute criterion for recognizing a species as a unit has been found, however. As Darwin said, different species of animals are different kinds of animals, and it is as difficult to define kind as species. Certain limitations may be suggested: A group of organisms sufficiently alike to have had the same parents belongs to one species; in other words, the extent of difference, morphological or physiological, is within the range of individual variability. Within a species of wide geographic range the variation may be so great that the extremes would not even be considered of the same species did they not intergrade with each other. This is another test of species: Members of the same species freely interbreed, while those of different species do not, except rarely, and therefore do not show intergrades.

THE BINOMIAL SYSTEM OF NOMENCLATURE

Following the *Binomial System of Nomenclature,* the general adoption of which dates from the work of Carolus Linñaeus (eighteenth century), each organism is known by two names. These are: (1) the name of the *genus* to which it belongs, always written with the initial letter capitalized; and (2) the *specific* or *trivial* name, its initial letter never capitalized. These two words constitute the scientific name of the *species*. (Examples: man, *Homo sapiens;* house sparrow, *Passer domesticus*.) It is customary to print scientific names in italics. The names are of Latin form, for two reasons: (1) when the system was adopted Latin was the international language of scientists, (2) since Latin is a "dead" language its forms are not subject to change.

CATEGORIES OF CLASSIFICATION

Although the species is the working unit of the biologist, for convenience in treating modifications within a species *subspecies* and *variety* names are sometimes employed. These constitute the third part of a *trinomial*. (Example: *Turdus migratorius propinquus* is the scientific name of the Western Robin; in the name of the Eastern Robin, which corresponds to the originally described species, the subspecific name is merely a repetition of the species name — *Turdus migratorius migratorius*.) With this exception, the species is the smallest category in classification. Species form a genus; genera, a *family;* families, an *order;* orders, a *class;* and classes are combined into *phyla*. Each succeeding category is more inclusive and larger than the preceding one. In addition, a class may be divided into *subclasses,* each containing several orders; or a family may, with other families, constitute a *superfamily,* the order containing more than one of these. Other intermediate steps in classification may be inserted wherever they may clarify the complexities of animal or plant relationships. The criteria of these categories are not established, i.e., a beginner in taxonomy has no way of knowing just how different animals must be from each other to constitute different genera rather than species, or families rather than genera. This even puzzles experts, and the absence of quantitative standards for the different categories is one of the weaknesses of taxonomy. However, the criteria in a limited group of animals tend to be more or less uniform. These are based on the experiences and opinions of individual taxonomists—specialists in particular fields. For examples of scientific classification see page 48.

CERTAIN ESSENTIAL RULES OF NOMENCLATURE

The Form of the Scientific Name. The genus name is a noun of Latin form, a singular nominative. The specific name is usually an adjective, which must be of Latin form and in agreement with the genus name in number, case, and gender. The specific name may, however, be a noun in apposition with the genus name; or it may be a noun in the genitive. When a species is named in honor of some one, the ending is in *-i* if the person honored is a man, in *-ae*, if a woman.

Publication. A new species for which a name is being proposed must be described in connection with its name or the latter is not valid.

Avoidance of Duplicate Names. The scientific name of a new species must be such that the organism will not be confused with another. The name must differ from all other species names in the same genus; and there must be no duplicate generic names among animals.

Priority. The first name of a species is given preference if it is later described under another name, the later name for the same species being called a *synonym*. The name of the author is ordinarily printed after the scientific name (but not in italics) to avoid confusion over synonyms. (The name of Linnaeus is commonly abbreviated Linn., or simply L.; and other, frequently occurring names, are also abbreviated.) If subsequent study suggests that a species was placed in the wrong genus, or that the original genus should be subdivided, the genus name is corrected but the original species name is retained; and the original author's name is also retained but in parenthesis. (See page 48).

REVIEW QUESTIONS

1. Define taxonomy, and explain its purpose.
2. What is a species; a subspecies?
3. Give the complete classification of some animal.
4. What are the principle rules of zoological nomenclature?

Chapter XXIV

GEOGRAPHIC DISTRIBUTION

THE GEOGRAPHIC RANGE OF ANIMALS

The animal geographer approaches his study with the assumption that but for certain factors every animal species should exist everywhere. One of the factors is, of course, lack of adaptability, *e.g.,* the climate of a given region prohibits existence of certain species there. An animal may, however, be completely absent from a perfectly suitable habitat because in its movements it has been unable to get there. Certain organisms have been known to thrive even better outside than in their native homes, *e.g.,* the English sparrow in America, the rabbit in Australia, the mongoose in Jamaica. In general, it is assumed that the ancestral home is within the present geographic range, and that the longer the species has existed the more extensive will be its range (Age and Area theory, Chap. XXVI). It is not always true that the place of origin is in the present range. The range itself may be discontinuous, suggesting that the species may have become extinct in part of its range. Discontinuous distribution may also be due to accidents of transportation, however. To explain these anomalies of distribution a knowledge of geology is necessary— changes in the earth's surface, appearance and disappearance of land bridges. All such knowledge must be correlated with the facts of paleontology. The presence and absence of topographic and climatic barriers to distribution, and the histories of these barriers, are of extreme importance in any analysis of present day animal or plant distribution.

DISPERSAL OF ANIMALS

The present distribution of a given animal species is the resultant of its tendency to increase its range and the inhibiting influence of *barriers*. An increasing geographic range is accompanied by a *dispersal* of the species — a migration. The factors of dispersal are here summarized:

Causes of Dispersal.

1. POPULATION PRESSURE, due to the fact that the food supply is inadequate for the number of progeny normally produced.
2. CHANGING HABITAT, this becoming unfavorable for the continued existence of the species in the same locality.

Means of Dispersal.

1. BY AIR: through powers of flight; or by being carried passively, as in a high wind or hurricane.
2. BY WATER: through swimming; or by being carried passively by water currents or on floating debris.
3. BY LAND: through active movements of the species involved.
4. BY HUMAN AGENCY: accidental or intentional transportation.

Barriers to Dispersal.

1. CLIMATIC BARRIERS: conditions of temperature, moisture, light.
2. EDAPHIC BARRIERS: conditions of the medium, e.g., soil constituents, as they may effect burrowing animals.
3. GEOGRAPHIC BARRIERS: obstacles such as oceans, rivers, mountains, deserts.
4. BIOLOGICAL BARRIERS: habitats in which the migrating species cannot maintain itself, for lack of food or the presence of enemies.

ZOOGEOGRAPHIC CLASSIFICATION

Attempts at zoogeographic classification, whether based upon animals or environmental factors, have marked limitations.

They have been useful, however, in providing a vocabulary for description of geographic ranges.

Zoogeographic Regions. Various attempts have been made during the last seventy-five years to classify the earth into areas characterized by peculiar faunas. The best known of these is that of A. R. Wallace (Fig. 90 and Table VIII), but the six regions he proposed have been variously condensed by subsequent students, as follows:

Nearctic	} Holarctic	
Palaearctic		} Arctogaea
Ethiopian		
Oriental		
Australian		Notogaea
Neotropical		Neogaea

Life Zones. In the United States, a frequently used classification of regions is that of Life Zones (of C. H. Merriam), based on the assumption that temperature and humidity are the major factors determining the extent of these biological regions.

ANIMAL MORPHOLOGY
AND GEOGRAPHIC RANGE

In general, certain correlations seem to exist between geographic range (as characterized climatically) and animal morphology. In a cold region, cold-blooded animals are generally smaller than closely related forms in a warmer region, whereas warm-blooded animals (birds and mammals) are usually larger. The latter, however, have smaller appendages (legs, ears, tails, wings) in a cold climate than in a warm one. It also seems to be generally true that desert animals are light in color, whereas animals of very humid regions tend to be of much darker color.

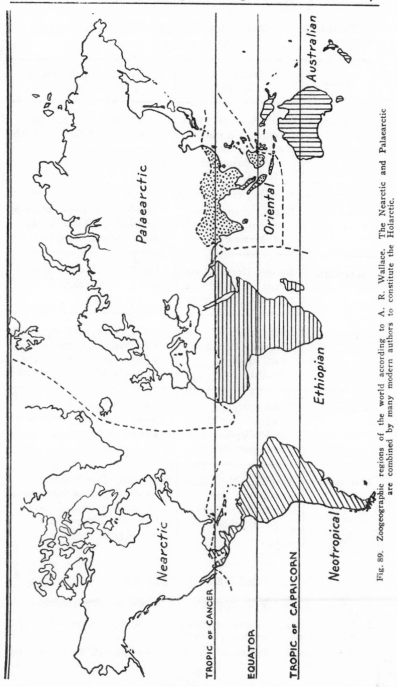

Fig. 89. Zoogeographic regions of the world according to A. R. Wallace. The Nearctic and Palaearctic are combined by many modern authors to constitute the Holarctic.

TABLE VI. ZOOGEOGRAPHIC REGIONS, ACCORDING TO WALLACE

Name	Geographic Range	Characteristic Mammals and Birds
NEOTROPICAL	South America, West Indies, Central America north along coasts of Mexico.	Sloths, armadillos, puff-birds, toucans, motmots, tinamous, hoatzin, macaws.
NEARCTIC	North America south into the highlands of Mexico.	Prong-horn antelope, musk-ox, prairie-dogs, turkeys, blue-birds, juncos, song-sparrows.
PALAEARCTIC	Europe, North Africa, Asia north and west of the Himalayas.	Camel, yak, chamois, several genera of warblers (Sylviidae).
ETHIOPIAN	Africa south of Sahara, Madagascar, southern Arabia.	Gorilla, chimpanzee, hippopotamus, numerous species of antelopes, ostrich, secretary-bird, plantain-eaters, colies.
ORIENTAL	South-eastern Asia, and adjacent islands to Philippines, Borneo, and Bali.	Orang-utan, gibbons, mouse-deer, broad-bills, numerous genera of babblers.
AUSTRALIAN	Australia, New Zealand, and East Indies from Celebes and Lombok east.	Marsupials (one family in America), monotremes, birds-of-paradise, honey-suckers, lyre-birds, cockatoos, cassowaries.

REVIEW QUESTIONS

1. What are the general principles involved in a study of animal geography?

2. In what ways may an animal increase the size of its geographic range, and in what ways are its movements limited?

3. Name, locate, and characterize the principal Zoogeographic Regions according to Wallace.

Chapter XXV

ECOLOGY

DEFINITION OF ECOLOGY

Ecology is the study of the relations between organism and environment. The ecology of a single organism is *autecology*; the ecology of a group of organisms is *synecology*. One means, by the environment, not only topographic and climatic factors in the surroundings but organisms other than the one or ones being considered.

FACTORS OF THE ENVIRONMENT

The Non-living Environment.

1. THE MEDIA IN WHICH ORGANISMS LIVE.

   a. *Soil.* The chemical composition of the soil is a factor in determining the presence of plants and certain animals (e.g., snails, earthworms). The texture is important in relation to moisture conservation and availability, and to the presence of burrowing animals. Angle of slope and exposure to the sun are important factors affecting drainage and the absorption of heat from the sun.

   b. *Water,* always present in protoplasm, is essential to life. It is important in preventing rapid temperature changes, as a solvent for many compounds, as a medium for ionization, and in possessing high surface tension. Its unusual property of expanding as it cools just before freezing is of paramount importance in insulating water under ice, and in aerating the water in the bottom of deep lakes.

   c. *Air.* The earth's atmosphere consists chiefly of nitrogen (about four-fifths) and oxygen (about one-fifth); a small amount of carbon dioxide is also present. The oxygen is essential to life; were it not for photosynthesis in green plants the oxygen would be replaced by carbon dioxide. The density of air, and therefore the partial pressure of its several constituents, decreases with increasing altitude.

d. *Bodies of Other Organisms.* Internal parasites must be able to obtain oxygen under extremely unfavorable conditions, and, if they are parasites of the digestive tract, to resist the action of digestive enzymes. They are protected from most enemies; and, in general, they have a more constant environment than do many free-living forms.

2. CLIMATE. The most important climatic factor is radiation from the sun — which includes heat, visible light, and ultra-violet radiations. Solar radiation, particularly that of longer wave-lengths, in heating the soil, in evaporating water, and in causing the air to expand (in conjunction with variable topography and rotation of the earth) produces such climatic variations as winds and rains.

The Biotic or Living Environment.

1. OTHER ORGANISMS OF THE SAME SPECIES — INTRA-SPECIFIC RELATIONS.

a. *Reproduction.* In sexual reproduction of dioecious organisms two or more individuals are always involved.

b. *Assistance.* This involves protection or rearing of young by parents, and assistance rendered parents by the young. It is cooperation in an animal society.

c. *Competition over Food.* This may be passive (due merely to numbers) as well as active.

d. *Definite Hostility.* Conflicts over territorial rights occur, as well as over mates. There may be elimination of the sick or maimed. The devouring of one mate by the other, or of the young by the parents, may occur.

2. INDIVIDUALS OF OTHER SPECIES—INTER-SPECIFIC RELA-
   TIONS.

   a. *Competition for Food.* This may be active, or merely
      a reflection of the absence of a sufficient quantity of
      food for the numbers present.

   b. *Prey-predator Relations.* Many organisms feed upon
      others. The success of the predator in maintaining its
      population obviously depends upon the presence of
      its prey.

   c. *Host-parasite Relations.* A parasite lives partly or
      wholly at the expense of its host; it may be complete-
      ly dependent upon its host, and definitely injurious
      to it. The most successful parasite is, however, the
      one which does least harm to its host.

   d. *Commensalism.* This is a close association of organ-
      isms, mutually beneficial, in which neither is depend-
      ent upon the other.

   e. *Symbiosis.* This is a close association between or-
      ganisms mutually dependent, e.g., termites and their
      intestinal protozoa.

   f. *Slavery.* Social animals may capture and use for
      service other animals.

3. SPECIAL RELATIONS BETWEEN PLANTS AND ANIMALS.
   Aside from relations suggested above: insects and birds
   pollinate many flowers; many animals aid in seed dispersal; galls are plant structures resulting from insect
   stings; certain plants capture, kill, and digest animals.

THE MAJOR HABITATS

The Ocean.

1. CHARACTERISTICS. The salt concentration is high, with
   little variability — about thirty to thirty-seven parts of
   salt per thousand. The temperature range is slight, about
   35 degrees Centigrade. Although there are regular ocean
   currents, and tidal fluctuations (of great importance to
   shore animals) occur, the ocean offers the most constant
   environment of the three major habitats.

2. DISTRIBUTION OF LIFE IN THE OCEAN.

  a. *Littoral Organisms.* Those living in the intertidal zone (between high and low tides) are adapted to alternate drying and wetting, to periodic feeding, to rapid temperature fluctuations, and, in many cases, to the impact of waves and a shifting substratum. Those below low tide are subject to fewer variables; the depth at which they live depends chiefly on the distance light penetrates — since that determines the presence of vegetation carrying on photosynthesis.

  b. *Pelagic Organisms.* The floating or drifting plankton, and the actively swimming nekton, together constitute the pelagic organisms.

  c. *Benthic or Bottom Organisms* occur at all depths of the ocean. Light is absent, except that from the luminescense of organisms.

Fresh-water.

1. CHARACTERISTICS. The low salinity (therefore low osmotic pressure) makes necessary the presence of organs for regulating the osmotic pressure of the organisms. Greater fluctuations in temperature and in concentration of gases in solution occur than in the ocean; other important differences from the ocean are periodic drying up, stagnation, high turbidity, rapid currents.

2. DISTRIBUTION OF LIFE IN FRESH-WATER. Distribution of organisms varies with the nature of fresh-water bodies — organisms of rivers being different from those of lakes, and these in turn differing from those of swamps and bogs. (See references of Pearse and Chapman).

Land.

1. CHARACTERISTICS. The land habitat has much the greatest fluctuations in climate. Both temperature and moisture vary greatly with seasons, with latitude, and with

altitude. The extremes recorded for soil and air tempera-
tures are more than 120 degrees Centigrade apart.

2. DISTRIBUTION OF LIFE ON LAND. Subterranean organisms are least subject to variations in climate. Above
ground, animals may live in direct contact with the soil,
or in various strata in the vegetation, *e.g.*, on grasses, in
shrubs, in trees. Some animals are aerial for long periods; such are, of course, fundamentally terrestrial.

PARASITISM

Those animals that live in or on the bodies of others, and
more or less at the expense of their hosts, have many remarkable
adaptations for the parasitic mode of life. They often possess
structures for attachment, such as hooks and suckers; and firmly
attached forms may completely lose all organs of locomotion.
Internal parasites have reduced sensory and nervous systems. If
they live in the digestive tract, they may lack an alimentary canal
of their own, obtaining their food by absorption through the body
wall. Reproductive organs, on the other hand, are usually highly
developed. Hermaphroditism and self-fertilization are common,
and enormous numbers of eggs are produced; but of course the
mortality of parasites is greater than of free-living forms. The
life cycle may be extremely complex, involving several hosts. In
general, the reproductive system is highly developed in parasitic
animals, whereas the other systems are less significant than in
free-living ones.

THE COMMUNITY

The most important concept of synecology is the *community*,
which is a group of organisms bound together by various factors.
The constituent organisms may be dependent on similar climatic
and edaphic conditions, but they are also related through a complex of biotic interrelationships — one of the most important of
which is probably the *food-chain* or *food-cycle* (Fig. 90). When
to the food cycle are added the parasites as well, the extreme
complexity of a community is apparent. In the food chain or cycle,
the largest organisms are not only the last links in the chain but
they are the species represented by fewest individuals. This prin-

ciple has been named "the *pyramid of numbers*," the whole food-chain being visualized as a pyramid in which the number of smallest organisms determines the area of the base, the number of the largest organisms, the apex. Communities of different size (extent) are recognized. Various elaborate terminologies for these have been devised, no one of which is universally accepted by ecologists. The literature of ecology frequently implies that

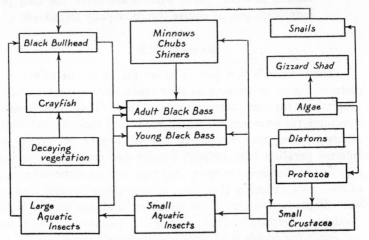

Fig. 90. Diagram illustrating a food-cycle in a Kansas lake stocked with black bass. Arrows point from prey to predator. (Data from H. H. Hall).

there are such things as plant or animal communities. As a matter of fact, relations between organisms are so close, and they are so interdependent, that, logically every community is a *biocoenosis* — a community of plants and animals combined.

THE ECOSYSTEM CONCEPT

The organisms of a biotic community do not constitute an independent complex. They cannot be considered apart from their non-living environment. The biotic community and the abiotic environment form an interdependent complex, the *ecosystem*. The energy necessary at all levels is provided by sunlight, which is used by green plants, the *producers*, in the synthesis of organic material. The producers provide food for *primary consumers* (herbivores), and these in turn provide food for *secondary consumers* (carnivores). The different nutritional levels in the food chain are referred to as *trophic levels*. Organisms of a given trophic level are dependent upon those of the preceding level for their energy, therefore; but there is always some loss from one level to the next. Metabolic activities of all these organisms, plus the actions of *decomposers* working on their dead bodies, release the essential inorganic compounds to the atmosphere and soil to be used again by the producers in the manufacture of new organic material. Thus we have in an ecosystem various *biogeochemical cycles*. Not only are the organisms affected by their environment; the environment is also affected by the organisms in it. This concept is basic to the idea of the ecosystem.

THE REGULATION OF POPULATION

An organism produces more offspring than can survive. The environment sets the limits on survival. Chapman has simplified this relationship in an analogy with Ohm's Law in physics, as follows:

$$\text{Population} = \frac{\text{Biotic potential}}{\text{Environmental resistance}}$$

In other words, the *population* of a species at a given time is determined by the ratio of the *biotic potential* (rate of reproduction) to the *environmental resistance*. As the latter increases, the population obviously will decrease; as the resistance becomes less (e.g., in a "favorable year"), the population will increase. Pearl has pointed out the fact that a given population tends to increase most rapidly at first, tending later to reach a level of relative stability, the rate of increase following what is called a logarithmic curve.

SUCCESSION

In each large area of the earth's surface, where conditions tend to repeat themselves year after year, a characteristic group of plants and animals develops. This is referred to as a *climax community*. (Examples: the grasslands of the central States, with their prairie-dogs and bison; the evergreen forest of central Canada, with its snow-shoe rabbits and moose.) If such a climax community is destroyed in a given area, and that area is then left undisturbed, it will return to the climax condition through a series of changes which constitutes a *succession.* A succession may proceed from a water environment to one of average moisture conditions, a *hydrosere,* or from a dry environment to one of average moisture conditions, a *xerosere.* Or, in a stream, the succession

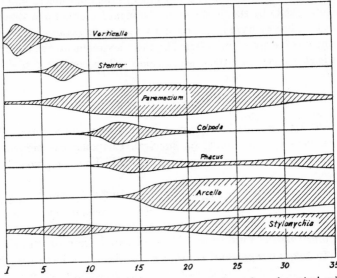

Fig. 91. Succession of predominant protozoa at the surface of a mixed culture made from pond water. The first day, and every fifth day thereafter, after preparation of the culture, are indicated by the vertical lines. The thickness of each band is proportional, over the period represented by the graph, to the relative abundance of the protozoa named.

proceeds from a community characteristic of shallow, swift water to one associated with deep, sluggish water. Or in a laboratory culture of mixed protozoa, the fauna and flora changes as rapid bacterial decomposition gives way to a period of quasi-stability—the latter condition constituting the environment of the climax community of this microcosm. (Fig. 91). These are all successions in time. One may observe succession in space also, *e.g.,* around the shores of a lake which is gradually filling up, or along the edges of a disintegrating rock mass. In fact, the concept succession has many meanings:

Succession	In Time	Geological.
		Seasonal (Annual).
		Daily.
	In Space	Horizontal — in latitude, or in small areas.
		Vertical — in altitude, or in vegetational strata.

Horizontal succession may correspond in space to geological succession in time; altitudinal succession may correspond to latitudinal succession — higher altitudes being similar to higher latitudes.

REVIEW QUESTIONS

1. Define ecology, autecology, synecology.

2. What are the characteristics of soil, water, and air of most importance in considering them as media in which organisms live?

3. Discuss intra- and inter-specific relations between animals.

4. Characterize the three major habitats.

5. In what ways do parasitic animals ordinarily differ from free-living ones?

6. Explain trophic levels and biogeochemical cycles in terms of the ecosystem.

7. Explain the relations between population, biotic potential, and environmental resistance.

8. What is succession? Give examples of different types of succession.

Chapter XXVI

ORGANIC EVOLUTION

DEFINITION OF ORGANIC EVOLUTION

Organic evolution is the progressive development of animals
and plants from ancestors of different forms and functions. It
is a very slow process, being measured in geological time. The
general term evolution is applied to any increase in complexity
through time — as the evolution of the solar system, the evolution
of human society, etc.; use of the adjective, organic, implies
evolution of plant and animal species.

EVIDENCE FOR ORGANIC EVOLUTION

Most evidence for organic evolution is indirect, its validity
being supported by many different lines of evidence all pointing
to the same explanation. This evidence is such that the only
scientific justification for much that we observe in nature is organic evolution. One of the best evidences for a common ancestry
of organisms, though indirect, is their fundamental similarity. In
spite of many adaptive differences, protoplasm and cells, and their
manifestations of life — metabolism, growth, and reproduction,
are essentially the same in all organisms. The survey of the
animal kingdom, Chapters VI-XXI inclusive, brings out a host of
structures which imply evolutionary change. Different degrees of
complexity, such as are involved in increase in germ-layers,
formation of a coelom, formation of a complete alimentary canal,
differentiation of such organ systems as the excretory, nervous,
sensory, and circulatory, all imply relationships of descent. It is
natural to interpret these fundamental similarities, which are
accompanied by different degrees of complexity, as due to common
ancestry. This, the evidence from comparative morphology, is
the most significant for the average biologist; but there are other
lines of evidence as well, and, whether direct or indirect, they
converge on this concept.

Lines of Indirect Evidence.

1. EVIDENCE FROM PALEONTOLOGY (Study of Fossils). Remains of previously existing organisms or any indications of their presence are fossils. These fossils exist in various types of rock and soil formations. Just as in a lake bottom, the mud on top has been most recently deposited, so in rock strata, the strata on top are more recent than those beneath if they have not been secondarily folded. With this in mind, the geologist is able to construct a chronological series of fossils, associating them with particular periods of geological time. It has been known for a long time that fossils demonstrate the presence of many animals and plants in the past that no longer exist. When the fossils are arranged in a chronological series, faunal and floral changes are found that can only be explained logically by a series of progressive changes, viz., organic evolution. (Table VII).

2. EVIDENCES FROM COMPARATIVE MORPHOLOGY.

   a. *Analogy and Homology.* Many rather unlike organisms have organs of similar function. If they are fundamentally unlike except in function they are said to be *analogous*. Analogous structures indicate no close relationship except in habit or habitat, and hence are of no significance in judging evolutionary relationships. (Examples: Tail fin of lobster and flukes of whale; wings of fly and bird). Organs fundamentally the same in structure, but perhaps modified for widely different functions, suggest a common plan that can only be explained through a common ancestry. (Figs. 86 and 92). Thus, the arm of a man, the wing of a bird, the wing of a bat, the flipper of a seal, and the fore-leg of a dog all have the same type of skeleton. Many of the bones correspond directly from one animal to another; all would, if it were not for the evident loss of certain ones. This fundamental similarity is called *homology*. The criteria of homologies are (1) similarity in embryonic origin, (2) similarity in structure, (3) sim-

TABLE VII. GEOLOGICAL TIME SCALE

NOTE. Geological time-tables are so constructed as to show the oldest **periods** at the bottom and the youngest periods at the top. *To get the proper order and sequence of events always read from the bottom to the top.*

Era = Time Group = Rocks	Period = Time System = Rocks	Life Record (Fossils) Both Animals and Plants
CENOZOIC Age of mammals and modern flora	QUATERNARY TERTIARY upper lower	Periodic glaciation and origin of man (Pleistocene). The transformation of the ape-like ancestor into man may have begun in the Pliocene. Culmination of mammals (Miocene). Rise of higher mammals (Oligocene). Vanishing of archaic mammals (Eocene).
MESOZOIC Age of reptiles	CRETACEOUS JURASSIC TRIASSIC	Rise of the archaic mammals in the interval between the Mesozoic and the Tertiary. This ERA is remarkable for the great development of the ammonites which became extinct at the end of the Cretaceous. The molluscs are more highly developed in this ERA than in the preceding one. Culmination and extinction of most reptiles (Cretaceous). Rise of flowering plants (Comanchean); birds and flying reptiles (Jurassic); dinosaurs (Triassic).
Upper PALEOZOIC Age of amphibians and lycopods	PERMIAN CARBONIFEROUS	Periodic glaciation and extinction of many Paleozoic groups during and after the Permian. Rise of modern insects, land vertebrates and ammonites (Permian); primitive reptiles and insects, (Pennsylvanian); ancient sharks and echinoderms (Mississippian).
Middle PALEOZOIC Age of fishes	DEVONIAN SILURIAN	First known land floras (Devonian) not very different from those of the Carboniferous. Earliest evidence of a terrestrial vertebrate in the form of a single footprint from the Devonian of Pennsylvania. Rise of lung-fishes and scorpions (first terrestrial air-breathers) in the Silurian.
Lower PALEOZOIC Age of higher (shelly) invertebrates	ORDOVICIAN CAMBRIAN	Rise of nautiloids, armored fishes, land plants and corals. Also the first evidence of colonial life (Ordovician). First known marine faunas; dominance of trilobites; rise of animals with hard shells or exoskeletons (Cambrian).
PROTEROZOIC Primordial life ARCHEOZOIC Most ancient life	PRECAMBRIAN	Fossils almost unknown except for a few problematical forms in the Proterozoic. Fossils unknown in the Archeozoic.

Reprinted by permission from *An Outline of the Principles of Geology*, by Richard M. Field, published by Barnes and Noble, Inc.

ilarity in function; the first is of most importance, the last is of least. The presence of homologies, as brought out in studies of comparative morphology, can only be explained logically by a theory of organic evolution.

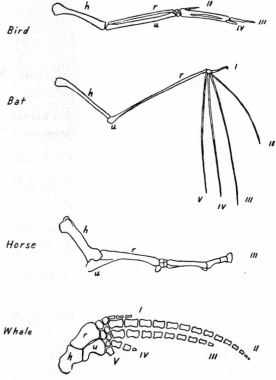

Fig. 92. Homologies of bones of the pectoral limb in the bird and three mammals; h, humerus; r, radius; u, ulna. Roman numerals refer to the elements of the primitive 5-digit appendage present in each. (Modified from various authors).

b. *Vestigial Structures.* Various organisms possess non-functional structures which, in other organisms, have essential functions. The coecum of the rabbit and other animals is homologous with the coecum and vermiform appendix of man. In man the structure is not only of no value but its presence may be harmful, whereas in the rabbit it is a very important functional part of the digestive system. In man its presence may best be explained on the grounds that it is a structural vestige, something which functioned in man's ancestry but exists now only as a useless relic. The vestigial muscles at the base of the human ear, the caudal vertebrae (coccyx), and other human structures may be explained only in this way. Many embryonic structures, as the arterial gill arches of the human embryo, may be understood likewise only as vestiges from a distant ancestor.

3. Evidence from Physiology. Just as homologous structures exist, homologous functions also occur. Various types of chemical tests show close similarity between the body fluids of animals, serum precipitation tests on mammals indicating, for example, a much greater chemical kinship between man and apes than between man and swine. Another interesting line of chemical evidence is the remarkable similarity in proportions of constituent salts between the blood of vertebrates, and sea-water. This supports the theory that the ancestors of terrestrial vertebrates were inhabitants of the sea.

4. Evidence from Embryology.

   a. *General Nature of Evidence.* From the earliest stages of development are found remarkable similarities between organisms. In both plants and animals, for example, the formation of gametes is accompanied by a reduction in chromosome number. Among animals, the stages of cleavage, blastula, and gastrula formation are fundamentally the same in such dissimilar animals as starfish and frog, earthworm and man. The nearer the relationship of adult structures, too, the greater is the similarity in course of development.

   b. *The Biogenetic Law.* The above stated observation led to the formulation of a theory which, though doubtless largely true, has probably been too widely applied — the *Biogenetic Law.* It may be expressed: Ontogeny repeats Phylogeny; or, the development of the individual recapitulates the development of the race. Among vertebrates, all embryos pass through a stage in which gill-like structures and their associated blood vessels are present. In fishes, the condition is adult; gills function in some adult amphibia but only in the tadpole stage of higher forms; in reptiles, birds, and mammals these gill structures are never functional, but nevertheless are always present in the embryo. In the embryo there are six pairs of arterial gill arches. Of these, relics of three persist even in adult birds and mammals. These are the third, as the carotids; the fourth, as the systemics; and the sixth, as the pulmonary arteries. The fact that they are derived from the embryonic arches is of no significance; it is rather a morphological accident; for there is no morphological necessity for such a transitional stage in the embryo. Evolution explains the presence of such an apparently unnecessary stage in development on the grounds that the embryonic gills of higher vertebrates are vestigial organs. This means that the ancestors of reptiles, birds, and mammals possessed gills, and were, therefore, aquatic. The heart shows similar relationships, the fish heart having one auricle and one ventricle, hearts of amphibians and reptiles having two auricles and one ventricle, and hearts of birds and mammals having two auricles and two ventricles. In embryonic development, birds and mammals pass through all these stages, and in the order just given. The similarity between embryonic stages and what appear to be the natural relations between existing animals therefore offers another evidence for evolution.

5. EVIDENCE FROM TAXONOMY. The principle of homology, and the Biogenetic Law, are the chief concepts used in taxonomy; the major purpose of the taxonomist is to so classify animals that their genetic relationships are best brought out. The evidences from taxonomy are, then, the evidences from comparative morphology and embryology.

6. EVIDENCE FROM GEOGRAPHICAL DISTRIBUTION. In groups of islands, the plants and animals of nearby islands are more alike than those of distant islands, whereas all organisms of such an island group show certain affinities with those of the nearest continental land-mass. The simplest explanation of such an observation is that, with isolation, due to the appearance of barriers, evolution has proceeded from a common starting type in gradually diverging lines. In conjunction with paleontology, good evidence for evolution may be deduced from the present and past distribution of camels and tapirs. The former are represented today only by the true camels of the Old World and by the llama and its relatives in South America. Tapirs occur today only in South and Central America and in Malaya. Fossil camels and tapirs have, however, been found in the intervening territory. The natural assumption is that the forms occurring in the intervening territory have become extinct, leaving only the descendants in the extremes of the range. The existence of a land bridge between present Alaska and Siberia, and a milder climate there formerly than now, are requirements of the theory, but for both conditions there is abundant geological evidence. (For a general discussion of geographic distribution see Chapter XXIV).

Lines of Direct Evidence.

1. EVIDENCE FROM GENETICS. Animal and plant breeders have long been able to develop domestic forms of desired characteristics by selective breeding; students of genetics, similarly, have been able to obtain evidence for evolution through controlled experiments. Spontaneous inherited changes or mutations (see Chapter XXII) have been observed; and mutations have actually been artificially induced by X-rays, radium, and more recently by treatment with alkaloid colchicine. One of the most striking evidences from genetics has come from the artificial synthesis of existing or new species by controlled hydridization; this evidence comes from plant breeding.

2. EVIDENCE FROM OBSERVATION IN NATURE. If large numbers of specimens of one or a few species are collected in a given locality, and the collection is repeated after a long interval of time, one may sometimes detect evolutionary changes which have taken place. Such changes have been found by Crampton, studying land snails of the genus *Partula* from Moorea. His collections, which were extremely large, were separated by an interval of only fourteen years. Such observations are not likely to be made during one man's lifetime, however, unless the organisms studied are well isolated and incapable of rapid migration.

EXAMPLES OF EVOLUTIONARY SERIES

Evolution of the Horse. The most ancient horse known, *Eohippus,* existed in the Eocene Epoch. It was about the size of a medium-sized dog, with somewhat the proportions of a modern horse. Its muzzle was shorter than that of a modern horse, however, and its teeth were low-crowned — better adapted for browsing than grazing. The fore feet bore four functional toes and the rudiment of a fifth; the hind feet had three, and the rudiments of others. The ancestor of *Eohippus,* not yet found, probably had five functional toes on each foot. In subsequent evolution, the number of toes has been progressively reduced through the stage of three on each foot to the modern condition in which only the middle toe is present. (The second and fourth are, however, represented by the "splints".) In the skull, the muzzle has become progressively longer, and the teeth have developed high crowns with ridged surfaces — adapted for grazing. All along, the fossil series, which is very complete, shows gradual increase in size. Horses began their evolution in North America, but completed it in the Old World, becoming extinct on this continent and not returning until introduced by the first Spanish explorers.

Evolution of Man. Fossil types of man are now known in relatively large numbers and from many localities in the Old World (Table VIII). The earliest known humanoid, tool-making types are represented by *Zinjanthropus* (by some considered in the genus *Paranthropus*) in East Africa, *Pithecanthropus* in Java, and *Sinanthropus* in China. *Australopithecus* and *Paranthropus* of South Africa may have been tool-making; they probably were tool-using. If *Zinjanthropus* is in the line of human evolution, man's evolution as a tool-making and speech-using animal has probably occupied little more than a million years. *Pithecanthropus* and *Sinanthropus* lived about a half million years ago. Neanderthaloid types, which are considered members of the genus *Homo* and which appeared considerably later, were widely distributed in Europe, Asia, and Africa. No fossil men, of this or earlier types, are known from the Western Hemisphere or Australia. Modern man, *Homo sapiens*, has apparently been the only hominoid type for the past 25,000 years or more. One of the best known fossil races of *Homo sapiens* is Cro-Magnon man, whose remains are known from caves in southwest Europe.

In general, human evolution, beginning in the early Pleistocene, has involved the following developments, some of which are illustrated in Fig. 93:

1. Increase in brain size — judged by increase in capacity of cranium.

2. More erect posture.

3. Disappearance of prominent supraorbital ridges.

4. Development of a vertical face.

5. Formation of a chin.

6. Shortening of the jaws in an antero-posterior direction.

THEORIES OF THE METHOD OF ORGANIC EVOLUTION

Historically there have been three great evolutionary theories, but these are not mutually exclusive. The views of most modern biologists combine the second and third of these. There is no experimental evidence for the first theory, that of Lamarck.

The Theory of Lamarck — Inheritance of Acquired Characteristics.

1. Structural variations are due to functional needs—to "use and disuse." Use of a structure increases its size, failure to use it results in its disappearance.

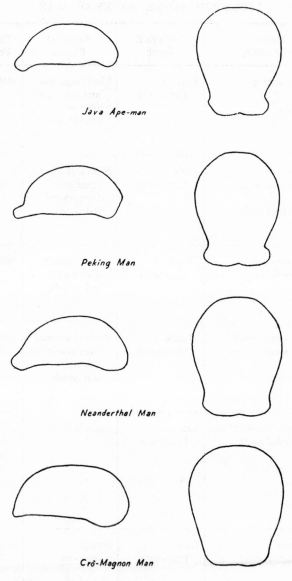

Fig. 93. Profiles of the brain case in four fossil species of man; in the left column, from the side; in the right column, from the top. The progressive increase in size, heightening of the forehead, and decrease in supraorbital ridges, are clearly shown. All drawings to the same scale. from casts. (Compare with the data in Table VIII.)

TABLE VIII. FOSSIL RACES OF MAN

Name and Locality	Geological Epoch	Nature of Fossils	Cranial Volume
Australopithecus sp. South Africa	Early Pleistocene	Skull fragments and other bones from many individuals	600 cc.
Paranthropus sp. (and *Zinjanthropus boisei*) South and East Africa	Early Pleistocene	Skull and other fragments from several individuals	up to 900 cc.
Pithecanthropus erectus (Java ape-man) Java	Middle Pleistocene	Skull fragments from four individuals	900 cc.
Sinanthropus pekinensis (Peking man) Northern China	Middle Pleistocene	Skeletal material from more than a dozen individuals	850 to 1300 cc.
Homo neanderthalensis (Neanderthal man) Europe, Asia, Africa	Late Pleistocene	Many skeletons	up to 1600 cc. (equal to modern man)
Homo sapiens (Cro-Magnon man) France, Spain	Late Pleistocene	Several skeletons	up to 1800 cc. (equal to modern man)

2. These variations (now referred to as "acquired characteristics") are inherited. This phase of Lamarck's theory finds no supporting evidence in modern biology. There is, of course, inheritance of acquired knowledge in human society, made possible by man's invention of speech and written language, and it is this type of inheritance of something acquired that has made the evolution of human culture so rapid in contrast to the evolution of human physique. If organic evolution took place by the inheritance of acquired characteristics it would be a much more rapid process than it is.

The Theory of Darwin — Natural Selection.

1. Organisms are prodigal in their production of offspring, far too many being produced to survive.
2. This results in competition, or a struggle for existence—actually more of a struggle to escape being destroyed.
3. This leads to natural selection of the most fit through death of those less fit to survive.
4. The progeny of the organisms most fit to survive inherit the characteristics of their parents—namely those characteristics which have made their parents most fit.

The Theory of De Vries — Mutation. Evolution has not taken place through the accumulation of fortuitous variations; it has been due to the appearance of a series of changes in the germ-plasm, *mutations*. These may be very pronounced or minor, but they are not equivalent to individual variations.

Modifications and Corollaries of the Principal Theories.

1. ISOLATION, as a factor in the development of new forms, has probably played a major role. The formation of barriers within the range of a species prevents interbreeding between organisms of different localities. Of equal or even greater significance are the genetic barriers which prevent reproduction between a new stock and the ancestral population.
2. AGE AND AREA. According to the concept of Age and

Area, organisms having widest geographical ranges are, other things equal, usually the oldest geologically. Hence, within a given genus, the species having the widest ranges are probably most like the ancestral type, while those of very limited range are probably of recent origin.

3. HYBRIDIZATION, or cross-breeding between species, may have produced much of the variation in nature through the introduction of new combinations. The evidence for this does not seem to be great. Unless accompanied by isolation of the hybrids, permanent effects of evolutionary significance are not likely to ensue.

4. ORTHOGENESIS. Some students of evolution, particularly paleontologists, observe that fossils forming an evolutionary series suggest that progress has been in a definite direction—the unsuccessful forms necessary to the theory of natural selection being absent. This theory that evolution proceeds in definite directions, from the directing tendency or limitations of internal structures, is orthogenesis. It finds little support today.

Modern Interpretations. Present day theories of the method of organic evolution come from observations and experiments in several fields of biology, particularly *population genetics*. These theories recognize, basically, the necessity for modification of the germ-plasm and preservation of such modifications if evolution is to occur, and they also recognize the fact that evolutionary units are intrabreeding populations. Modern theories require some understanding of ecology as well as genetics, for they emphasize, particularly, the role of isolation. These theories are essentially refinements of the general concepts of natural selection and mutation. They begin with recognition of what is called the *Hardy-Weinberg principle*, which states that in a population whose members mate purely at random the genes remain, generation after generation, in the same relative proportions (frequencies) with reference to each other. This principle is theoretically true. It means that evolutionary change cannot be induced merely by new combinations of existing genes. Modifications in gene frequencies must occur if evolution takes place, and it is the methods by which these modifications of the Hardy-Weinberg principle take place that provide our modern theories of the method of evolution. There are four possible ways in which these population frequencies may change. These modifications of the Hardy-Weinberg principle are all potential methods by which evolution can occur:

1. DIFFERENTIAL MUTATION RATE. If a gene mutates more frequently in one direction than back to its original form gene-frequencies change.

2. GENE SELECTION. If a mutation confers an advantage on an organism it is more likely to be preserved (by natural selection) than is the original gene.

3. MIGRATION. If possession of a certain gene or combination of genes is related to movement into or out of a given population this produces gene frequency changes in the population.

4. GENETIC DRIFT (SEWALL WRIGHT EFFECT). In small populations chance survival or loss of a mutation is more likely to occur than in large populations. Thus the chance variation associated with small samples may be responsible for evolution in a small population.

REVIEW QUESTIONS

1. How might a comparative study of animal structures lead one to a theory of evolution?
2. What are the evidences for organic evolution?
3. Give the principal tendencies of structural change in the evolution of the horse.
4. Discuss the extinct races of man in relation to human evolution.
5. Discuss the various theories of the method of organic evolution, and their corollaries.
6. How has modern genetics contributed to our knowledge of the method of organic evolution?

PART FOUR

HISTORICAL SUMMARY

———

CHAPTER XXVII

HISTORY OF ZOOLOGY

CHRONOLOGICAL SUMMARY, BY PERIODS

Prehistoric Biology. The beginnings of biology are lost in antiquity. Man began as a hunter, undoubtedly, and his occupation forced him into a knowledge of nature. The thoroughness of his knowledge is reflected in the cave painting and sculptures left by the Cro-magnon race. Domestication of plants and animals was followed by a still more intimate acquaintance with nature. Crude medical practise involved a certain amount of human anatomical knowledge, just as use of animals for food gave primitive man a certain superficial familiarity with their structures.

Zoology in the Ancient Historic World.

1. ZOOLOGY IN ANCIENT BABYLON, EGYPT, ISRAEL, AND THE FAR EAST. In Babylon, the priesthood knew something of anatomy (particularly of sacrificial animals) and medicine, the latter sadly involved in astrology, however. The medicine of ancient Egypt was more practical. The ancient Jews contributed to our modern conceptions of hygiene in their laws. In the Far East, knowledge of nature and medicine was not so far advanced as other aspects of the culture.

2. ZOOLOGY IN ANCIENT GREECE. Scientific medicine began, practically, with Hippocrates (*cir.*, 460-377 B.C.), his method empirical. Aristotle (384-322 B.C.) was the first great organizer of biological knowledge, his best known biological treatise being *Historia animalium*. The Greek tradition continued in the *Museum* of Alexandria until about 30 B.C., but under Roman rule steadily declined.

3. ZOOLOGY UNDER THE ROMAN EMPIRE. There was progress in anatomy and physiology through the work of Galen (A.D. 130-200), the first great physiologist; otherwise nothing of note.

Zoology in the Middle Ages. From about the time of the death of Galen until the thirteenth century works of Greeks and Romans were recopied, both texts and drawings, with no recourse to sources in nature. They progressively acquired more and more errors. During the latter part of this period the chief centers of culture were in the Arabian Empire. Arabian scientists preserved and interpreted the finest of ancient Greek science, and with the revival of learning in western Europe this came into western Europe from the Arabs.

Zoology during the Renaissance. This revival expanded into the Renaissance. Art became more naturalistic, and involved a thorough study of subjects (*e. g.*, by Leonardo da Vinci, 1452-1519). In 1543, Vesalius' great work on human anatomy appeared; natural histories of animals were printed in the same century; and, in 1628, appeared Harvey's work on the circulation of the blood.

Zoology in the Seventeenth and Eighteenth Centuries. The attitude of scientific men began to change—they looked to nature herself for information. The period of geographic exploration expanded their vision; the invention of the microscope intensified it. The first scientific societies and journals were founded. Detailed studies on the anatomy of small organisms and parts of larger ones were pursued, and cells were discovered and named, (Hooke, Malpighi, Grew, Swammerdam, Leeuwenhoek). Schemes of classification were devised, following the stimulus of explorations, (Ray, Linnaeus).

Nineteenth Century Zoology.

1. MORPHOLOGY. Anatomy became not only more detailed, but comparative. Cuvier (1769-1832) founded comparative anatomy; he studied extinct as well as modern vertebrates. Lamarck (1744-1829), his contemporary, best known today for his theory of evolution (Chap. XXII),

was a thorough student of plants and animals. The cell theory was propounded in 1839 (Chap. III). The doctrine that protoplasm is a universal characteristic of life was accepted within another thirty years. Studies on mitosis, the history of germ-cells, fertilization, embryology, characterized the last of the century.

2. PHYSIOLOGY. At the beginning of the century, the discoveries of the identity of combustion and respiration, and the formation of oxygen by green plants (Lavoisier and Priestley), gave an impulse to the application of chemical knowledge to organisms. The first organic compound to be synthesized, urea, was prepared by Wöhler (1828). Liebig (1802-1873) applied chemistry to living phenomena, especially in plants. Claude Bernard (1813-1878) was the great chemical physiologist of the century. The germ-theory of disease was developed, and biological control of disease begun (Pasteur, Koch, Lister). Johannes Müller (1801-1858), extremely versatile, applied comparative anatomy, chemistry, and physics in physiology. Ludwig (1816-1898) also approached physiology from the standpoint of physics; he invented some of the most widely-used laboratory apparatus of today.

3. EVOLUTION. Lamarck's doctrine of use and disuse, with inheritance of acquired characteristics, came at the beginning of the century. It was opposed by Cuvier, whose influence was great, with the result that it found little favor. Evolution was not widely accepted until after 1859, in which year was published *The Origin of Species* by Charles Darwin (1809-1882). August Weismann (1834-1914) brought out, toward the close of the century, the importance of the germ-plasm and the non-inheritance of acquired characteristics.

4. GENETICS. The experiments of Gregor Mendel (1822-1884), performed in the 1860's, were not appreciated until 1900. Statistical methods were applied by Francis Galton (1822-1911) to studies of human inheritance.

Twentieth Century Zoology. The present century has been characterized by a more intensive application of experimental methods. The application of physical chemistry in zoology has become prominent; other aspects have attained considerable recognition, e. g., ecology. But the twentieth century has been the period of greatest advance in genetics, primarily. The mutation theory was proposed in 1901 by Hugo de Vries (1848-1935), and marked achievements have come in the study of the mechanism of heredity, particularly by T. H. Morgan and his associates.

BRIEF BIOGRAPHIES OF GREAT BIOLOGISTS

Aristotle (384-322 B.C.). The Father of Biology; founder of the Lyceum at Athens. Organized the knowledge of his period. Chief contributions on the natural history, anatomy, and reproduction of animals.

Andreas Vesalius (1514-1564 A.D.). Belgian, who became professor of anatomy at Padua, Italy. Published first scientific treatise on human anatomy, beautifully illustrated (1543).

William Harvey (1578-1667). English physician, educated at Padua, Italy. Published first accurate account of the course of the blood in the human body (1628) ; in embryological studies (1651) emphasized origin of both viviparous and oviparous forms from the egg.

Carolus Linnaeus—Carl von Linné (1707-1778). Swedish botanist and zoologist. Established on a firm basis the binomial system of nomenclature (1758, the date of publication of the tenth edition of his *Systema Naturae,* is the base date for zoological nomenclature).

Charles Darwin (1809-1882). Naturalist of the *Beagle* on trip around the world 1831-36. On return established notebook on the change of species. *Origin of Species* published in 1859— in its effect on human thought the most significant book of the century. Published many other works, not all in the field of evolution.

Gregor Mendel (1822-1884). Monk, and later abbot, of a monastery in Austria; discoverer of the laws of inheritance now called Mendel's Laws (Chap. XXVI).

Louis Pasteur (1822-1895). French chemist and bacteriologist. Simultaneously with Robert Koch, German, demonstrated the bacterial origin of disease. Developed a method of attenuating (weakening) a disease-producing organism so that it could be used in developing immunity. Established inoculation against .rabies or hydrophobia.

August Weismann (1834-1914). German zoologist, proposed the theory of the continuity of the germ-plasm. Made first important scientific denial of the inheritance of acquired characteristics.

Hugo de Vries (1848-1935). Dutch botanist. His early experiments in plant physiology formed a basis for the theory of electrolytic dissociation. Founder of the mutation theory of evolution.

Thomas Hunt Morgan (1866-1945). American zoologist. His experiments with *Drosophila,* coupled with those of his students and associates, have been the basis for the gene-theory of heredity.

Hans Krebs (1900-   ). British biochemist who was awarded the Nobel Prize for his research in cell respiration. The Krebs cycle received its name in recognition of his discoveries.

REVIEW QUESTIONS

1. Trace the progress of zoology from prehistoric times to the present.
2. What have been the major trends in zoological research since the Renaissance?
3. Give the essential contributions of a representative number of great biologists, including Aristotle, Vesalius, Harvey, Linnaeus, Darwin, and Mendel.

APPENDICES

APPENDICES

AN ABRIDGED CLASSIFICATION OF ANIMALS

Phylum Protozoa. Unicellular animals.
Class Mastigophora (Flagellata). Flagellate protozoa.
Class Sarcodina (Rhizopoda). Amoeboid protozoa.
Class Sporozoa. Spore-producing protozoa.
Class Ciliata (Infusoria). Ciliate protozoa.
Class Suctoria. Suctoria.

Phylum Porifera. Sponges.
Class Calcarea. Sponges with lime spicules.
Class Hexactinellida. Sponges with glass spicules.
Class Demospongia. Commercial sponges.

Phylum Coelenterata (Cnidaria).
Class Hydrozoa. Hydroids.
Class Scyphozoa. Jellyfishes.
Class Anthozoa. Corals and sea-anemones.

Phylum Ctenophora. Comb-jellies or sea-walnuts.

Phylum Platyhelminthes. Flatworms.
Class Turbellaria. Planaria and relatives.
Class Trematoda. Flukes.
Class Cestoda (Cestoidea). Tape-worms.
Class Nemertea (Nemertinea). Ribbon-worms.

Phylum Nematoda. Roundworms.

Phylum Acanthocephala. Spineheaded worms.

Phylum Nematomorpha. Hair-worms.

Phylum Rotatoria. Rotifers.

Phylum Gastrotricha. Gastrotrichs.

Phylum Tardigrada. Water-bears.

Phylum Chaetognatha. Arrow-worm.

Phylum Bryozoa. Moss animals.

Phylum Brachiopoda. Lamp-shells.

Phylum Echinodermata.
> *Class Crinoidea.* Sea-lilies.
> *Class Asteroidea.* Starfishes.
> *Class Ophiuroidea.* Brittle-stars, serpent-stars.
> *Class Echinoidea.* Sea-urchins, sand-dollars.
> *Class Holothurioidea.* Sea-cucumbers.

Phylum Annelida. (See Chapter XII.)
> *Class Archiannelida. Polygordius* and relatives.
> *Class Polychaeta. Nereis* and relatives.
> *Class Oligochaeta.* Earthworms and relatives.
> *Class Hirudinea.* Leeches.
> *Class Gephyrea. Phascolosoma* and relatives.

Phylum Onychophora. *Peripatus.*

Phylum Arthropoda. (See Chapter XIII.)
> *Class Crustacea.* Crayfish, crabs, barnacles, water-fleas.
> *Class Diplopoda.* Millipedes.
> *Class Chilopoda.* Centipedes.
> *Class Insecta.* Insects. (See Chapter XIV for Orders.)
> *Class Arachnida.* Spiders, ticks, mites, scorpions.

Phylum Mollusca.
> *Class Amphineura.* Chitons.
> *Class Gastropoda.* Snails, slugs.
> *Class Scaphopoda. Dentalium* and relatives.
> *Class Pelecypoda.* Clams, mussels, oysters.
> *Class Cephalopoda.* Squids, octopus, nautilus.

Phylum Chordata.
> *Subphylum Enteropneusta* (Hemichorda). Balanoglossus.
> *Subphylum Tunicata* (Urochorda). Sea-pork, sea-squirts.
> *Subphylum Cephalochorda* (Leptocardii). *Amphioxus (Branch-iostoma).*
> *Subphylum Vertebrata* (Craniata). Vertebrates.

Superclass Pisces. Fishes.
  Class Agnatha (Cyclostomata). Hagfishes, lampreys.
  Class Chondrichthyes. Sharks, rays, chimaeras.
  Class Osteichthyes. Ganoids, bony-fishes, lung-fishes.
Superclass Tetrapoda. Amphibious and terrestrial vertebrates.
  Class Amphibia. Salamanders, frogs.
  Class Reptilia. Lizards, snakes, turtles, crocodiles.
  Class Aves. Birds.
  Class Mammalia. Mammals: moles, dogs, bats, whales, man.

ALTERNATIVE CLASSIFICATIONS

Among widely accepted modifications of the above should be noted in particular the following (all referred to at appropriate places in the text):

Phylum Nemertea or Nemertinea, considered a distinct phylum rather than a class under the Phylum Platyhelminthes.

Phylum Aschelminthes, including most pseudocoelomate animals. The Phyla Nematoda, Acanthocephala, Nematomorpha, Rotatoria, and Gastrotricha are considered classes in this phylum.

Phylum Bryozoa, comprising two quite distinct groups of animals, the Phylum Entoprocta and the Phylum Ectoprocta (the latter being the Phylum Bryozoa in the limited sense).

Phylum Hemichordata, considered a distinct phylum rather than a subphylum under the Phylum Chordata.

A few distinct animal types do not fit well into any of the ordinarily accepted phyla. One such group, comprising extremely simple parasites apparently intermediate between Protozoa and Porifera in complexity, is now recognized as constituting the Phylum Mesozoa.

GLOSSARY

The following definitions are intentionally brief, suggesting merely the ordinary significance of each term as used in biology. Terms of special and limited usage, defined where they occur in the text, are omitted.

Abdomen: the major body division posterior to head and thorax.

Acquired characteristic: a trait acquired by an individual in response to its environment.

ADP: adenosine diphosphate.

Afferent: leading to or toward the organ of reference.

Allantois: an embryonic membrane of higher vertebrates arising as an outgrowth of the hind-gut.

Allelomorphic: the relation between two or more alternative genes.

Alternation of generations—metagenesis.

Amino acid: an organic acid containing the $-NH_2$ group.

Amitosis: direct nuclear division, usually not followed by cell division.

Amnion: a membrane surrounding the embryo of reptiles, birds, and mammals.

Anabolism: metabolic activities involving the synthesis of compounds.

Anaerobic: in the absence of free oxygen.

Analogy: superficial resemblance — due only to similarity in function. (See *homology*.)

Anatomy: the study of visible or gross structure.

Antenna: a slender, flexible appendage on the head.

Anterior: toward the forward end.

Antibody: something produced in the body to combat the injurious effect of a foreign substance (antigen).

Antigen: a foreign protein which causes the production of an antibody in an organism.

Antimere: one of the two or more segments of an animal which correspond with reference to the axis of symmetry.

Anus: the outlet of the digestive tract.

Aorta: a large artery.

Artery: a vessel which carries blood away from the heart.

Asexual reproduction: reproduction by one individual, independent of gamete formation.

Assimilation: the manufacture of protoplasm.

ATP: adenosine triphosphate.

Atrium: a chamber of the heart in which blood is received.

Auditory: referring to the sense of hearing.

Auricle: 1, ear; 2, a heart chamber—atrium.

Autecology: the ecology of an individual organism or species.

Autonomic nervous system: a system of nervous coordination independent of the higher brain centers, its ganglia located outside the brain and spinal cord.

Autotrophic: the type of nutrition in which the organism manufactures its own food from inorganic compounds.

Axial skeleton: that portion of the vertebrate skeleton in the body axis — skull, vertebrae, and thoracic basket.

Basal metabolism: metabolic activity required simply to maintain life.

Biogenetic law: the principle that the development of the individual repeats the development of the race.

Biogeochemical cycle: interrelations of chemical elements in an ecosystem.

Biotic potential: an expression of the rate of reproduction.

Biramous: with two branches.

Blastula: an early stage of the embryo, which consists essentially of a hollow ball of cells.

Book-gill: an aquatic respiratory organ made up of leaves of sheet-like tissue.

Book-lung: an air-breathing respiratory organ made up of leaves of sheet-like tissue.

Botany: the science of plant life.

Brachial: referring to the pectoral appendage.

Branchial: referring to the gills.

Caecum: a blind sac.

Capillary: a small, thin-walled blood vessel through which diffusion may readily take place.

Carbohydrate: a compound of carbon, hydrogen, and oxygen, the last two typically in the proportions of water; sugars and their condensation products.

Cardiac: 1, referring to the heart; 2, referring to the anterior end of the stomach.

Catabolism: metabolic activities involving the breakdown of compounds.

Cell: the unit of structure and function in organisms.

Cell membrane: the living membrane forming the external boundary of the animal cell. (Not *cell wall*.)

Cell wall: a rigid, non-living envelope surrounding the cell membrane, typical of plant cells.

Centriole: a structure, present in cells of animals and lower plants, from which radiate the spindle fibers during mitosis.

Cephalothorax: a body division consisting of head and thorax combined.

Cervical: referring to the neck.

Chlorophyll: the pigment of green plants, involved in photosynthesis.

Chloroplast: a plastid containing chlorophyll.

Chondrocranium: a cranium consisting of cartilage.

Chromatin: a nuclear constituent staining readily with basic dyes; the material of chromosomes.

Chromosome: a structure formed from chromatin, which appears in cells during mitosis; the bearer of hereditary determiners, or genes.

Cirrus: a slender, usually flexible appendage.

Citric acid cycle: Krebs cycle.

Cleavage: cell division characteristic of early stages of the embryo.

Cloaca: the common channel for digestive, excretory, and reproductive systems in vertebrates; the terminal portion of the digestive tract in certain invertebrates.

Coelom: the true body cavity; a large space in which the viscera lie, lined with mesoderm.

Colony: a group of organisms of the same species living together.

Community: a group of organisms related together by environmental requirements.

Complete metamorphosis: metamorphosis in which successive stages may be very different from each other.

Compound eye: an eye made up of many separate optical units.

Conduction: broadly, the transmission of an impulse through living cells; in zoology, usually, the transmission of a nerve impulse.

Contractile vacuole: an intracellular excretory organelle.

Contraction: decrease in length, as of a muscle; not accompanied in living tissue by a decrease in volume.

Corpuscle: a blood cell.

Cranial nerve: a nerve arising in the brain.

Cranium: that portion of the skull enclosing the brain.

Crop: a thin-walled division of the alimentary canal, usually near the anterior end, primarily for food storage.

Cross-fertilization: union of egg cell from one individual with sperm cell from another individual.

Cuticle: a thin external covering.

Cytology: the study of cells.

Cytoplasm: the protoplasm between the cell membrane and the nucleus.

Decomposer: an organism whose metabolism involves the breakdown of compounds of a dead organism.

Decarboxylation: removal of carbon dioxide in a metabolic process.

Deficiency disease: an abnormal condition due to inadequacy of a vitamin in the diet.

Dehydrogenation: removal of hydrogen in a metabolic process.

Diapause: a period of dormancy in the development of an insect.

Digestion: preparation of food for absorption and assimilation; chemically it is hydrolysis.

Digit: one of the terminal divisions of an appendage (in tetrapods).

Diploblastic: derived from two embryonic germ-layers, ectoderm and endoderm.

Diploid: the normal number of chromosomes in the cells of a particular organism.

Dissimilation: the oxidation of food with the release of energy.

Distal: away from the point of attachment or place of reference.

DNA: deoxyribose nucleic acid.

Dominant: the one of two alternative characters which appears in a heterozygous individual. (See *recessive.*)

Dorsal: toward the back.

Duodenum: the first division of the small intestine.

Ecology: the study of relations between organism and environment.

Ecosystem: a complex of interrelated organisms and non-living environmental factors.

Ectoderm: the outer layer of cells of the early embryo.

Efferent: leading away from the organ of reference.

Egestion: the discharge of unabsorbed food from an animal.

Egg cell: a female gamete.

Embryo: the inactive stage in the early development of an organism.

Embryogeny: the process of development of the embryo.

Embryology: the study of development.

Endocrine gland: a gland of internal secretion (ductless gland); a gland which produces a hormone.

Endoderm: innermost layer of cells in the gastrula stage of the embryo.

Endoplasmic reticulum: a network of vesicles extending throughout the cytoplasm.

Endoskeleton: an internal supporting structure.

Enzyme: a catalyst characteristic of living organisms.

Epidermis: a layer of cells covering an external surface.

Epithelium: a layer of cells covering a surface or lining a cavity.

Erythrocyte: a red blood corpuscle.

Esophagus: the portion of the alimentary canal leading from the pharynx to the stomach or crop.

Evolution, Organic: the development of organisms of complex nature from simpler types of life.

Excretion: the discharge of waste products formed in metabolism.

Exoskeleton: an external supporting structure.

Fertilization: the union of two gametes to form a zygote.

Fibrin: the fibrous material of a blood clot.

Fission: reproduction by division into equivalent parts.

Flagellum: a thread-like or whip-like organ of locomotion occurring in certain protozoa.

Flame cell: a ciliated terminal cell of the excretory system in certain invertebrates.

Food chain: a series of organisms in which each succeeding organism feeds on its predecessor.

Food vacuole: an intracellular digestive organelle.

Gall bladder: the sac in which bile is stored.

Gamete: a mature germ cell; sperm cell or ovum.

Gametogenesis: the process of the formation of mature germ cells; maturation.

Ganglion: a concentration of nerve cells.

Gastrovascular cavity: a cavity which functions in both digestion and circulation.

Gastrula: an early stage of the embryo which consists essentially of an invaginated blastula.

Gene: an hereditary determiner — located in a chromosome.

Genetic code: the sequence of nitrogenous bases in DNA that affects the synthesis of particular proteins.

Genetic drift: chance preservation of mutant genes, which is more probable in a small population than in a large one.

Genetics: the science of heredity.

Genital: referring to the reproductive organs.

Genotype: the type of an individual determined by its fundamental hereditary (genetic) constitution. (See *phenotype*.)

Germ cell: a reproductive cell.

Germ-layer: one of the three embryonic cell layers of multicellular animals.

Germ-plasm: the gametes and the cells from which they are formed, considered as a unit.

Gill: a respiratory organ for gaseous exchange in water.

Gill slit: an opening in the wall of the pharynx, between gills.

Girdle: the skeletal connection between axial skeleton and the skeleton of a pair of appendages.

Gizzard: a heavily muscled division of the alimentary canal.

Glycogen: a complex carbohydrate, a polysaccharide; "animal starch."

Golgi body: a group or network of vesicles localized in the cytoplasm; related to intracellular metabolism.

Gonad: an organ in which gametes (ova or sperm cells) are produced.

Haemal arch: the ventral arch of a vertebra, enclosing the blood vessels.

Haemocoel: a body-cavity reduced in size and functioning as part of the blood-vascular system.

Haploid: the reduced chromosome number; half the diploid number, the chromosome number characteristic of the body cells of an organism.

Hardy-Weinberg principle: the ratios of genes in a population do not change if mating is at random and if the genes themselves are not changing.

Hepatic: referring to the liver.

Hepatic portal system: a system of veins leading into the capillaries of the liver.

Heredity: transmission of characters from parent to offspring.

Hermaphroditism: the condition in which gonads of both sexes occur in the same individual.

Heterotrophic: the type of nutrition in which an organism derives its food from other organisms.

Heterozygous: said of an individual which has unlike or alternative genes (allelomorphs) for any character being considered. (See *homozygous*).

Hexose: a sugar containing six carbon atoms.

Histology: the study of tissues.

Holozoic: type of nutrition in which solid food is ingested.

Homology: fundamental similarity — based primarily on development and structure. (See *analogy*).

Homozygous: said of an individual which has duplicate genes for the character being considered.

Hormone: a chemical regulator; a substance which serves in the chemical coordination of the body.

Immunity: resistance to disease.

Incomplete metamorphosis: metamorphosis involving stages which do not differ markedly from each other.

Instar: any one of the successive stages in the life history of an insect.

Irritability: the capacity to respond to a stimulus.

Kidney: an excretory organ; the term may be limited to the metanephros, the excretory organ of reptiles, birds, and mammals.

Krebs cycle: a cycle of metabolic reactions constituting part of the process of cellular oxidation.

Lacteal: a lymphatic vessel of the intestinal drainage.

Larva: an active, early developmental stage.

Larynx: the voice box.

Leucocyte: a colorless blood corpuscle.

Linkage: the condition in which characters are inherited together due to the presence of their genes in the same chromosome.

Lipid: a true fat or related compound.

Liver: a digestive, storage, and excretory organ.

Lymphatic system: a system of vessels leading from the intercellular spaces to the large veins near the heart; part of the circulatory system.

Malpighian tubule: a blindly-ending excretory duct, characteristic of arthropods.

Mammary gland: a milk-secreting gland.

Mantle: the membrane lining the respiratory cavity of mollusks.

Maturation: gametogenesis.

Medusa: the bell or umbrella body-form of a coelenterate, as typified by a jelly-fish.

Meiosis: cell division in which the chromosome number is reduced from diploid to haploid.

Mendelism: the principles of heredity discovered by Gregor Mendel, in particular segregation and independent assortment.

Mesoderm: the cells between ectoderm and endoderm in animal embryos; typically these cells are in two layers, one next the ectoderm, one next the endoderm.

Mesonephros: moderately complex type of vertebrate kidney, with numerous tubules.

Messenger RNA: the nucleic acid that transfers information from the gene to sites of protein synthesis in the cytoplasm.

Metabolism: the chemical processes characteristic of protoplasm.

Metagenesis: alternation of sexual and asexual methods of reproduction.

Metamerism: segmental repetition of organs or organ systems.

Metamorphosis: pronounced change in form during the course of development.

Metanephros: the most complex type of vertebrate kidney (the "true kidney"), with a great many tubules.

Metazoa: 1, all animals other than Protozoa; 2, all animals other than Protozoa and Porifera.

Micron: unit of length, $\dfrac{1}{1000}$ millimeter.

Mitochondrion: a granular or rodlike cytoplasmic inclusion involved in cellular oxidation.

Mitosis: cell division in which the nuclear constituents are divided equationally; indirect cell division.

Morphology: the study of structure.

Mutation: an inherited change due to a modification of the germ-plasm.

Myotome: a muscle segment.

Natural selection: the process leading to the survival of the best adapted (most fit) in the competition in nature.

Nephridium: an organ of excretion; a kidney unit.

Neural arch: the dorsal arch of a vertebra, enclosing the nerve cord.

Neurohumor: a secretion of a nerve ending.

Notochord: a gelatinous, stiffening, axial support characteristic of all chordates.

Nucleic acid: a complex compound made up of a chain of nucleotides.

Nucleolus: a more or less spherical body within the nucleus; it is a region of RNA concentration.

Nucleotide: one of the "building stones" of nucleic acid; it consists of phosphate, pentose sugar, and a purine or pyrimidine.

Nucleus: a definite controlling body within a cell, containing chromatin and surrounded by a membrane.

Nymph: a juvenile stage of an insect that has incomplete metamorphosis.

Occipital condyle: an articular surface on the skull with which the first vertebra of the neck articulates.

Ocellus: a simple eye.

Oesophagus: esophagus.

Olfactory: referring to the sense of smell.

Ommatidium: a single optical unit in a compound eye.

Oögenesis: the process of maturation of egg cells.

Optic: referring to the sense of sight.

Organ: a group of cells or tissues functioning as a unit.

Organelle: a specialized structure of a unicellular organism or a single cell.

Organism: a single animal or plant, one that behaves as a unit.

Organ system: a group of organs functioning together.

Orthogenesis: evolutionary progress in a definite direction.

Ostium: an opening; usually applied to an opening, guarded by valves, into heart or pericardium.

Ovary: the gonad of the female, producing ova.

Oviduct: the tube by which the eggs leave the body of the female animal.

Oviparous: the condition in which the young hatch from eggs outside the parent's body.

Ovipositor: an organ for the deposit of eggs.

Ovoviviparous: the condition in which the young hatch from eggs in the uterus, and are born alive.

Ovum: an egg cell; a female gamete.

Palp: a small, flexible appendage on the head.

Pancreas: a digestive and endocrine gland of vertebrates.

Parapodium: a soft, lateral appendage typical of polychaet annelids.

Parasite: an organism which lives at the expense of another.

Parazoa: animals of the form of sponges (Phylum Porifera).

Parthenogenesis: reproduction involving development from an unfertilized egg cell.

Pathogenic: disease producing.

Pectoral: referring to the anterior paired appendages and girdles of vertebrates.

Pelvic: referring to the posterior paired appendages and girdles of vertebrates.

Penis: a copulatory organ for conveying sperm cells to the genital tract of the female.

Pentose: a sugar containing five carbon atoms.

Pericardium: the cavity enclosing the heart; also the membrane lining the cavity and covering the heart.

Peristalsis: rhythmic muscular contractions which pass along a tubular organ.

Peritoneal cavity: that portion of the coelom of vertebrates exclusive of pericardial and pleural cavities.

Pharynx: the portion of the alimentary tract immediately back of the mouth; it may be an important part of the respiratory system.

Phenotype: the type of an individual determined by appearance, without regard to its hereditary constitution. (See *genotype.*)

Phospholipid: a fatlike compound in which a fatty acid is replaced by a phosphorus-containing group.

Phosphorylation: the combination of a compound and a phosphate group from ATP; an energy-supplying process.

Photosynthesis: synthesis with energy from light; specifically, the synthesis of carbohydrates by green plants in the presence of sunlight.

Physiology: the study of function.

Placenta: the organ in mammals through which exchange of diffusable substances occurs between embryo and mother.

Pleural cavity: the cavity enclosing a lung.

Polyp: the cylindrical body-form of a coelenterate, typified by the sea anemone.

Population: an intrabreeding group of organisms.

Posterior: toward the hinder end.

Predator: an animal which obtains its food by preying on other animals.

Producer: an organism that manufactures its own food.

Pronephros: the simplest type of vertebrate kidney, consisting of a few tubules, draining the coelom.

Protein: a compound of carbon, hydrogen, oxygen and nitrogen, which is made up of amino-acids.

Protoplasm: the physico-chemical system which constitutes living matter.

Proximal: toward the point of attachment or place of reference.

Pseudopodium: a flowing extension of protoplasm, used in cell locomotion.

Pulmonary: referring to the lungs.

Pyloric: referring to the posterior end of the stomach.

Pyramid: the relationship between the small number of organisms at the apex of a food chain and the larger number constituting its base.

Rectum: the terminal portion of the intestine.

Renal: referring to the kidneys.

Renal portal system: a system of veins leading into the capillaries of the kidney.

Reproduction: the maintenance of a species from generation to generation.

Respiration: broadly, all steps involved in taking in oxygen and giving off carbon dioxide; cell respiration is oxidation.

RNA: ribose nucleic acid.

Saprophytic: type of nutrition in which the organism absorbs food through its body wall.

Sciatic plexus: the interlacing nerve fibers supplying the pelvic limb.

Scientific name: the name given a species of animal or plant, consisting of generic name and specific name; the form is Latin.

Segregation: the separation of paired determiners in the gametes.

Self-fertilization: union of egg cell with sperm cell produced in the same individual.

Serum: the liquid remaining after the formation of a blood clot.

Seta: a bristle.

Sewall Wright effect: genetic drift.

Sexual reproduction: reproduction involving gametes of opposite sex.

Simple eye: an eye consisting of a single optical unit.

Sinus: a cavity of irregular shape.

Sinus venosus: a cavity of the heart which receives blood from the large veins (exclusive of the pulmonary).

Somatic: referring to the body cells as opposed to the germ cells.

Species: a natural population of intrabreeding organisms isolated from other such populations; a "kind" of animal or plant.

Spermatogenesis: the process of maturation of sperm cells.

Spermatozoan: a male gamete; a sperm cell.

Sperm duct: the tube through which sperm cells leave the body of the male.

Spiracle: 1, an opening into a trachea; 2, the vestigial first gill slit in some fishes.

Spiral valve: a spiral fold of tissue inside a portion of the alimentary canal.

Spore: a cell capable of developing independently into a new individual.

Sternum: the breast bone or bones.

Succession: a natural sequence of changes in type of community.

Supraorbital ridge: a skeletal ridge over the orbit of the eye.

Synecology: the ecology of community relations.

Systemic circulation: the portion of the circulatory system not directly involved in respiration.

Tarsus: 1, the terminal division of the insect leg; 2, the ankle of the higher vertebrate.

Taxonomy: the science of plant and animal classification.

Tentacle: a flexible, elongated appendage, usually near the mouth.

Testis: the gonad of the male, producing spermatozoa.

Thorax: the major division of the animal body next posterior to the head.

Tissue: a group of cells having the same structure and function.

Trachea: an air tube.

Transfer RNA: a nucleic acid molecule that moves an appropriate amino acid into position during protein synthesis.

Triploblastic: derived from three embryonic germ layers — ectoderm, endoderm, and mesoderm.

Trochophore: a larval form, bilaterally symmetrical but somewhat ovoid, bearing an equatorial band of cilia.

Trophic level: the nutritional level of an organism with respect to its position in a food chain.

Tympanic membrane: a vibrating membrane involved in hearing.

Ureter: the duct of the metanephros or true kidney.

Urethra: the urinary duct leading from the urinary bladder to the outside of the body.

Urinary bladder: a sac in which urine is temporarily retained.

Uterus: an enlargement of the posterior portion of the oviduct, in which the developing young may be retained.

Vacuole: a relatively large globule of liquid suspended in the cytoplasm.

Vagina: the terminal portion of the genital tract of the female.

Vein: a vessel which carries blood toward the heart.

Vena cava: a large vein carrying blood into the heart.

Ventral: toward the lower side, away from the back.

Ventricle: a chamber of the heart from which blood is pumped.

Vertebra: one of the cartilage or bone elements in the axial skeleton of vertebrates.

Visceral skeleton: the skeleton of jaw and gill-arches, and its derivatives.

Vitamin: an accessory food factor; an essential constituent of the diet which, however, may be required only in minute quantities.

Viviparous: the condition in which the young develop in the uterus and are born alive.

Water-vascular system: the locomotor system of echinoderms, consisting of tube-feet whose movements are produced by changes in hydrostatic pressure.

Wolffian duct: the duct of the mesonephros.

Zoogeography: the study of the distribution of animals throughout the earth.

Zoology: the science of animal life.

Zygote: a fertilized egg.

APPENDIX C

REFERENCES

Books to which students are here referred for supplementary reading are classified in three main groups. These correspond to (1) the Introduction and Part I; (2) Part II; and (3) Parts III and IV of this Outline. Cross references to textbooks of General Zoology (not included below) may be found in the Quick Reference Table. Magazine articles are not included below; the student will find many particularly valuable references in recent volumes of *Scientific American*. One important series of books now being published but not listed, the *LIFE Nature Library*, published by Time, Inc., includes a number of volumes on zoology.

PRINCIPLES OF ORGANIZATION OF THE ANIMAL BODY

Barry, J. M. *Molecular Biology*. Prentice-Hall, 1964.

Barth, L. G. *Embryology*. Holt, Rinehart & Winston, 1953.

Bloom, W., and Fawcett, D. W. *A Textbook of Histology*. Saunders, 1962.

Bonner, J. T. *The Ideas of Biology*. Harpers, 1962.

Brachet, J., and Mirsky, A. E. (eds.) *The Cell—Biochemistry, Physiology, Morphology*. 5 vols. Academic Press, 1959-1962.

DeRobertis, E.D.P., Nowinski, W. W., and Saez, F.A. *General Cytology*. Saunders, 1960.

Downes, H. R. *The Chemistry of Living Cells*. Harpers, 1962.

Gerard, R. W. *Unresting Cells*. Harpers, 1961.

Giese, A. C. *Cell Physiology*. Saunders, 1962.

McClung, C. E. (ed.) *Handbook of Microscopical Technique*. Hafner, 1950.

McElroy, W. D. *Cellular Physiology and Biochemistry*. Prentice-Hall, 1961.

Oparin, A. I. (trans. by Morgulis, S.) *The Origin of Life*. Dover, 1953.

Scheer, B. T. *General Physiology*. Wiley, 1953.

Schrader, F. *Mitosis*. Columbia University Press, 1953.

Shumway, W., and Adamstone, F. B. *Introduction to Vertebrate Embryology*. Wiley, 1954.

Sussman, M. *Animal Growth and Development.* Prentice-Hall, 1960.

Swanson, C. O. *The Cell.* Prentice-Hall, 1960.

Wilson, E. B. *The Cell in Development and Heredity.* Macmillan, 1928.

THE ANIMAL KINGDOM

General References and Invertebrates

Borradaile, L. A., et al. *The Invertebrata.* Cambridge University Press, 1961.

Brues, C. T., and Melander, A. L. *Classification of Insects.* Bulletin, Museum of Comparative Zoology (Harvard), 1932.

Buchsbaum, R. *Animals without Backbones.* University of Chicago Press, 1948.

Chandler, A. C., and Read, C. P. *Introduction to Parasitology.* Wiley, 1961.

Coe, W. R. *Echinoderms of Connecticut.* State Geological and Natural History Survey, Connecticut, 1912.

Hall, R. P. *Protozoology.* Prentice-Hall, 1953.

Huxley, T. H. *The Crayfish: An Introduction to the Study of Zoology.* D. Appleton-Century, 1880.

Hyman, L. H. *The Invertebrates. Vol. I. Protozoa through Ctenophora. Vol. II. Platyhelminthes and Rhynchocoela. Vol. III. Acanthocephala, Aschelminthes, and Entoprocta. Vol. IV. Echinodermata. Vol. V. Smaller Coelomate Groups.* McGraw-Hill, 1940-1959.

Jahn, J. T. *How to Know the Protozoa.* Wm. C. Brown, 1949.

Kudo, R. R. *Protozoology.* Thomas, 1960.

Lutz, F. E. *Field Book of Insects.* Putnam, 1935.

Parker, T. J., and Haswell, W. A. *A Text-book of Zoology.* 2 vols. Macmillan, 1960.

Pearse, A. S. (ed.) *Zoological Names.* Durham, N. C., 1948.

Pennak, R. W. *Fresh-water Invertebrates of the United States.* Ronald, 1953.

Prosser, C. L., and Brown, F. A., Jr., *Comparative Animal Physiology.* Saunders, 1961.

Ricketts, E. F., and Calvin, J. *Between Pacific Tides.* Stanford University Press, 1962.

Ross, H. H. *A Textbook of Entomology.* Wiley, 1956.

Schmidt-Nielsen, K. *Animal Physiology.* Prentice-Hall, 1960.

Snodgrass, R. E. *Principles of Insect Morphology.* McGraw-Hill, 1935.

Swain, R. B. *The Insect Guide.* Doubleday, 1948.

Ward, H. B., and Whipple, G. C. (Edmondson, W. T., ed.) *Freshwater Biology.* Wiley, 1959.

Vertebrates, including Man

Best, C. H., and Taylor, N. B. *The Physiological Basis of Medical Practice.* Williams & Wilkins, 1961.

Carlson, A. J., and Johnson, W. *The Machinery of the Body.* University of Chicago Press, 1962.

Ditmars, R. L. *Reptiles of the World.* Macmillan, 1926.

Frohse, F., Brödel, M., and Schlossberg, L. *Atlas of Human Anatomy.* Barnes & Noble, 1957.

Gray, H. (Goss, C. M., ed.) *Anatomy of the Human Body.* Lea & Febiger, 1959.

Hamilton, W. J., Jr. *American Mammals—Their Lives, Habits, and Economic Relations.* McGraw-Hill, 1939.

Holmes, S. J. *The Biology of the Frog.* Macmillan, 1927.

Lanham, U. *The Fishes.* Columbia University Press, 1962.

Noble, G. K. *The Biology of the Amphibia.* McGraw-Hill, 1931.

Orr, R. T. *Vertebrate Biology.* Saunders, 1961.

Parshley, H. M. *The Science of Human Reproduction.* Norton, 1933.

Patten, B. M. *Human Embryology.* McGraw-Hill, 1953.

Romer, A. S. *The Vertebrate Body.* Saunders, 1962.

Ruch, T. C., and Fulton, J. F. *Medical Physiology and Biophysics.* Saunders, 1960.

Steen, E. B., and Montagu, A. *Anatomy and Physiology.* 2 vols. Barnes & Noble, 1959.

Turner, G. D. *General Endocrinology.* Saunders, 1961.

VanTyne, J., and Berger, A. J. *Fundamentals of Ornithology.* Wiley, 1959.

Welty, J. C. *The Life of Birds.* Saunders, 1962.

BIOLOGICAL PRINCIPLES AND HISTORY

Allee, W. C., et al. *Principles of Animal Ecology.* Saunders, 1949.

Bates, M. *The Forest and the Sea.* Random House, 1960.

Bonner, D. M. *Heredity.* Prentice-Hall, 1961.

Clarke, G. L. *Elements of Ecology.* Wiley, 1954.

Darlington, P. J., Jr. *Zoogeography.* Wiley, 1957.

Dobzhansky, T. *Genetics and the Origin of Species*. Columbia University Press, 1951.

Dodson, E. O. *Evolution: Process and Product*. Reinhold, 1960.

Hall, T. S. *A Source Book in Animal Biology*. McGraw-Hill, 1951.

Henderson, L. J. *The Fitness of the Environment*. Peter Smith, 1959.

Herskowitz, I. H. *Genetics*. Little, Brown, 1962.

Hesse, R., Allee, W. C., and Schmidt, K. P. *Ecological Animal Geography*. Wiley, 1951.

Hough, J. N. *Scientific Terminology*. Rinehart, 1953.

Jaeger, E. C. *A Source-Book of Biological Names and Terms*. Thomas, 1959.

Locy, W. A. *The Growth of Biology*. Holt, 1925.

Mayr, E. *Animal Species and Evolution*. Harvard University Press, 1963.

Mayr, E., Lindsley, E. G., and Usinger, R. C. *Methods and Principles of Systematic Zoology*. McGraw-Hill, 1953.

Montagu, A. *An Introduction to Physical Anthropology*. Thomas, 1960.

Odum, E. P. *Ecology*. Holt-Rinehart-Winston, 1963.

———. *Fundamentals of Ecology*. Saunders, 1959.

Ross, H. H. *A Synthesis of Evolutionary Theory*. Prentice-Hall, 1962.

Simpson, G. G. *The Meaning of Evolution*. Yale University Press, 1960.

———. *Principles of Animal Taxonomy*. Columbia University Press, 1961.

Sinnott, E. W., Dunn, L. C., and Dobzhansky, T. G. *Principles of Genetics*. McGraw-Hill, 1958.

Snyder, L. H., and David, P. R. *Principles of Heredity*, Heath, 1957.

Stern, C. *Principles of Human Genetics*. Freeman, 1960.

Wallace, A. R. *The Geographical Distribution of Animals*. 2 vols. Harpers, 1876.

Wallace, B., and Srb, A. M. *Adaptation*. Prentice-Hall, 1961.

Winchester, A. W., *Heredity*. Barnes & Noble, 1961.

APPENDIX C
SAMPLE FINAL EXAMINATION

The following examination is intended to provide examples of the different types of questions used on an objective examination. In contrast to a question calling for an essay-type answer, an objective question requires little or no organization of material. It can be answered with symbols, words, or phrases. It does require a critical understanding of the vocabulary, however, and it may demand a full understanding of the relations among various phenomena.

The variety of material on an objective examination appears almost unlimited. This sample examination should be studied, therefore, mainly for the suggestions it gives on kinds of questions. One type of question frequently used has been omitted. That is the one based on a drawing, usually from a laboratory exercise, for which the student is expected to supply the appropriate labels.

Answers are given at the end of this section. Some advantage may be gained from taking the complete examination and checking the answers afterward.

Essay-type questions as given on final examinations are well illustrated by the questions at the end of each chapter in this *Outline*. A compilation of the more comprehensive or inclusive of these will constitute for the student a sample final examination of the essay-question type.

Multiple Choice. In each of the following sentences two or three alternative words or phrases are included in parentheses. In each case only one of these words or phrases can be used correctly. Underline the correct expression in each sentence:

1. Two organisms of different species living together in a mutually dependent relationship are (parasitic, symbiotic).
2. A structure which persists as a useless relic of an ancestral condition is called (atavistic, vestigial, ontogenetic).
3. A group of organisms living together constitutes (a cosmos, a community, an environment).
4. (Trypsin, Lipase, Diastase) acts in the digestion of protein.
5. The human ovum after ovulation first enters the (ovary, Fallopian tube, uterus).
6. Organisms must be better adapted to temperature fluctuations in fresh water than (on land, in the ocean).

7. In a food chain the (smallest, largest) organisms provide food for the rest.

8. The factor which inhibits population growth is (biotic potentential, environmental resistance).

9. Darwin's theory of evolution is known as the theory of (mutations, acquired characteristics, natural selection).

10. The climax community which develops as an aquatic environment and is transformed into one of average moisture conditions is the result of a (xerosere, hydrosere, mesosere) succession.

11. Structures alike in function but not in structure or origin are (homologous, analogous, phylogenetic).

12. The ocean as a habitat for organisms differs from land and fresh water in its greater (stability, variability).

13. There are (two, three, four) separate cavities of the human coelom.

14. The cavity of the vitreous humor is (behind, in front of) the lens of the eye.

15. Bowman's capsule functions by (secretion, filtration, evaporation).

Matching. Each of the characteristics or conditions listed in the first column is appropriate to one (and one only) of the Phyla in column two. Place the number of each characteristic in front of the name of the Phylum to which it applies:

1. Stinging cells	1 _____ Coelenterata
2. Lophophore	2 _____ Porifera
3. Eight rows of paddle plates	3 _____ Ctenophora
4. Flagellated collar cells	4 _____ Platyhelminthes
5. Pharyngeal gill slits	5 _____ Bryozoa
6. Metameric coelom	6 _____ Echinodermata
7. Mantle, enclosing mantle cavity	7 _____ Annelida
8. Chitinous exoskeleton, with jointed appendages	8 _____ Chordata
9. Triploblastic, with gastrovascular cavity	9 _____ Mollusca
10. Tube-feet	10 _____ Arthropoda

Completion. In the following paragraphs certain essential terms have been omitted, their places being taken by numbers in parentheses. In the spaces provided, insert the appropriate terms.

The science dealing with all living things is called (1) _____, its subdivision dealing with animals being (2) _____. The subdivision of the latter which has to do with the study of function is (3) _____; that which deals with structure is (4) _____.

(*The following statements apply to man.*)

The location of a muscle is given by naming the place of attachment of each end, the end moving less during contraction being the (5) _____, the end moving more being the (6) _____. In the biceps muscle these two ends are attached respectively to the (7) _____ and the (8) _____. The action of the biceps is (9) _____ of the arm at the (10) _____, illustrating a (11) _____ class lever. The opposing action is accomplished by the (12) _____ muscle, operating as a (13) _____ class lever, the end with greater movement being attached to the (14) _____.

In the recovery phase of contraction the chemical process of oxidation is involved. This requires the presence in the muscle of the gas (15) _____ carried to it in blood cells called (16) _____ in which it is carried in combination with a pigment, (17) _____. In the process of oxidation in the cell two waste products are formed, (18) _____ and (19) _____. These are transported to the heart, where they empty into the (20) _____ atrium, thence passing into the (21) _____. Blood flows from the heart to the lungs in the (22) _____.

A foreign protein in the blood, an (23) _____, may be precipitated by the action of (24) _____ formed by the blood. Foreign particles may be engulfed by certain types of blood cells, the (25) _____, by the process called (26) _____.

The nervous system is made up of specialized conducting cells, the (27) _____, each consisting typically of: a part containing the nucleus, the (28) _____; an extension over which impulses in a reflex arc are received, the (29) _____; and an extension which carries the impulse as it leaves the cell, the (30) _____.

True-False. Place a plus sign (+) in front of each true statement, a minus sign (—) in front of each false one. Remember that if any part of a statement is false the whole statement must be considered false.

1. _____ Protoplasm is a definite chemical compound.
2. _____ Protoplasm contains at least one chemical element found only in living matter.
3. _____ Proteins are made up of amino-acids.
4. _____ Digestion is the process by which food is hydrolyzed to simpler molecules.

5. _____ A single cell may be as much as an inch in diameter.
6. _____ A cell wall is a typical constituent of animals cells.
7. _____ Chromatin is nuclear material which stains with basic dyes.
8. _____ The cell membrane is freely permeable to all substances in solution.
9. _____ Mitosis typically results in the equal division of each chromosome in the cell.
10. _____ A group of cells of similar structure and function is a tissue.
11. _____ A true coelom is lined with mesoderm.
12. _____ In asexual reproduction the progeny are derived from a single parent.
13. _____ The process of meiosis involves two successive cell divisions.
14. _____ In the process of meiosis the haploid chromosome number becomes diploid.
15. _____ An hermaphrodite is an animal in which eggs develop without fertilization.
16. _____ In animal classification Orders are combined to form Families and Families to form Genera.
17. _____ Malaria is caused by a protozoan.
18. _____ Paramecium reproduces by both sexual and asexual methods of reproduction.
19. _____ Sponges are restricted in distribution to the ocean.
20. _____ Commercial sponges have skeletons of silica.
21. _____ Hydra has a medusa stage which reproduces sexually.
22. _____ Reef-forming corals are active reef-builders at all depths of coral reefs.
23. _____ Planaria is a free-living, ciliated flatworm.
24. _____ A cercaria is an active larval stage of a tapeworm.
25. _____ Echinoderms and coelenterates are both derived from radially-symmetrical larvae.
26. _____ The earthworm is fully metameric in all organ systems.
27. _____ The parapodia of Nereis bear setae.
28. _____ The millipede is a typical member of the Phylum Annelida.
29. _____ The appendages of the crayfish are modified from a biramous type.
30. _____ Biting and sucking mouth-parts of insects are derived from homologous structures.
31. _____ Complete metamorphosis of insects is development in which the hatched young are quite similar to the adults.
32. _____ One difference between the Hemiptera and the Coleoptera is in the type of mouth-parts.
33. _____ The segments of a typical insect leg are: coxa, trochanter, femur, tibia, tarsus.

34. _____ Insects have an open circulatory system.
35. _____ The larva of a fresh-water mussel is a parasite on fishes.
36. _____ A calcareous shell is characteristic of all types of mollusks.
37. _____ All Chordata have a dorsal, tubular nerve cord.
38. _____ Amphioxus has a nervous system with a specialized brain.
39. _____ All birds possess feathers.
40. _____ Mammals are the only vertebrates with three auditory ossicles.

Arrangement in Sequence. Trace the blood through the path it must follow by the *shortest route* in each of the following cases, naming all heart chambers, arteries, veins, and capillary systems in order.

a. In the frog, lung capillaries to mesonephric capillaries:

1. lung capillaries
2.
3.
4.
5.
6.
7.
8.
9. mesonephric capillaries

b. In man, inferior vena cava to common iliac artery:

1. inferior vena cava
2.
3.
4.
5.
6.
7.
8.
9.
10. common iliac artery

Lists:

1. Give four developments that took place in human evolution.
2. Name in order the four phases of mitosis.
3. Give the complete classification of one kind of animal, including six categories and the scientific name.
4. Name and locate the six Zoogeographic Regions according to Wallace.

Genetic Problems:

a. In guinea pigs black or pigmented hair (P) is dominant over white (p), the unpigmented condition; and rough hair (R) is dominant over smooth (r). A female with smooth white hair has a litter of five young, two of these black with rough hair and the other three with white rough hair. Give genotypes of both parents and the five young:

Parents: Male: Female:
Progency: 2:
            3:

b. "Blue" Andalusian fowls are the heterozygous progeny of homozygous black (BB) and homozygous splashed white (bb) parents. Give the expected phenotypic and genotypic ratios of progeny in the following crosses:

b^1 Blue   X   White

Progeny:

b^2 Blue   X   Black

Progeny:

b^3 Blue   X   Blue

ANSWERS

Multiple Choice: 1. symbiotic. 2. vestigial. 3. community.
4. trypsin. 5. Fallopian tube. 6. in the ocean. 7. smallest. 8. environmental resistance. 9. natural selection. 10. hydrosere. 11. analogous. 12. stability. 13. four. 14. behind. 15. filtration.

Matching: 1. Coelenterata. 2. Bryozoa. 3. Ctenophora. 4. Porifera. 5. Chordata. 6. Annelida. 7. Mollusca. 8. Arthropoda. 9. Platyhelminthes. 10. Echinodermata.

Completion: 1. biology. 2. zoology. 3. physiology. 4. morphology (or anatomy). 5. origin. 6. insertion. 7. scapula. 8. radius. 9. flexion. 10. elbow. 11. third. 12. triceps. 13. first. 14. ulna. 15. oxygen. 16. erythrocyte. 17. hemoglobin. 18-19. carbon dioxide and water. 20. right. 21. right ventricle. 22. pulmonary arteries. 23. antigen. 24. antibodies. 25. leucocytes. 26. phagocytosis. 27. neurons. 28. cell body. 29. dendron (or dendrite). 30. axon.

True False:

True: Nos. 3, 4, 5, 7, 9, 10, 11, 12, 13, 17, 18, 23, 27, 29, 30, 32, 33, 34, 35, 37, 39, 40.

False: Nos. 1, 2, 6, 8, 14, 15, 16, 19, 20, 21, 22, 24, 25, 26, 28, 31, 36, 38.

Arrangement in Sequence:

a. 2. pulmonary veins. 3. left atrium. 4. ventricle. 5. truncus arteriosus. 6. systemic arch. 7. dorsal aorta. 8. renal arteries.

b. 2. right atrium. 3. right ventricle. 4. pulmonary arteries. 5. lung capillaries. 6. pulmonary veins. 7. left atrium. 8. left ventricle. 9. aorta.

Lists:

1. See page 217.
2. See pages 22-23.
3. Examples on page 48.
4. See page 226 and map on page 227.

Genetic Problems:

a. Parents: Male: PpRR   Female: pprr
   Progeny: 2: PpRr
            3: ppRr
b. b¹ Progeny: 1 Bb : 1 bb
   b² Progeny: 1 BB : 1 Bb
   b³ Progeny: 1 BB : 2 Bb : 1 bb

INDEX

Page references to definitions in the Glossary are not included.